# Gardening Under Glass

# GARDENING UNDER GLASS

## An Illustrated Guide to the Greenhouse

by JEROME A. EATON

*Macmillan Publishing Co., Inc.*
NEW YORK

*Collier Macmillan Publishers*
LONDON

Photos courtesy of Ralph S. Bailey, 91, 139; Chapin Water-
matics Inc., 35; Dr. O. Wesley Davidson, 109, 114, 116B,
117, 118, 120B; Gottscho-Schleisner, Inc., 4-5, 8, 12T, 13,
14, 43T, 58, 68, 71, 151, 178, 187, 212, 215, 222, 223, 226,
243, 253, 272, 288, 289, 292; M. R. Harrison, Rutgers
University, 116T; Humex Ltd., 34, 43B, 45; Janco Greenhouses, 10; Lord and Burnham, 2, 6, 16, 17T, 18, 19, 28,
29T, 41R, 52, 53, 54, 63B, 66, 77; *Popular Science,* 22;
University of Illinois, 21; Dr. Leonard Weinstein (Boyce
Thompson Institute), 119, 120T.

Macmillan Publishing Co., Inc.
866 Third Avenue, New York, N.Y. 10022
Collier-Macmillan Canada Ltd.

Library of Congress Catalog Card Number: 75-189678

Fourth Printing 1974

Printed in the United States of America

*To the late* RALPH S. BAILEY, *a great humanist—whose imagination was captured by the earth out of gardening —and whose skill with the word and the pen enabled it to be shared by many*

# Acknowledgments

Looking back upon the various periods in writing this book, I find that it has been anything but the result of my efforts alone. Risking the inevitable oversights, I cannot go further without acknowledging the considerable assistance of others: Elizabeth Aleinikoff for pushing me into sound writing techniques and pulling me out of editorial dilemmas; Dr. O. Wesley Davidson, who helped me to simplify and capsulize the complex subjects of soil, nutrition, and plant pathology; the late Herbert Kastl for his up-to-date data on spray chemicals; Ester Asheroff for wrestling with my scribbled manuscript over long periods until it was finally in order; my daughter, Carol Eaton, for great help in research; Laura Lane for extensive and expert editorial assistance in pulling all the loose ends together. Both thanks and apologies are due Don Richardson and Dr. Carl L. Withner for permitting interruptions and providing me with invaluable assistance. Thanks to my son, Tom, whose criticism of various ideas never left doubt as to their value.

After working alone for many hours at a time, the most valuable and necessary assistance was that of a valid reaction to my written thoughts. My wife, Shirley, has not only provided these reactions, but also the thoughtful alternatives that have been folded into every chapter.

# Contents

## III. WHAT WILL YOU GROW?

# Introduction

THIS BOOK IS directed both to people who are thinking about buying a greenhouse and to those who already own one but would like
to enjoy it more. While, in part, this is a *how*-to-do-it book, it is
even more a *why*-to-do-it book. Knowing *why* prepares you, the
gardener, for almost every step of growing plants under glass.
Armed with predictability, you are in better control of what is
going to happen. When you come to recognize what I often refer
to as the "balance of conditions" and the "feel" of plant life, your
own life will be enriched by the discoveries you will make in the
greenhouse every day.

Recalling my own decisions and qualms, successes and failures,
pleasures and disappointments, I have recorded in the following
pages the important aspects of greenhouse culture in much the
same order as you will confront them.

## A Greenhouse Transcends Geography

With the proper site and structural design, the modern greenhouse can duplicate the conditions of an alpine hillside, a desert floor, a tropical forest, an orchard, or a vineyard. Becoming aware of the broad and fascinating life supported by each of these ecological areas is part of the attraction of greenhouse gardening. Bright flowering plants with heady perfumes in the dead of winter, cut flowers anytime, a head start on the summer vegetable garden— these are among the diverse pleasures in store for you.

The experienced greenhouse grower may appear casual about his exotic plants and flowers, but his methods and procedures are not haphazard. For example, when he feels the soil or lifts a pot, he makes a dozen or more observations and interrelated judgments. This kind of familiarity does not come to the grower overnight or without its setbacks, but experiences eventually add up to giving him the "feel" of the house. In time, each practitioner acquires the detailed knowledge that helps him achieve a predictable result by routine measures. The fundamentals that, with experience, will make you master of the greenhouse form the fabric of this book.

## Cycle of the Seasons

The renaissance of spring, the full flowering of summer, and the dormancy of winter are all parts of the uniform cyclic reactions of most of our outdoor garden plants. In the greenhouse, however, the plants are likely to have growth cycles independent of one another. This is because they originated in widely scattered regions. In such cases of mixed seasons, if not mixed climates, you may not immediately recognize which plant is resting, which is in active growth, which is completing its cycle, and which is about to start into growth. But knowing and recognizing the needs of each, and segregating them accordingly, are essential to your success. The South African calla-lily and Persian cyclamen, for example, both rest in a dormant state all summer with no water other than the moisture in the atmosphere. They start into growth in the fall and reach full flower during the winter. The lily of the Nile (*Agapanthus africanus*), on the other hand, flowers in the summer and spends the winter months in a state of inactivity. Normal watering during its dormant period, when there is little need for it, would be worse for the plant than insufficient water during regrowth. It is too much to ask that you know the peculiarities of the growth cycle of every plant, but it is possible to become familiar with those in your own greenhouse.

### Four Factors in Plant Growth

The atmosphere of your greenhouse can be thought of as an envelope of climate—any climate you choose. The components, balanced to make up this artificial atmosphere, are water, heat, light, and air. A *hothouse*, created by adding heat to a glass enclosure, is not a greenhouse until you provide and control all four climate components.

Plants are unable to adapt to changes in environment without some signs of distress. In the greenhouse, these "symptoms" give

*Milwaukee incorporated the newest engineering techniques in developing its conoidal greenhouses.*

# HOTHOUSES FOR THE MILLION.

## SAMUEL HEREMAN

BEGS TO INFORM THE PUBLIC THAT HE HAS BEEN APPOINTED SOLE AGENT FOR THE MANUFACTURE AND SALE OF

# THE NEW PORTABLE AND ECONOMICAL HOTHOUSES,

INVENTED AND PATENTED BY

## SIR JOSEPH PAXTON, M.P.

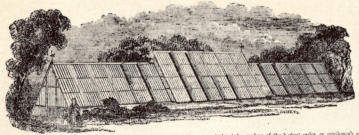

These Buildings are of unparalleled cheapness, and being composed of simple parts can be enlarged, removed, or adapted to any Horticultural purpose by ordinary labourers.

They are calculated for gardens of the highest order, or gentlemen's gardens generally, for market gardens where they may be made to cover any extent of surface, and also for suburban, villa, and cottage gardens.

The moderate cost of these houses not only places within the reach of persons of limited means a luxury hitherto confined to the wealthy, but offers immense advantages to all who have garden walls already standing—as from their peculiar construction they can be formed into ranges of lean-to houses with a facility and at a cost hitherto unheard of.

Whilst they are adapted for permanent structures they are also particularly

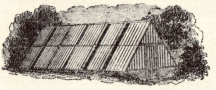

suited for persons having temporary or limited tenures, as they can with ease be packed up and removed at the expiration of the tenancy.

The above engravings show some of the uses to which this invention can be adapted, and the forms it can be made to assume. It will be seen that no houses, however costly, can be turned to more useful purposes or more effectually fulfil all

the requirements of Horticultural operations. Although the chief aim of the inventor was to reduce the cost of such structures, and to place them within the reach of all classes, yet by varying the arrangements and dimensions of the several parts, ornamented buildings can easily be formed. The prices of these houses with water troughs, doors and ends complete, are as follows :—

| | 8 Feet Lights. | 10 Feet Lights. | 12 Feet Lights. |
|---|---|---|---|
| 30 feet in length | £33 0 | £42 5 | £53 0 |
| 40 feet in length | 41 16 | 53 17 | 66 15 |
| 50 feet in length | 51 5 | 65 10 | 80 10 |
| 60 feet in length | 69 12 | 77 0 | 94 5 |
| 70 feet in length | 69 5 | 87 10 | 106 5 |
| 80 feet in length | 78 12 | 99 3 | 120 10 |
| 90 feet in length | 87 18 | 111 0 | 139 0 |
| 100 feet in length | 90 15 | 121 5 | 147 0 |

The above lengths are given in round numbers, but from the nature of their construction the houses will practically in all cases exceed these measurements.

**HEATING APPARATUS** of the best description can be supplied and adapted if required.

It is intended to supply purchasers according to the rotation in which their orders are received, the sale having commenced on Monday, January 9, 1860.

Letters prepaid addressed to S. HEREMAN, 7, Pall Mall East, S.W., will receive immediate attention.

Printed by William Bradbury, of 13, Upper Woburn Place, and Frederick Mullett Evans, of No. 7, Queen's Road, West, both in the Parish of St. Pancras, in the Co. of Middlesex, Printers, at their Office, Lombard St. Precinct of Whitefriars, City of London; and published by them at the Office, No. 5, Upper Wellington St., Parish of St. Paul's, Covent Garden, in the said Co.—Saturday, February 4, 1860.

*Above: After designing conservatories for Britain's royalty, Paxton directed his efforts toward the needs of the populace in 1860. Opposite: The typical Victorian greenhouse, more a folly than a practical structure.*

the signal that you should rebalance the various growth factors, lest they soon become limiting factors instead.

An understanding of the phrase, *limiting factor*, is essential. If any one of the four major factors (heat, light, water, or air) is in either short or overabundant supply, growth will be limited to the extent of the imbalance.

A considerable portion of this book is devoted to those techniques that make the limiting factors easier to recognize, adjust, and maintain. Although in former days an old hand in the greenhouse could sense the moisture on his cheek, the heat on his lips, and the light at a glance; much of this kind of monitoring is now done with automatic devices, which are programmed to make the necessary adjustments themselves.

Every change in one of the four factors has some effect on the other three. If you open the ventilators wide in winter, you will have to add heat. If you add heat, the air will become drier and require additional moisture. And so on. When any of these changes causes you to react automatically to keep the various levels in proper balance, you are well on your way to complete greenhouse enjoyment.

## Our Debt to History

Many of the basic practices I describe in this book are actually of ancient origin, and it is only their adaptation that is new. For example, the luxury of growing fruit and vegetables out of season

was not uncommon in the aristocratic society of the Roman era. The Pompeiian "specularia" was a forcing house, incorporating heat ducts within its walls and translucent sheets of mica in its roof. Seneca's first-century glasshouse was heated by hot water and supported many rare and out-of-season fruits; he grew grapes and cucumbers, as well as a number of decorative plants. Many structures, which today would be called root cellars, cold frames, hotbeds, and even conservatories and greenhouses, were devised for similar purposes. Horticultural techniques to obtain early ripening within these special structures were spelled out in Columella's *De Re Rustica*, the classic Roman work on agriculture.

The use of heated glass enclosures was brought to France and England by the Romans and, although each century shows an evolution of design, the forcing house remained, understandably, almost exclusively a plaything of the leisure class until the eighteenth century. It was then that the great orangeries of France and the English stove houses (for growing pineapples and bananas) enabled the small landholder to enjoy an early salad or a few flowering plants out of season.

Once the idea of such pleasures challenged the ingenuity of the countryman, developments came at a quickened pace. White Dutch tiles were used to reflect the light from the solid walls. Portable stoves, built on wheels, provided heat when it was needed and left maximum working space at other times. As an understanding of the physics of hot water grew, new heating methods were produced. In Iceland, ingenuity long ago improved the local economy, as well as the menus, by utilizing the natural underground hot springs as a free source of constant heat in huge greenhouses. And today, Iceland produces a full range of table crops, from the commonplace tomato to the exotic banana.

By 1850, every ancient technique and device for controlling the glass-enclosed environment of plants had been exploited and refined. The useful features of the large conservatories had been brought down to the scale of the now-popular home greenhouse. All this experience plus adaptations of new scientific findings and technical advances, have made the greenhouse ready once again for a new era of popular acceptance and use.

Today's greenhouse gardener controls automatically the climate he has chosen, but he owes a debt to his predecessors who discovered the *whys* and *hows* that this book explains in detail.

# I. First Decisions

*Proper siting can shield the greenhouse from prevailing winds.*

# 1

# The Site

WHERE YOU PUT your greenhouse depends on how your property is used at present and on your plans for its future. Naturally, you do not want to infringe on the children's play area, unless necessary, or plunk your greenhouse down in the middle of the front lawn. But you can attach it to any room in the house or place it on your residential property wherever you can meet the chief requirements for a site.

Four considerations have to be taken into account right at the start. One is the factor of available light. The second is the direction and force of prevailing winds—in both winter and summer. The third is the drainage of the site—both on the surface and underground. The fourth is simply your own convenience. More often than not, once you resolve the first three considerations, convenience will be paramount.

Next, you probably will have to decide whether your greenhouse would be best attached to your house or separate from it. I would vote in favor of attaching a lean-to to your house or putting up a freestanding model nearby, since a greenhouse is little pleasure if you must trudge through the snow or rain to get to it, no matter how perfect it might otherwise be. Properly planned and planted, with an inviting walk leading to it, your greenhouse should enhance your garden rather than be a purely utilitarian building surrounded by broken pots and mounds of compost.

Situating a greenhouse is often full of compromises; however, you can overcome or compensate for most of them in one way or another. In terms of light, experts mainly agree that the ideal site is unobstructed toward the south. But opinion is divided on which directions the ends of the greenhouse should face. If the ends face north and south, all the plants will get a substantial amount of light as the sun moves across the sky. Should the ends face east and west, the plants on the north side of the house will always enjoy a degree of shading. I say "enjoy" because plants should be

segregated according to their sensitivity to and need for sunlight. In no case, however, should heavy shade be cast upon the glass on either side. I favor an east-west orientation because it enables more of the beneficial light rays to penetrate the glass.

One benefit of the freestanding greenhouse is early- and late-day sun during all seasons of the year—extra insurance for the successful growth of a wide choice of plants. But almost any exposure with at least three hours of sunlight each day will give reasonably good results. Only when there is excessive sunlight as a result of unobstructed southern exposure, will you need to provide mechanical means of shading, such as roller blinds of either wood slats or plastic netting. When there is insufficient sunlight from the south, you will need to provide more light. Judicious pruning, or removal, of an offending tree is often the simple solution. If the shade is cast by a house or another immovable object, you may

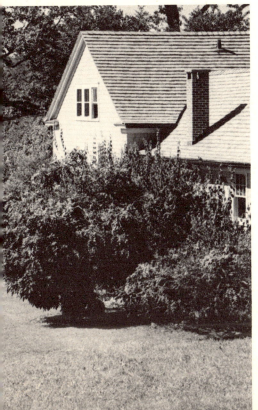

*The best site includes maximum light, drainage, protection from wind, and convenience. Here, the convenience of proximity is outweighed by the conveniences of the potting shed.*

have to go along with the situation. When a north light is all that is available, you will need to choose plants that grow even in that extreme situation. Also, a few strips of fluorescent lights, properly placed, can alleviate the lack of sunlight considerably.

*Why not have a greenhouse off your bedroom?*

While a completely unobstructed site provides excellent light, the prevailing winds may prove to be a problem in keeping your greenhouse warm enough. A hedge or group of shrubs, 10 to 15 feet away from the most vulnerable side, will cut down the speed of the wind if the branches are not too dense. (A *solid* hedge or fence actually causes the air to increase its velocity after it passes over the top, much as a roller coaster does after it reaches the crest of a rise.) In the winter you will need to be aware of the cooling action of fast-moving air across the glass surface.

A low area, into which surrounding slopes direct a flow of cold air, creates a refrigerator. To avoid this, provide a protective planting, but assure maximum air drainage by creating openings in two sides of the fence or group of shrubs. In the summer, warm breezes coming through these slots will circulate the air and keep temperatures from building up.

In a low area you have the added possibility of accumulated groundwater. However, the situation need not be serious if you install perforated drainage tiles to carry off the excess water that collects below the surface.

Too many people are frightened away from constructing a greenhouse because of the false impression that *all* the conditions of a site must be perfect. Actually, it is often a unique characteristic—one that is less than ideal—that results in a greenhouse of special merit. If this were not so, there probably would not be the large number of greenhouses on rooftops and terraces high above the streets of New York City, some with fine collections of orchids. Nor would you see so many pit houses built into unpromising hillsides. These pit houses often lead to the establishment of diverse and interesting collections of alpines, cacti, and other specialties.

To sum up, you will, of course, look for the best site, but you will have to use whatever is available. And you can use whatever is available if you make the necessary adaptations.

*The well-planned even-span greenhouse, attached at one end, can be made an integral part of the overall architecture.*

# 2

# Greenhouse Types and Construction

THE MASS EXODUS from the cities to the suburbs after World War II gave the greenhouse industry a shot in the arm. Whole new groups of materials came into being. The aircraft industry found aluminum extrusions and plastics to be components which are economical and easy to work with. Fiberglass, electronic sensors, and other new developments rapidly became as commonplace as the heavy, wooden-framed greenhouse and hand-cranked ventilators of earlier times.

The era of large estates, when greenhouses were located in the service area with large piles of coal nearby, is largely a thing of the past. Times and the scene have changed, and the greenhouse has become an adjunct of the living wing of the house—often it is an extension of the living room itself. You can enjoy Sunday afternoon on the garden terrace in pleasant, quiet, and verdant surroundings the year-round—*if* you have a properly planned greenhouse.

## Types of Greenhouses

The only uniform description of all home greenhouses is "too small." Other than that, they vary greatly—in size, in shape, and in construction materials, depending mainly on the site available and the owner's horticultural interests.* In the following paragraphs, we consider the major types of greenhouses, their uses, and their locations.

The *lean-to greenhouse* has good reason for being the most popular type. Attached to, and having at least one wall in common with, your house, the lean-to receives insulation from the cold and accessible utilities can be extended to it with a minimum of expense. Even hot water is feasible in this type of greenhouse, a very helpful asset in the care of many kinds of plants. A greenhouse of this type can be a most decorative addition to you home, especially when you view it from your living room through a picture window. The greenhouse will look most dramatic when it is lighted in the evening, with a few well-displayed flowering plants in the foreground.

* See Appendix for a list of manufacturers of all types of greenhouses and greenhouse accessories.

*Even a greenhouse with glass to the ground, such as the lean-to greenhouse shown here, requires a solid footing.*

The house wall is a perfect surface on which to train climbing plants, either flowering or fruiting, with their roots directly in the ground. This should leave plenty of room for a walk and a long elevated bench on which to grow potted plants. Caution—when you build your lean-to, be certain that a window necessary for home ventilation, such as one in the kitchen, is not obstructed by the greenhouse.

The exposure you have may put limitations on the lean-to. A north-facing lean-to will limit you to those plants with low light requirements. Chill winds and absence of warming sun will make the cost of heating a factor to consider. A southern exposure is most desirable and will permit you to grow a wide variety of plants. However, the excessive buildup of heat on sunny days will call for a dependable, automatic ventilating system along the ridge. Whether you choose solid walls (about 3 feet high) or a model with glass-to-ground walls depends on the severity of your climate and/or on the architectural compatibility with your home.

You may want a *glass-to-ground greenhouse* if you are particularly interested in growing plants that need headroom, such as sweet peas sown in ground beds or in tubs. Fuchsias, geraniums, lantanas, and chrysanthemums also fit into this category. Rhododendrons, azaleas, and even grapes will benefit from the additional light in a glass-to-ground structure, if you have room for a few specimens.

The *even-span greenhouse* has both sides of the roof of equal size, and its interior floor space gives you the maximum area for growing plants. You can either erect it as a freestanding unit or attach it to one end of an existing building, such as a potting shed. A freestanding unit permits the greatest amount of light and ventilation, but is more difficult to provide with the necessary utilities (water, electricity, and gas or oil). Attaching one end of an even-span greenhouse to your home provides advantages similar to those of the lean-to—maximum light and ventilation, accessibility to the needed utilities, and handiness to the house. If a potting shed is within your budget, attach it to the northern end of your greenhouse. You can build both lean-to and even-span greenhouses with low masonry walls for cold climates or with wooden ones in milder areas. The insulation of solid walls usually is a welcome economy.

*Above:* When positioning a freestanding greenhouse, consider the accessibility to utilities as well as exposure. *Below:* A pit greenhouse is ideally suited to growing alpine plants and is good for propagation purposes.

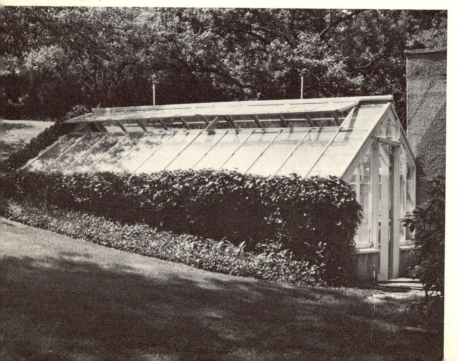

*A top ventilator on a window greenhouse will prevent the buildup of excessive heat on sunny days.*

Variations of the lean-to and even-span greenhouses are available in prefabricated sections for assembly to suit any specialized requirements. A *propagating house* can easily be constructed with prefab sections. You can fit an even-span roof directly upon 4-foot-high solid walls, but you will need to lower the path a foot or two to give sufficient headroom. The area underneath the benches is ideal for the heating units or pipes used to provide the necessary soil warmth. A *pit house* is almost entirely underground. It has an even-span roof and its walls and walk are below grade. The pit house is especially useful for growing alpine plants, as well as other species that benefit from cool conditions. The insulation provided by the surrounding soil permits the growth of plants native to high elevations with a minimum of artificial heat.

*A window greenhouse* will give you an introduction to greenhouse gardening if a full-scale structure is impractical at this time. Stock sizes are available to fit most standard windows, and components can be cut to order for any special situation. A window

*Opening into the living room, a window greenhouse creates a pleasant indoor garden effect.*

greenhouse can open fully to the room where it is located in order to use the existing heat, and you can install an electric heating cable as a supplement. But remember, the smaller the greenhouse, the faster the buildup of temperature and the quicker it will cool off. The window greenhouse, therefore, will do best if you can take time to provide a cooling spray or add a bit of heat during the day.

## Construction

*Foundations* can vary according to local climatic conditions. A solid base to support the walls should go down at least 1 foot below the frost line. In the middle-Atlantic, northwest, and plains states, 3 feet below grade is adequate, while 4 feet might be necessary in New England and the north-central states. Check your local building code. In southern states you can avoid deep foundations and provide merely a solid base to which you attach the frame.

Concrete blocks are the easiest to use for the foundation, but poured concrete or brick and mortar are also satisfactory. If you do not use a deep foundation, bury a coarse galvanized screen (hardware cloth) from wall to wall to keep out rodents.

The *walls* above ground level can be constructed of a great variety of materials, ranging from concrete block and brick through redwood and fiberglass. Mainly you will need to consider what is most compatible with the surrounding architecture and what gives the best insulation.

Greenhouses are being made currently of all kinds of materials— wood, aluminum, steel, polyethylene plastic, and fiberglass. Each has its advantages as well as its drawbacks for specific uses. Greenhouses built of *wood framing* offer a uniform atmosphere, since

*A typical brick foundation is not difficult to build, but be sure the walls are square and level. Each layer of bricks will accentuate any errors.*

*Aesthetically, stone walls seem just right in a woodland setting.*

they do not cool off as quickly or lose their atmospheric humidity as readily as a less absorbent material. Every year you should scrub the interior of any greenhouse to keep down the growth of algae and insects, so a wooden structure is likely to lose its protective coat of paint after a few years. However, redwood and cypress are both long-lasting, rot-resistant woods.

Greenhouse gardeners (usually gadget-oriented people) enjoy the ease with which they can attach things to a wooden frame with no more than screws and a screwdriver. More rigid materials, such as aluminum, call for a metal drill, nuts, bolts, and sometimes a special bracket to mount a shelf or an electric device.

In spite of the relatively low cost and other advantages of wood, the *aluminum greenhouse* is the most practical in the long run. It almost never needs structural maintenance and even the glass is held in place with strips of plastic that seem to last forever. You can order aluminum sections in widths of 2½ feet to complete a house of any length.

*Properly insulated wooden walls will contain the heat and often suit the surroundings better than concrete.*

*Brick walks drink in moisture at watering time and release it slowly to the atmosphere (left), but wooden slats are easier on the feet (below).*

*Above: A prefabricated greenhouse requires a certain amount of adaptation to the site. Below: Then, the walls are fitted in place.*

*Above: The roof panels are installed next.*
*Below: The finished job is a full day's work.*

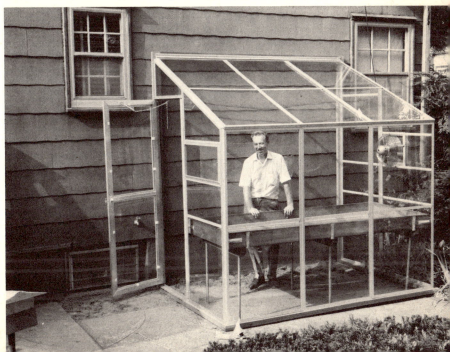

The manner in which the *roof* of a greenhouse is built is only in part governed by the necessary headroom, snow load, and the aesthetics of its shape. The overriding factor is the best angle at which to capture the maximum rays of the sun.

*Glazing* of the modern greenhouse varies little from the technique used in the Victorian era. The ideal is still the largest size of pane that the design will allow, positioned nearly right-angled to the sun during the growing season. Thickness should be governed by the force of winds and weight of any snow load that the glass might carry. All of these factors—size, strength, transmission of light—are considered in the various manufactured greenhouses.

A good professional plumbing installation will assure your greenhouse of a constant water supply regardless of the temperature outdoors.

Fiberglass and rigid plastic, as glazing substitutes, are holding up well and producing fine results after years of testing. They have the advantage of combining good light transmission with great structural strength. The large panels need few overhead supporting members; they allow evenly diffused and virtually shadowless light that is well suited to a wide range of greenhouse plants.

The design of plastic greenhouses has become a major project of departments of many state colleges of agriculture. Engineering

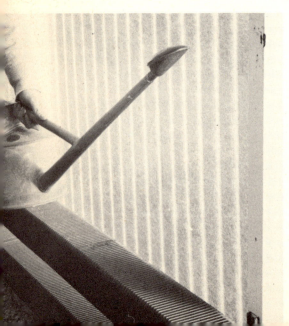

*Fiberglass provides a strong siding and permits the entry of sufficient light for good plant growth.*

*Experimental designs are constantly being developed with an eye to cost, materials, and practicality of use.*

departments have joined in this search for an attractive greenhouse with ingenious design and ease of construction at modest cost. Most of these inventive plans (often free upon request) call for a wood frame placed upon a footing of either poured concrete or cement blocks. Prices estimated by most universities often do not include the cost of the footing or of utilities. Therefore, a "$300 greenhouse" might cost a total of $700 after you add a heating

*This geodesic model can be put up for seasonal use. Further information can be obtained by writing* Popular Science.

unit, frostproof footing, electricity, and water. Of course, the severity of the weather in your locality will be an important factor in these added costs.

Greenhouses for do-it-yourself construction range from traditional designs to the most avant-garde. In most cases the designer has made maximum use of modular units and strong but lightweight materials. This cuts down considerably on the need for professional help in putting the greenhouse together.

Each year new materials and new greenhouse designs are developed for home use and once you have cut through the superficial aspects of their appearance and weighed each of the "working features" for its practicality you will make a choice based on the following: adaptation to your site, adaptation to your climate; durability of materials; ease of use based on layout, dependability, and economy of utilities; and number of automatic monitoring devices.

Even after your greenhouse is in full operation, you would do well to keep your name on file with the various greenhouse manufacturers so that you can receive their catalogs and other periodic publications. In this way, you can keep abreast of new devices for your greenhouse.

*Costs* vary considerably, as they do for most structures. However, roughly speaking, you can buy on a do-it-yourself basis a 13-foot automatically ventilated lean-to (excluding the foundation and heating) for as little as $500. Others of the same length, offering more architecturally pleasing lines and greater usable space (as is found in the freestanding models), are available at $800 to $1,500. Fortunately, most of the larger manufacturers can provide stock parts that you can assemble to fit almost any special requirement of architecture or terrain. Turning a second-floor deck off a bedroom into a plant room-solarium is no more difficult or costly than erecting the more conventional lean-to off the living room or sinking a sun-heated pit house (for growing alpine plants) into a hillside.

The great variety of greenhouse structures allows you to consider your needs and your wants, match them with what is being manufactured, and then come up with the model best suited to you.

# 3

# A Built-in Climate

ONE POPULAR MISCONCEPTION about gardening under glass is that you are attempting to grow plants just as well as they grow under natural conditions. Actually, under natural conditions they really do not grow *that* well. The competition among plants is great, and periodic insect infestations take their toll or reduce the vigor of a great number of plants that inhabit any one ecological niche. So in the greenhouse your goal is actually to improve upon nature and grow a plant to its optimum capacity—something it seldom does in its native, competitive environment. To meet your goal, you must understand the crucial components of the greenhouse environment.

Upon determining the climate you wish to re-create (tropical, temperate, alpine, etc.), you must control four major factors. *Heat* is one factor; you may need it year-round. Whether heat is artificial or from the sun, a thermostatic device is necessary. *Water*, as a part of climate, refers to the humidity of the atmosphere, as well as to the moisture in the soil. Like heat, the humidity must be applied, automatically measured, and controlled. An optimum amount of *air* is also needed for plant growth. *Light* is one of the most difficult factors to measure. Light is not just a matter of brightness; it contains a spectrum of colors (or wavelengths), each having its own special value and each obtainable in a different way. The degree to which you alter any one or more of these factors in relation to the others varies the greenhouse climate. The variation may be of little consequence or it may be one of such importance that it affects growth or even survival of a plant. We will consider each of these factors in this chapter.

I will assume at this point that you have completed the construction of your new greenhouse and have installed the various devices necessary to maintain your plants. The heater and thermostat, the ventilators and their thermostat are all in working order.

If your greenhouse is to operate at a minimum nighttime temperature of 60° for tropical and subtropical plants, the relative humidity will probably be in the vicinity of 65 percent. If the temperature should rise, as it will during the day, you will have to add humidity to the atmosphere, since heat has a drying effect. You can add this needed humidity manually by damping down the walk and under-bench areas with a hose or you can accomplish this automatically with a humidifier preset at the specific requirement. Air, as it cools, holds a decreasing amount of moisture. This moisture, once suspended in the atmosphere, forms droplets on glass, on plant leaves, or on any surface cooler than the air itself. Any sharp drop in temperature will bring about an excess of moisture, which, if left on plant leaves overnight, will soon produce a rash of fungous diseases. Whether you maintain a cool or a warm greenhouse makes little difference. The principle is the same and the reactions are identical—only they occur at different temperatures and you must; therefore, deal with them on a somewhat different schedule.

Here are two tests that you can make for yourself that will result in a better understanding of your greenhouse atmosphere. The flow of air is often too subtle to be felt, but it is easily *seen* if you place a piece of smoldering wood or rope in a tin can at one end of the house. You can observe the course of the smoke when the greenhouse is closed and again when the vents are open. This intimate knowledge of the air movement in your greenhouse will be particularly useful when you position plants that are sensitive to drafts and to temperature changes (which often result from increased ventilation).

Next, record the readings of a few thermometers placed at various locations from one end of the greenhouse to the other, some high above the benches and some close to the floor. The differences in temperatures of three or four thermometers will influence your decisions on which plants to grow and where to grow them. They will also help you determine the changes which are necessary in the environment you are creating.

The addition of light to provide optimum growing conditions is equally critical. Large groups of people live in widely varying conditions around the world, and, to the casual observer, seem to be thriving. However, there is little doubt that a slight change in their diet or living conditions would result in a dramatic change in their metabolism. Likewise with other living forms, such as plants, a varying amount or quality of light can make a world of difference. Each plant species has its own requirements and tolerances based upon its adaptability to its native environment. In many cases, however, a plant can be pushed beyond this point and, with even more light (in proper balance with the other three factors), it can increase its tempo of food manufacture, and therefore grow beyond its norm. Yes, we can improve upon nature if we understand the factors governing plant growth and their interdependence.

## Heat

You want a greenhouse free of worry. That means one which allows you to be away for a holiday in midwinter without wondering if the cold snap killed off your orchids or nipped the buds of your lilies. So, an adequate and dependable heating system is essential.

This glassed-in room represents a climatic microcosm; it can support only that plant life which can complete its entire growth cycle within the conditions you provide. Therefore, you must decide in favor of one of three types of greenhouse—the warm, intermediate, or cool greenhouse. Economics or a proclivity for a certain group of plants determines which you choose.

The *cool greenhouse* is maintained at a minimum nighttime temperature of 45° to 50° and a maximum of 55° during the day. The *intermediate* or *compromise greenhouse* is kept at a minimum nighttime temperature of 50° to 55° and a maximum of 65° during the day. A *warm greenhouse* runs at 60° to 70° at night, with daytime temperatures climbing into the 80's. These are winter limits and you will need the proper heating devices to achieve them. However, too much heat is as fatal as excessive cold, and therefore it sometimes is necessary to install special cooling devices in order to keep temperatures from exceeding safe limits. Fortunately, each range of temperatures has many plants compatible with it—plants which run the gamut of form, texture, and color—so, whatever type of greenhouse you choose can be satisfying. If you have not already made an irrevocable decision with regard to the kinds of plants to be grown, consider the various heating methods and their long-term economics.

Most manufacturers of greenhouses rate the heat requirement of each greenhouse in terms of Btu's (British thermal units). Any greenhouse dealer or heating contractor in your locality can provide you with the Btu output you will need, if you give him the temperature range you must maintain and all the dimensions of your greenhouse. His answer will determine the size of heating unit you need. It does not matter what kind of heater it is—oil, coal, gas, or electric—as long as the hot water or hot air it produces generates the rated number of Btu's.

When you have an idea of the amount of heat you will need, you have to determine what kind of system will produce it most efficiently and economically. The system you end up with should be able to maintain a minimum nighttime temperature 10° above the minimum needs of your plants as a safety factor. Such a system should also have sufficient output to allow for the possible future expansion of your greenhouse.

There are a number of ways of generating greenhouse heat, all of them practical under specific conditions. But, first consider that the method by which the heat is generated in a burner or furnace is separate from the form in which heat is delivered into the greenhouse itself. Oil, gas, electricity, and coal are all heat-producing fuels, available at varying cost depending upon your location. I will rule out *coal* as a home greenhouse fuel for all but those who are close to a supply—and do not mind the soot. *Oil* is often used today in heating greenhouses and can be fed automatically to heat any number of dependable and compact boilers. You can set up such units independent of your home heating system or as an extension of it, with its own set of controls. You will also need access to electricity to activate these controls. In areas where the climate is mild and *electricity* is both

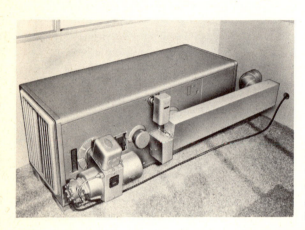

*Left: Modern oil burner units are capable of controlling a warm air system efficiently, at moderate cost. Below: The electric heater is useful for the small cool greenhouse.*

*Below: Gas heaters vent all fumes outdoors and, on the inside, they take up a minimum of space.*

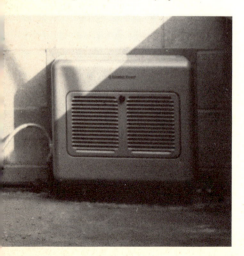

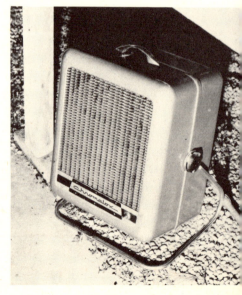

inexpensive and dependable, electric heaters provide the simplest method of heating. In such instances, heating is used to take the extreme chill out of the air and out of the soil at night during four or five months of the year. The fuel gaining most favor today in many areas around the country is *gas*. It is clean, dependable, relatively inexpensive, easy to install (either by a feeder pipe from the local utility company or with tanks of liquid gas), and it will produce heat quickly.

There was a time when gas heat for greenhouses was taboo. The gas fumes were too toxic for plants. However, new units have been developed in recent years which operate on either natural gas or bottled liquid gas, with the combustion chamber sealed off from the rest of the unit in such a manner that the fumes are expelled outside the greenhouse (with no chimney necessary). Low-voltage controls for these gas units operate automatically after you set them at the required levels. The hot air-producing gas heaters do require service from time to time. You also must figure on replacing the unit every few years, since the parts are fairly short-lived, especially in the moist greenhouse atmosphere.

All of these fuels can deliver heat through pipes or ducts to your greenhouse in the form of hot water or hot air. Some do this more efficiently and with less installation cost than others. Hot water, heated by natural or bottled gas or by oil, can be forced through fin-tube radiation throughout the greenhouse and recirculated back to the boiler for reheating. The heat thrown off by a pipe depends only in part upon the temperature of the water running through it. The amount of surface that the pipe exposes is of almost equal importance. For this reason, heat pipes are most often manufactured with a continuous series of fins running along their lengths. With the surface thus increased, they throw off considerably more heat into the greenhouse atmosphere. Fin-tube radiation has the advantage of delivering heat uniformly along the entire length of the pipe and it cools off very slowly. You can incorporate various automated controls in an installation of this kind and thus be set up to handle a reasonable degree of expansion a few years hence. You must also figure into the cost of the system a water tank or boiler, unless you use the system you use for heating your home. If you utilize the existing system, you will need to add some independent controls.

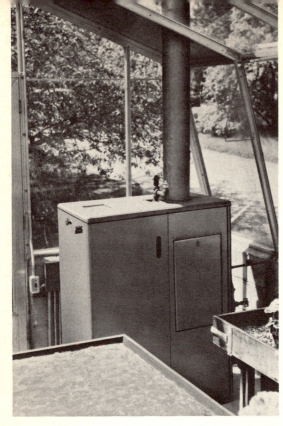

Left: Compact hot water heating systems can be fired either by gas or by oil. Below, left: Fin-tube radiation increases the heating surface, warming the air faster than conventional pipes. Below, right: A thermostatically controlled fan blows across hot water pipes inside this unit, forcing the warmed air into all parts of the greenhouse.

Hot air heating is fast becoming the most favored for use in the home greenhouse. It does not require a water tank or expensive piping. Heated by gas or oil, the air is pulled by means of a fan, either through a metal or plastic duct to the greenhouse or directly from the heat-generating unit situated right in the greenhouse.

Hot air heat eliminates the need for pipes but it creates the need for supplementary humidification. The drying effect of warm, moving air can be offset by a pool of water at the point where the air is expelled or by an automatic humidifier set to operate by its own humidistat. Recirculating waterfalls also can supply this needed humidity and add to the decoration and charm of the greenhouse as well.

Steam boilers are seldom used today in residential heating, and I do not recommend their installation either as a new system for a greenhouse or as an extension of an existing system.

Almost invariably you will come back to considering whatever heating system you use for your home. This is logical, since it is usually cheaper to extend an already existing system to the greenhouse than to install a new one from scratch. (This is especially true when you heat a lean-to or an attached even-span greenhouse.)

Even the best heating system with automatic controls is susceptible to failure. Lack of fuel, a broken electric line, or a sticky valve are but a few reasons for breakdown that make *an emergency alarm system* advisable. If the temperature falls to a dangerously low level on a winter night, or should the ventilator not open on a sunny day when the heat reaches the 90's, a bell hooked up to dry cell batteries will quickly alert anyone at home to the problem.

In the case of a loss of heat, you will need a portable standby heater to take care of the crisis until the necessary repairs are made. Since electric heaters do not operate independently of your house current, they do not meet many of the emergency situations and are useful only as a supplement to your regular system on especially cold nights. For emergencies involving power failure, kerosene or catalytic heaters do the trick.

## Water and Humidity

Water thoroughly but do not overwater; water plants when they become dry. These seem like reasonable statements until you stand there in the greenhouse, watering can in hand, faced with a decision. Then you ask yourself, "How do I know when I'm overwatering?," "How much is thoroughly?," "How do I know whether it's dry?"

You cannot consider watering, as an element of growth, without considering the plant. For example, as most people know, a cactus will not tolerate continuously wet soil. Thus, knowledge of each plant's natural habitat and habit of growth is essential to success. Investigation will reveal the amount of rainfall the plant requires and a still closer look into an encyclopedia of plants will describe the kind of soil it prefers. So, when you pick up the watering can, you should be aware of the needs of the plant, the capacity of the soil, and the variations of both brought about by changes in temperature and light.

**Food travels via water.** Plants require water in order to transport the necessary soluble nutrients from the soil through the roots to the leaves. It is here in the leaves that the additional processes of food manufacture are achieved. An undersupply of water will result either in wilting (which can be quickly overcome by the application of water) or in the plant's death (if the condition of drought is allowed to continue). In most species wilting takes place soon after the level of moisture within the plant drops below normal. This is a visual warning and ordinarily is not dangerous.

Overwatering is a more sinister danger because its effects are not immediately obvious above ground. By the time you see the plant's reactions, some roots have rotted away and the soil, deprived of its aeration, often has become rampant with fungous disease. It is a good idea to tap a plant out of its pot once in a while to inspect the roots and the soil around them. See if the soil mass is moistened throughout (this is what the various electronic moisture-testing devices do, only in a more complicated way).

**Water According to Need.** On bright, sunny days, moisture evaporates through the leaves and is replaced continuously by water being pulled out of the soil through the roots. If replacement moisture is not readily available, wilting will occur. Since it is necessary to pour more heat into the greenhouse during cold weather (cloudy or bright), it is imperative to be alert to the resulting drying effects. However, the plant's slower moisture consumption on mild, cloudy days might call for skipping a day between waterings. Therefore, a set schedule of watering can be dangerous and only a daily appraisal of conditions can tell you what is safe. With experience, you will consolidate all the variable factors into a single, all-inclusive observation.

Fortunately, you can handle most plants pretty much alike— watering them thoroughly when they are dry, but giving them only slightly more water than necessary to moisten the entire soil mass. Too little water will cause an accumulation of soluble salts, which will damage plant roots, while too much will carry nutrients away through the drainage hole, along with the excess water. Certain plants with special water needs, such as orchids, bromeliads, and cacti, will be discussed in the sections devoted specifically to them.

There are a number of ways, both old and new, to tell when and how much to water, but, unless you are running a one-crop greenhouse, they all have some shortcomings. One of the simplest methods of learning when to water is to tap the side of each pot

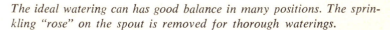

*The ideal watering can has good balance in many positions. The sprinkling "rose" on the spout is removed for thorough waterings.*

with a small wooden mallet—or your knuckle will do. A dull sound indicates sufficient water content, while a ringing sound indicates that the soil is dry. An even more primitive method is the practice of lifting each pot and judging by weight. A dry pot feels lighter than a moist one. This kind of judgment can come only with constant practice. The tensiometer, once feasible only for commercial greenhouses, is now available to everyone in a simplified, inexpensive form. Insert its stem into the soil of a pot and, through an electronic reaction (although no battery or electric current is necessary), the dial indicates wet, moist, or dry soil conditions.

**Watering Devices.** There are a number of watering devices worth having, either as full-time aids or as tools to put in the hands of a neighbor's boy who will take care of your greenhouse when you're on vacation.

*Bench watering systems* are sold in kit form for plants growing directly in the bench soil rather than in pots. A plastic pipe, clamped to the perimeter of the bench, has nozzles which can easily be inserted every 2½ inches. The system is completely automatic and is activated by an electric water valve which, in turn, is controlled by a clocktimer. Thus you can control the number of minutes you water as well as the days of each week.

The *Watermatic system* will do the work for you if a bench contains pot plants exclusively. A hose, constituting the main source of water, has a series of smaller subsidiary tubes that drip small quantities of water into the soil surrounding each potted

*Simple tensiometers translate the moisture content of pot plants.*

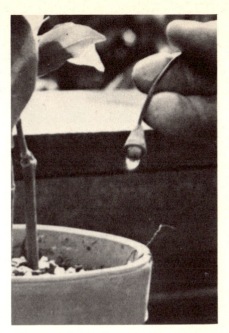

*Below: Automatic watering systems can be set up with spaghettilike tubes leading from a main hose to each pot. Right: When the main water valve is open the perforated lead weight in each pot allows the slow, steady droplets of water to thoroughly moisten the soil.*

plant at a uniform rate and all at the same time. A lead weight keeps the tube in place.

The *constant-level method* of watering flowering plants that are planted directly in the bench is well worth the trouble of construction for the busy person. This technique works upon the capillary principle. The greenhouse bench is constructed with a V-shaped bottom and is waterproofed with plastic or made wholly of cement. The bench is then filled to the top of the "V" with a porous type of gravel—slag does the job nicely. On top of this, add 1 inch of sand and then 4 inches of prepared soil (⅔ garden loam, ⅓ leaf mold or peat moss). Attach a tank next to the bench with a float valve to maintain the water up to the level of the sand. Capillary attraction will do the rest. If liquid fertilizer is needed, just pour it into the tank and it will automatically mix and flow into the bench.

A *watering tray* offers another method for taking care of valuable plants while you are away. This is no more than an oblong frame, 6′ × 2′, that is made of 1″ × 2″ lumber that is laid on edge and nailed together. Drape a sheet of 4 mil polyethylene plastic over this frame so that a trough is formed on the inside. Staple the plastic to the outside edge of the tray. Set it on a wooden shelf and fill it with vermiculite. Then saturate the vermiculite with water. If you place potted plants on the tray they will absorb moisture as it is needed by capillary attraction. A tray will usually hold enough water for about 10 days to 2 weeks. And it is easier for someone to fill a tray with water than to properly water each pot.

The *garden hose* is the easiest device for watering in the summer (when the temperature of the water in the pipes is only moderately cool) or in cases where large numbers of plants are involved. Until very recently, rubber was the only material for greenhouse hoses that did not get brittle when used with cold water. But now there are plastics that stay flexible even at low temperatures and are, therefore, easy to handle. A water breaker (a metal device) on the end of the hose will cut down the force of the stream and eliminate washing soil out of the pot or compacting it excessively. (Compaction reduces necessary aeration.)

Water a potted plant until the water begins to flow from the drainage hole. At this point, the entire soil mass should be moistened and the soluble salts reduced. More water would only create saturation, with water taking the space between the soil particles that should be occupied by air. This would stifle growth and leaves would soon begin to yellow. At times when thorough watering is unnecessary but a syringing is needed to keep up the humidity, replace the water breaker with a fogging nozzle.

Where you do not use mechanical devices, I suggest certain special steps in watering a variety of plant species in the green-house. First, segregate all plants with similar environmental needs, as well as those with the same growth cycle. Plants that normally grow very slowly consume little water, as do those which are native to arid regions. This is also true of plants just entering or in the midst of their dormant periods. Broadly speaking, most cacti bloom, rest, and start into growth at the same time of the year. It is easier to take care of all these plants with minimum water needs at one time and tend to the moisture-loving subtropical plants at another time and in still another area on the bench.

*Water breakers reduce the force of the stream while watering.*

*Above: A water mixer will allow you to use moderate temperatures in midwinter. Below: A quick-coupler allows you to attach lengths of hose in various locations with ease.*

**Winter Watering.** Fill the deep greenhouse sink or some other convenient container with water during the winter so that the next day's water supply will come to room temperature. In winter, water temperature drops sharply and the speed at which plants absorb moisture from the cold soil is reduced considerably. If you have too many plants to make hand watering practical, you will need close at hand a threaded mixing faucet which apportions the right amounts of hot and cold to produce tepid water. Any greenhouse over 12 feet long should have more than one faucet to which you can attach a hose. Couplers make moving the hose from one location to another a quick and simple matter.

**Related Factors.** Water, soil, ventilation, and temperature—all of these are interrelated. The texture of the soil will affect water retention. If your potting mixture contains too much coarse sand, the result will be rapid drainage and minimum retention. In time, all the nutrients will be leached from the soil and starvation will follow. Heavy soil which is not porous enough is equally damaging. A soil texture compatible with the plant's moisture requirements is a necessity.

The kind of pot you use also has a bearing. The nonabsorbent quality of a plastic pot, as compared to clay, makes it essential to segregate the two kinds in the greenhouse so that you can care for each separately. Peat pots, more often used for the first transplanting of seedlings, have much the same characteristic as peat moss used as a garden mulch. When kept moist, it is fine, but if allowed to dry out, it becomes almost impervious to water and roots cannot penetrate its walls as they should.

Ask your local water department to analyze a sample for acidity before you water your plants. If you have hard water—one with an alkaline condition, high in calcium and magnesium—add peat moss to your soil mixtures or add ¼ ounce of ammonium sulphate per gallon of water as a counteractant. *Do not use water softeners.* They merely exchange the undesirable excess of calcium and magnesium for sodium chloride (ordinary table salt), which is a far worse growth retardant. Some plants, such as azaleas, primroses, and certain orchids, prefer an even higher acid condition and call for a greater percentage of peat.

During dormancy a plant should receive only a minimum

*Leaves particularly susceptible to fungous diseases, such as ranunculus and anemones, can be kept off the damp soil by chicken wire supports.*

amount of water. But, with its renaissance, steadily increase the water to keep pace with quickening growth.

**Other Recommendations.** Arrange your plants so that the hose or watering can reaches all of them easily. Use the "rose," or sprinkler, on the spout of the watering can only for watering seed pans, seedlings, or other young or newly potted plants. Apply all other water directly from the spout to the pot, in order to insure filling the "reservoir" to the rim without getting water into the leaf crown. The space between the soil level and the topmost rim of the pot should be sufficiently deep to hold the water needed for one application. Do not spray or broadcast water from overhead. This is especially important in the winter, when water which stands in the plant's crown spells trouble in the form of disease and eventual loss. Also, many flowers are subject to spotting if watered overhead, particularly if the water temperature is lower than that of the greenhouse atmosphere. Even ferns, moisture-loving as they are, resent constant wetting from above. On warm days, it is helpful to wet down the walks and under-bench areas in order to keep up the level of humidity in the air.

Never water so late in the day that droplets remain on the leaves or in the crown of the plant during the evening when temperatures are lower. Such dampness promotes fungous diseases, as I mentioned earlier.

When a plant, for some reason, does not get watered and the soil and the pot itself become dry, it requires more than a thorough dousing. You will find that water will pour out of the bottom drainage hole, yet the soil mass will not be moist. You will need to give the plant two or even three sparse applications to re-create the necessary communication between soil particles and to restore movement of moisture throughout the pot. Remember, too, that a clay pot drinks water. When it becomes dry, the clay literally sucks water out of the soil; so, you must keep a close watch until a neglected plant is back on its regular watering schedule, with a normal amount of moisture in both the soil and the pot.

On hot days with considerable air movement, you will need to

*Left: A portable humidifier will provide ideal moisture content in the air surrounding a group of plants having similar requirements.*

*Right: A humidifier with a large distribution fan will maintain any desired level of humidity for the entire greenhouse.*

*A misting attachment will provide a moist atmosphere and cool down your plants without actually rewatering them.*

replace evaporated moisture by a second watering. This is true also of moisture-loving plants in their period of most active growth. In the summer, damping down the walks and areas under the benches will reduce the loss of water through plant leaves (transpiration) and often will prevent the necessity for a second watering.

## Air and Ventilation

The goal you strive for in ventilation is to provide the maximum amount of air without adversely affecting the temperature or humidity in the greenhouse. In order to insure a complete change of air and avoid a stagnant condition, you may have to add extra heat and moisture at times.

"Adequate air" means that enough of that gaseous ingredient, oxygen, is not only in the air but also in the soil, where it is essential for proper growth. Inadequate air is one of those "limiting factors" I have mentioned.

Of course you cannot "feel like a plant" in order to understand its physiology, but there is a "feel" that you develop in time. Men and plants both breathe, absorbing oxygen and releasing carbon dioxide. In plants, however, the respiration process is accelerated with increased ventilation and moisture must be replaced in order to perpetuate the food manufacturing process. Even in cold weather and at night, fresh air is necessary to promote the release of carbon

*Above: Manually operated ventilators require a "man on duty," but far more control can be exercised with them than with automatic devices. Below: Preset high and low temperature limits will activate ventilators automatically. A second thermostat controls the automatic heaters.*

dioxide into the atmosphere for subsequent use in the process of photosynthesis.

When you construct your greenhouse, be sure to install adequate ventilators—in excess of winter needs—so that you can dispel heat built up during summer days before damaging any plants. During daylight hours, light rays pass through the glass. They are absorbed in the form of heat by the many solid parts within the greenhouse (wooden bench frames, soil, and walks), and this heat is soon released into the atmosphere. Unlike the light rays, heat rays cannot pass out through the glass to escape. This makes adequate ventilation essential, and I recommend automatically controlled devices for the purpose. Even with the vents strategically located and efficiently activated, you will also need shading to reduce the buildup of high temperatures. On a sunny spring day more than 150 complete changes of air are required to maintain the greenhouse temperature at a safe level for plant growth.

You may want to install screens on the ventilators and doors because certain flowers have a great attraction for bees, moths, and butterflies, and, after pollination takes place, the individual blossoms begin to fade rapidly. Orchids, lilies, daffodils, and clivia are among those which are especially affected. This problem mainly concerns the operator of a commercial greenhouse, who figures each flower in terms of profit, but it also concerns the owner of a home greenhouse who has a colony of bees.

Simple hand-operated ventilators usually are alternated along the ridge of the greenhouse and along the sides just above the benches. This arrangement allows for opening only those vents on the leeward side on breezy days. In quiet weather, when cold drafts pose no danger, you can use the ventilators on both sides to provide an adequate change of air. However efficient the hand-operated devices are in avoiding drafts, those which are controlled automatically are certainly superior. They also make it possible for a house to be cooled before severe overheating takes place, since the vents are tied in electrically with a thermostat. When the sun goes down in the afternoon, the ridge vents will react to the lowering temperature and, in closing, will retain much of the accumulated warmth for the nighttime hours.

I am sure you would feel more comfortable if I could say that balancing the ventilation in a small greenhouse is an easy matter;

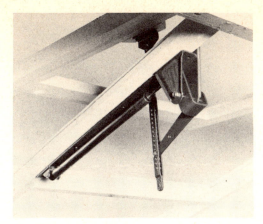

*Nonelectric automatic vent openers are a guarantee against plants being cooked by a hot sun.*

however, it just is not. The smaller the area, the more quickly it heats up and the more quickly it cools off. Much like a cork bobbing in the sea, it reacts violently to any change in conditions. But do not despair—there are mollifying devices and techniques in this age of automation. Even in locations where electricity is not readily accessible, you can install inexpensive automatic ventilators. These operate by the expansion of gases within a cylinder as the temperature increases. This pushes a rod which is attached to the greenhouse ventilator.

In locations where prevailing breezes often are blocked by a building, trees, or the terrain, you can install an exhaust fan (of the type used in kitchens) at one end of the greenhouse near the ridge. If you connect it to a thermostat, it will draw out the warm air quickly until a preset temperature is reached.

Circulating fans also are made especially for greenhouse use to insure the continual movement of air. This is a great deterrent to diseases.

The summer greenhouse is often thought of as a lost cause, for if you fight the hot sun with dense shading, you create leggy growth with a minimum of bloom. Hence, many greenhouse gardeners are turning to air conditioning. This is not the same kind of unit that you would put in your bedroom window. Its cost is comparable, but it works on a different principle. More accurately, it is an evaporative cooler in a metal cabinet, rather than an air conditioner. The entire unit measures approximately 2 feet square and

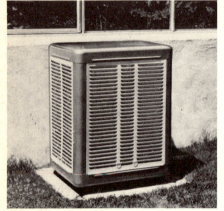

*Above: Air turbulators are designed to move air constantly without creating drafts. Left: Evaporative coolers are compact and virtually trouble-free.*

stands about 3 feet high. You can set the cabinet in the potting shed near an open window or position it outside the greenhouse. Its operation is really quite simple. A drum-shaped fan draws in the warm air from outdoors. It is then pushed through filters which are continually moistened by the constant dripping of cold water. Forced into one end of the greenhouse or under a bench, this now-cooled air replaces the hot summer air, which is pushed out of the top vent, which should be kept open 1 or 2 inches.

It is true that many tropical plants can make it through a hot summer in the greenhouse without much greater trouble or mortality than those at the headwaters of the Amazon. But those orchids found on the cool mountainsides of the Andes—or the hundreds of other plants that thrive upon cooling breezes—will grow and flower to a far greater degree of perfection with the aid of an air conditioner than if you leave them on their own in a hot, stagnant environment. Also, the cooled fresh air will not be as conducive to the breeding of aphids, mealy bugs, etc., as is the warm air.

## Light and Shade

If you have ever tried to grow a house plant in a not-too-well-lighted living room and found the leaves turning brown and dropping off one by one, you have had a fundamental lesson in the importance of sunlight to plant growth. You learn the next lesson, often equally frustrating, when you place the plant on a window sill for still more light. This time, too close to the glass, the plant either freezes or the chill temperature slows down its growth process to such an extent that it continues to lose leaves and soon enters into a dormant state. Once again, the decisive factors of plant growth (temperature, moisture, ventilation, light) have come into play. All these factors are so closely interrelated that it is impossible to consider the importance of one except in the presence of all the others. As I have said, recognizing the symptoms of any imbalance of these factors will help you make the necessary corrections.

The overall growth of a plant is controlled, to a great extent, by the intensity of the light provided. Since the growth-producing foods are created by carbon dioxide and water in the presence of sunlight and in sufficient warmth to stimulate the various reactions, the plant's ability to grow is restricted when the amount of light is restricted. The amount of light needed for proper growth varies greatly from one plant species to another. Some will grow satisfactorily in an environment somewhat different from their native surroundings, but it is a good rule of thumb to provide conditions similar to those found where the plant normally grows. *Plants which flower generally need double the light required by foliage plants.*

Insufficient light affects a plant's ability to utilize nutrients and to regulate its moisture supply. The symptoms of this imbalance do not always show up as clearly isolated deficiencies, but as a combined reaction. Individual symptoms of insufficient light are: elongation of the space between leaf nodes, light-green or yellow-green foliage, underdeveloped flowers, and too few buds.

Should your greenhouse provide insufficient light to satisfy the plants you grow, you can install fixtures with fluorescent tubes or incandescent bulbs to bring up the light level. If too much light is a problem, provide shading of one kind or another for the plants.

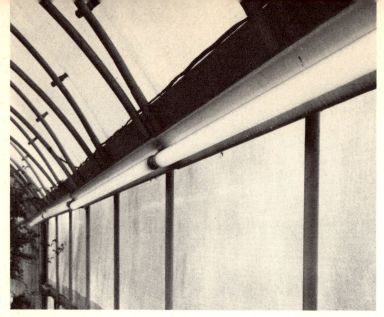

*A strip of fluorescent lights will improve the growth and flowering of plants in an otherwise poorly lit greenhouse.*

It is not difficult to understand that which can be seen or felt readily; for instance, it is relatively easy to detect a 20 percent drop in temperature in the greenhouse—from 60° to 48°—and make whatever adjustment is necessary. However, it is almost impossible to detect a 20 percent drop in light, since the eye usually is not sufficiently sensitive to distinguish between 500 and 400 foot-candles. Therefore, a knowledge of how to take full advantage of all available light often makes the difference between success and failure.

It is essential to recognize the maximum light potential as well as the light limitations of your greenhouse. An east-west-oriented greenhouse will transmit approximately 25 percent more light to the plants than one situated north-south, since it presents more of its surface to the sun at a right angle, and it is at this right angle that the fullest spectrum of the sun's rays passes through the glass to the plants and to the soil. You need to be aware of the arrangement of plants, in relation to the shading they cast upon other plants, and of greenhouse structural components and the shadows they cast (or the light they absorb) to obtain the maximum benefit of the available light. The gradual buildup of algae on the inside of the greenhouse glass, coupled with accumulated soot or dust on the outside, eventually will sacrifice as much as 40 percent of the light. Therefore, you will need to clean the greenhouse glass at least once a year—perhaps in the winter when light intensity is weakest—and even more often if your greenhouse is near a dusty, unpaved road. You can tackle cleaning inside the greenhouse a section at a time, at the season when each can be most conveniently cleared. In a lean-to greenhouse the solid wall will provide the most reflected light if you paint it white and wash it down periodically.

The more light admitted into the greenhouse, the higher the air temperature will be and, by reason of absorption, the higher the soil temperature. During the warmer months, you must give care to this temperature buildup by providing either adequate ventilation, an appropriate shading device, or both, as I have said elsewhere. In winter, the warmth retained by the solid walls and wood furnishings from the day's sunlight will pay dividends by requiring less heat at night. Here again, "balance" is the watchword. Too high a daytime temperature will dehydrate plants and interfere with their flowering. Therefore, the maximum beneficial light for the kinds of plants being grown should be balanced with adequate heat. You will also need to bear in mind that ventilation has both a cooling and drying effect on the atmosphere. Complicated? Perhaps so, but it would be a lot more frustrating to try to maintain this balance without understanding the role of each of its components.

It is helpful to understand certain qualities of light: two which affect plant growth are *intensity* and *duration*. The first, intensity, has to do with the amount of light available in a particular location at one specific time. This can be limited at the site by the surrounding trees, the terrain, or by soot and other air pollutants if you are near an industrial or highly populated urban area. Another limitation may be the position of the glass surfaces in relation to the sun. Light striking the glass at a right angle will pass through it almost intact, as I have mentioned. That is, nearly the full spectrum will be admitted. However, as the angle moves away from the perpendicular toward a parallel, more light will bounce off.

The duration of the light, in whatever intensity is available, is

*Shading compound can be scraped off in strips, which will provide 50 percent more light during the fall and early winter months.*

often determined by the position of your greenhouse in relation to surrounding buildings or by such unalterable conditions as your latitude.

Light intensity is quite a separate factor from light duration. While the former reflects itself in the general condition of a plant, the latter is the switch which, in most cases, triggers bud development or retards it.

Plants such as roses and carnations are insensitive to day length and will proceed with bud development at any time of the year that they reach the proper stage of maturity. Others, like chrysanthemums and camellias, "set," or develop, their buds with the arrival of short days in the fall. Still others, such as most annuals and some perennials, produce their buds with the advent of the long days of spring.

We can simulate these differences in light duration inside the greenhouse by artificial means, so there is no reason why you cannot grow any particular plant insofar as its lighting needs are concerned. I refer, of course, to the use of either the incandescent or fluorescent light. While neither one produces the full color spectrum, as does sunlight, a combination of both kinds produces a satisfactory substitute. Since the heat generated by incandescent bulbs has a drying effect, I recommend using them only in a 1 to

3 ratio with fluorescents. This combination will provide a sufficiently broad spectrum when used as the sole light source, as you might in growing African violets in the basement, or as supplementary light in making up a deficiency or extending day length to force a plant into bloom. When you use artificial light alone, experiment to match it to the needs of the plants you grow.

Rather than go through all the complicated mathematical rigmarole of adapting your photographic light meter to greenhouse use, take a light meter reading outdoors on a cloudless summer day. Then go into your greenhouse and take a reading. This will then become your "control figure," representing the maximum available light. Readings considerably less than this maximum will call either for supplementary artificial light, adjustments in water, amounts of nutrients, or all three.

## Shade

With the coming of spring, when the sun rises higher in the sky, you will need to give greater thought to providing the necessary amount of light and, at the same time, to protecting foliage from excessive dehydration and the burning that would inevitably follow. Shading will reduce evaporation and therefore cut down on the need for as much water, but do not use it as an easy substitute for watering. The sun's rays trigger many processes within the plant and, should sunlight be withheld, various nutritional benefits would also be withheld.

There are various techniques for providing shade to reduce the heat and limit the effect of the sun's rays. Those providing exact control require more of your time and attention. By far the easiest approach is the direct application to the glass of one of the commercial shading compounds or a solution of 4 pounds of white lead and ½ gallon of kerosene to which ⅛ pint of linseed oil has been added (the last ingredient acts as an adhesive and prevents rapid washing off). Apply this lightly as a spray or with a paintbrush in late winter, then add a heavier coating each month as the days lengthen. Then, toward fall, gradually remove the coating with a stiff brush or scrape it off, leaving a striped pattern. Or, if the material is not too tenacious, leave it to wear off in the seasonal rains.

Green vinyl plastic sheeting, for a uniform degree of shading throughout the hot months, is gaining favor. It is sold in rolls and you can cut it to the size of each pane of glass. Apply it by spraying water on the inside of the glass, laying the plastic sheet against it, and squeegeeing the surface to press it on and remove the excess water. These thin sheets remain in place and provide shade until they are peeled off for storage and subsequent reuse.

These foregoing methods have the inherent weakness of providing a constant degree of shading, day to day, in spite of any variance in the existing weather. The ideal, however, is to provide

*Flexible sheets of green plastic are affixed to the inside of the glass to shade the sunny side of greenhouse. The exhaust fan will go on only when heat becomes excessive.*

*Roller blinds can be adjusted according to the weather.*

the maximum available sunshine to plants on cloudy days and still be able to block out the excessive heat that comes with the sun in clear weather. You can accomplish this with a *roller-blind* made of narrow slats, each spaced with a link of chain. If you affix this to the outside top ridge of the greenhouse, you can raise and lower it by hand to the right position in order to get the maximum advantage from the weather. The cost of slatted roller-blinds has been increasing, however, and perhaps this has spurred on the use of saran and fiberglass *screening*. Low in cost, long-wearing, attractive in appearance, and suitable for do-it-yourself installation, these screens can be rigged with ropes and pulleys for easy operation. Ideally, you should leave an air space between an exterior blind and the glass to prevent the buildup of heat, which otherwise would be transferred from the glass to the interior of the greenhouse.

There is always the mechanically oriented gardener who will seek out the newest or the trickiest device to install. In solving the problem of shading, he can have his fun. For example, a per-forated plastic water pipe can be attached to the ridge of the greenhouse roof. A thermostat is then hooked up to an electric solenoid, which will turn on the water valve when the air in the greenhouse reaches any given temperature. A film of water from the pipe cools the glass and also breaks up the sun's rays which seek to enter. You can attach a similar device to venetian blinds to close them as the sun becomes stronger during the day.

Occasionally, one particular part of the greenhouse, such as the propagating bench or a few pots of tuberous begonias, needs more shading than another. Handle this special situation by hanging a piece of burlap or brown wrapping paper inside the greenhouse. Such interior shading does little to keep down the temperature but will effectively check the burning rays of the sun.

There is another way to shade plants by the judicious placement of one in the shadow of another. Often this simple procedure spells the difference between optimal and marginal growth. The crux lies in the accurate determination of the amount of light needed by any specific plant and in providing it. Plants, both in their native state and in the greenhouse, are constantly vying for their share of available light. In the greenhouse this competition normally is the result of three hard-to-overcome habits of the grower: sowing too many seeds (". . . there was a *whole* packet,

*Plastic screening stretched over the frame keeps heat from reaching glass.*

and what could I do with the excess, anyway?". . .), not discarding excess seedlings, and trying to grow a mélange of plants
which varies too greatly in cultural requirements. When the plants
cannot compete successfully with one another, light becomes a
limiting factor, resulting in spindly or stretched-out appearances.

If I did not have a shading device that could be adjusted to the
changes in the weather, I would prefer to shade my plants somewhat all day long and sacrifice a portion of light on dull days,
since no shade at all would surely spell disaster. It is here that a
matter of "degree" is important, for plants given excessive summer
shading will develop soft, thin leaves which will be unable to take
in moisture easily. Such plants often do not live through the winter.
This brings us back to the fact that the right amount of shading
is the minimum amount that your plants need to keep them free
from excessive water loss and burning. The only answer, therefore,
is in knowing your plants—their native habitats and growth cycles.

### Which Climate for Your Greenhouse—Warm or Cool?

This is a question you will need to answer before you begin construction. Your answer might be determined by economics.

In areas of low temperatures, it is more costly to build a warm
greenhouse, because you need walls that provide better insulation
from the cold. Also, if you choose a warm greenhouse you can
expect to spend more on the heating unit and on fuel.

Your plant preferences will be another factor. I suggest you
study the lists of "warm" and "cool" plants (see pages 168-173)
to find your favorites before you decide.

**The Warm Greenhouse.** A tropical atmosphere, created in the
greenhouse, opens the way to growing a large and most interesting
variety of plants. However, when the word "tropical" comes to
mind, naturally you may conjure up an image of warmth, humidity,
and sunshine. All of these are part of the tropical scene, but not
necessarily at all times or all together in one place. The tropics
have their rainy and dry seasons, and regions of tree-shaded forests
and sun-drenched savannahs. The variety of terrain and the climates associated with each are reflected in the indigenous plant
life. Your success in growing tropical plants, therefore, will depend

upon your willingness to learn about the requirements of each one and to cater to its needs.

A practical grouping also may include plants of the subtropics, those regions in both the northern and southern hemispheres that are immediately adjacent to the tropics. Their characteristic climate is more tropical in character than the temperate regions. The southern portions of Florida and California are good representative examples of subtropical regions, where a great variety of tropical plants have been introduced and cultivated successfully. This broadened aspect of the warm greenhouse includes minimum nighttime temperatures ranging from 58° to 70°; of course these lower limits are more subtropical than tropical. Daytime temperatures often can run into the 90's without harm if you provide shade, ventilation, and humidity as needed.

**The Cool Greenhouse.** In commercial greenhouses the "cool" house is the one that receives just enough heat to keep out the frost—its temperature sometimes gets up to 45° or 48°. If the temperature goes up to 55° it is called an "intermediate" house. In my listing on pages 168-173, I have combined plants which tolerate a cool and intermediate environment just as I combine tropical and subtropical plants for the "warm" greenhouse. Therefore, the cool greenhouse should be considered as having a temperature range from 45° to 57°.

The plants that you can grow in the cool greenhouse can be as equally exotic as those in warm temperatures. Consider the alpines, cacti, and orchids of the high-altitude regions and you will find just as diverse and fascinating a collection of plants.

No doubt you will come across a number of plants that could grow just as easily in a cool corner within a warm greenhouse as they could in a warm spot of a cool greenhouse. Such borderline cases eventually will tempt you to experiment—and perhaps suffer your share of failures by "pushing" a plant a bit too far. You can add such exceptions to your repertoire after you have gained a measure of experience with the clear-cut selections.

# 4

# Arrangements
# and Furnishings

As you plan the basic structure of the greenhouse, consider its interior layout. To a large measure this will be dictated by your horticultural interests and by the amount of time you can devote to actual gardening—the gratifying pursuits of scheduling, propagating, growing, arranging, and rearranging.

There are certain basic elements with which you must work—plant benches, plant stands, ground beds, walls, shelves, and brackets for hanging plants—all of which you can juggle to fit your situation. It should be possible to reach every plant easily and work with all of them from a comfortable position. Therefore, I recommend a bench width of 36 inches; the height will be governed by that which is most comfortable for you—32 to 36 inches is about right, depending upon how tall you are. An island bench (one that you can walk around) can be 4½ feet wide and still be fully accessible.

For benches, the materials currently available range from wood to cement to wire. Each has its advantages. Redwood is both long

*Of course, a roomy potting shed with storage space for soil, fertilizers, chemicals, tools, and pots makes chores easier.*

lasting and capable of holding considerable amounts of moisture. Transite (a cement product) will not rot and therefore is the most popular material in use today. Hardware cloth, a heavy wire mesh, is best for staging pots of orchids. The free movement of air through its open construction allows for the installation of a humidifier below the bench. Any excess from daily watering drains away easily through the wire mesh, which keeps insect nesting places to a minimum.

You can arrange *plant stands* as a grandstand or series of steps. Place them against a wall, presenting but one exposure to the sun, or, locate them on a center bench, where each side will receive its share of light. This device often makes a fine display table for plants currently in flower, although tall ones, such as fuchsias, clematis, geraniums, or trellis-trained tubbed bougainvillea, need the extra headroom afforded by a ground bed.

*Above: Redwood benches are still the most serviceable for pot plants.*
*Below: Transite, a cement product, makes an excellent rot-proof bench.*

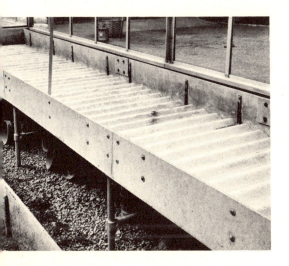

*A grandstand arrangement provides each plant with more light and allows closer inspection.*

*Above: Hardware cloth, instead of solid benches, insures air circulation and water drainage in otherwise warm greenhouses. Right: Walls are good for storing utilities and sundries.*

*Nasturtium is but one flowering vine that is useful in framing a doorway or screening a partition.*

You can create an atmosphere of permanence in the greenhouse by using vines, ground covers, and even a water feature emerging right out of the ground, such as a pool, a simulated stream, or a waterfall. Do not overlook the house wall of a lean-to or the end wall against a potting shed as a valuable support for permanent climbers—grapes, allamanda, or lapageria. Annuals, such as sweet peas or nasturtiums, display equally well on such a wall or can frame a doorway.

A variety of *shelves* helps "stretch" the greenhouse walls during the year's most active periods. Those made of wood, glass, or metal, supported with either permanent or temporary brackets, get the spring seedlings up to the light or make room for flats of daffodils forced in midwinter.

*If the plants are supplied with the proper soil, adequate nutrition, and daily watering, a hanging basket of great beauty will be sure to follow.*

*Hanging containers* are great for plants with a pendant, clambering, or trailing habit. They add beauty to otherwise unattractive overhead areas and they represent the best way to grow and display certain plants that usually choke out their neighbors. Wire baskets, tree-fern slabs, and redwood rafts are often used as planters; hang them between the ridge and the eaves, planted with bright flowers which often go unseen on the floor.

Who has not rearranged his living room at least once? Why not rearrange the greenhouse? A change will give rise to new inspiration

*Above: Slabs of tree fern are good anchors for orchid roots. Below: Temporary glass shelving takes care of extra plants without cutting down on the available light.*

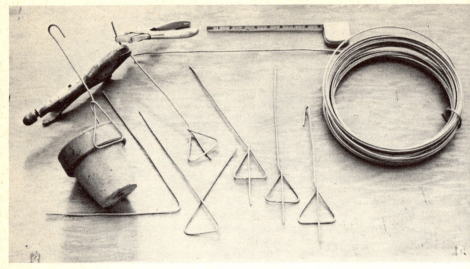

*Above: Two pairs of pliers and a coil of galvanized wire are all that is necessary to make a supply of handy hangers. Below, left: Wire hangers not only get plants above pot-filled benches but allow maximum air circulation. Below, right: Slip-on shelf brackets handle periodic overcrowding.*

and, indirectly, will introduce you to new groups of plants. I have gone through many stages, from the conventional three-bench, two-aisle arrangement with plants grown directly in the soil, to ground beds and a pool (which now permits me to play with some of the interesting aquatic plants). Whatever the arrangement you settle on, *do not* let the construction be so permanent that you cannot expand or follow a new approach in some entirely different direction.

## Supplementary Structures

Space soon becomes a premium commodity in any greenhouse, but before you expand beyond the greenhouse walls, consider the following possibilities.

**Can You Hang the Overflow from the Roof?** If you check the catalogs of leading greenhouse builders, you will find that fixtures are available to support overhead shelves. It is likely that you will only need to use these on a seasonal basis. That two-month period in the spring, following the germination of seeds in pans, finds wooden flats filled with neatly spaced transplanted seedlings waiting for the danger of frost to pass. It is in this preparation for outdoor planting that temporary shelves are most useful.

**Should You Build a Cold Frame?** This is the simplest auxiliary structure—a wooden frame set above ground level, with cement block or a similar impervious material below the soil level and a slanting, glazed top that is removable. I recommend that you position your cold frame facing south and adjacent to one wall of your greenhouse. This will protect it from the most severe winter winds and it will be convenient. Whether it is permanent or portable, the ideal size for one unit is about 3 feet wide by 6 feet long—not so large that lifting the top becomes a chore. Inside, the cold frame should be deep enough to provide headroom for plants of various sizes. A good average would be 12 inches at the front and 18 inches along the back. If you plan to winter-over taller plants, such as azaleas, there is no reason why a depth of 5 feet is impossible, provided there is adequate drainage. The sloping top will help achieve a better light-gathering angle. The pitch of the

*Above: Thick wood and a few extra inches in depth help to insulate a permanent cold frame—an invaluable asset in rooting hardwood cuttings and providing the necessary dormancy prior to flowering hardy plants and bulbs. Below: A lightweight portable cold frame helps "harden off" garden plants in early spring.*

top is never sufficient to lessen the snow load, nor is it necessary for a surface of such small size to do so.

Should you glaze your cold frame covers with plastic, use a rigid or semirigid material, such as Mylar or fiberglass, rather than polyethylene. This will make an easy-to-lift cover while providing the strength to withstand any snow, hail, rain, or falling twigs.

Your use of a cold frame will vary with your needs and ingenuity. It will provide additional space in the spring, when seedlings for the outdoor garden have been transplanted and need growing room as well as gradual hardening. If you use it with a cover of lath (instead of the glazed top) to reduce the effects of burning sunlight, you can summer a number of greenhouse plants in the cold frame. It is particularly useful as a storage place for potted bulbs, azaleas, hydrangeas, and other semiwoody plants— providing the dormancy necessary until new growth occurs or specially timed flowering is desired. Biennials, used as potted plants in the winter greenhouse, are best started from seed in late July. Then, after transplanting, you can grow them in the cold frame until you must bring them back inside in late November or when cold weather arrives. Pansies and English daisies are two that you can handle in this way.

A cold frame used during summer and fall will be subject to considerable changes in temperature and, therefore, you will have to open it often—sometimes raise the top a mere crack and other times remove it completely: You cannot use a shading compound on the glass or needed light will be lost on cloudy days, so keep a pail of sand handy and sprinkle a few handfuls over the glass when you need to reduce excessive sunlight. In dull weather, you can brush off or spill the sand easily by tipping the cover.

**Should You Transform a Cold Frame into a Hotbed?** You can use a hotbed effectively during the early spring and take the pressure off of the greenhouse, when a cold frame is not yet safe enough for flats of new seedlings. Use a hotbed again in the fall for biennials. Their active growth would stop in the cold frame, but they will thrive in a hotbed and allow you to bring into the greenhouse a few pots at a time for forcing.

Transforming a cold frame into a hotbed requires only the addition of an electric heating cable, with a self-contained ther-

mostat. Commercial greenhouses extend their steam pipes to provide heat within these frames; however, the lead- or plastic-covered cable is the least expensive heating method for the amateur. A $20 investment will give you several years of service. Bury the cable about 6 inches beneath the surface of the soil and cover it with a piece of heavy galvanized screen to prevent it from being cut accidentally with a trowel.

Remember, a hotbed is not supposed to be an intermediate or warm greenhouse for growing tropical plants. The cable will heat the soil so that it never freezes, but the air under the glass cover still will be chilly on a near-zero winter night, so a covering of some kind is necessary. Reed mats or quilted canvas mats are best.

**Should You Build a Lath House?** This is the structure I would least like to do without. It is a most helpful adjunct to the greenhouse during the hottest months of the year—it protects plants and spreads out the growing area.

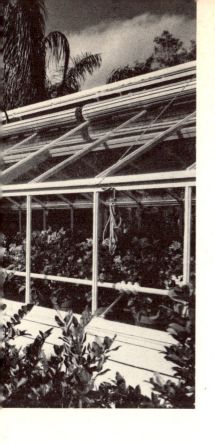

*A lath house can be the luxurious component of a greenhouse complex (left), a forthright, practical structure, nearby (below), or an extension at the end of the potting shed (bottom).*

A simple lath house need be only a few lengths of snow fence stretched over four stakes driven in the ground with enough head-room to give you easy access to your plants or you can make your lath house a decorative structure, with sitting room as well as plant room. The interior should include hooks for hanging baskets, stands for potted plants, shelves for flats, and graveled space for tubs. I like to keep plants off the ground so that they remain as free as possible from snails, slugs, and crawling insects. By keeping plants above the gravel, I can drench the ground heavily with an insecticide from time to time.

I enjoy my plants in my lath house during the summer in much the same way as I enjoy them in my greenhouse in the winter.

### The Greenhouse as a Sitting Room

Your greenhouse need not look like a production line for plants; it can be aesthetically pleasing. Thanks to the ingenuity of green-house manufacturers, a greenhouse owner need not necessarily be a greenhouse gardener. As inconsistent as this may sound, it *is* true. The number of solaria, conservatories, or just plain sun-rooms that have been attached to existing houses or planned into new ones increases each year. This renaissance of a Victorian custom makes it possible for us to enjoy our leisure in verdant beauty.

The greenhouse, as a sitting room, provides a scaled-down "piece of an environment" in which to read the Sunday paper, absorb the warmth of the sun on a winter afternoon, or entertain friends amid the fragrance of growing plants.

First, define your sitting area, making it large enough for two chairs and perhaps two pull-up stools, a round table or a small utility table. When you arrange the furniture, take into account the winter exposure to the sun—that will be important if you work into the setting a canopy of plants. You will need some convenient method of providing maximum sunlight in cold weather and shade in warm weather. This rules out shading compounds you apply directly to the glass and suggests the use of adjustable roller blinds.

*This is not a Moorish garden but a greenhouse sitting room.*

*A garden, a pool, and an entertainment area all under one greenhouse roof.*

Good ventilation is essential to your comfort in the sitting room and to the health and vigor of the plants you grow. This means you will need ventilators you can regulate by hand, as well as those which are automatically controlled. Specifically, you need to maintain a flow of fresh air and avoid drafts—hot and cold; so position your heating device, whether blower or pipes, to provide an even temperature without drying currents of air.

Turn next to the basic camouflage. The materials you use should be compatible with the majority of plants you will grow. Cork-bark wraps for posts and bench legs will make a far more suitable background for climbing tropical plants than preformed and color-toned concrete. For partial shade, make a "tree" of bent or welded pipe and cover it with cork bark. Stuff it with osmunda fiber and it will make an ideal support for bromeliads and orchids. Do not

*Above: It takes a little courage to tear things apart in order to create a greenhouse sitting room. Below: The planting takes a few months to take hold.*

*Left: A little
excavation, some
wire reinforcement,
a mixture of
waterproof cement
and . . . Below: . . .
presto—a garden
pool. Opposite: Add
a recirculating pump
and some plants to
the garden pool and
you can enjoy a
whole new tropical
environment.*

camouflage or conceal your thermostat too well! It operates accurately only when there is free air movement around it.

Do not settle for conventional arrangements of potted plants—row-upon-row on benches. Variations in heights are far more interesting, and you can achieve this by an arrangement of steps along with a ground bed. Add drama to the room with a small free-form pool surrounded by rocks and planting pockets.

You can create a wall of plants along the north side by providing height with appropriately shaped plants and by cascading

*An indoor garden is practical when proper materials are used. Note the brick wall to exclude excessive moisture from the living area.*

vines and hanging baskets from the rafters or ventilator supports. None of these effects need be accomplished with plants selected principally for their flowers. Use foliage plants as the predominant background, accenting it with the color of occasional flowering "gems." Place a fragrant plant here and there to add an extra dimension.

I suggest using the opposite wall (the south side of the greenhouse) in an even more vertical manner. Make a "sandwich" of moss, holding it together with chicken wire, and attach it to the

*Above: A lean-to opening into your living room easily creates the illusion of an indoor garden. Below: a mini-greenhouse also brings you closer to your plants.*

greenhouse wall. This contrivance offers the ideal conditions for a great many plants that enjoy a moist and shady situation. It helps transform your greenhouse into an exotic place.

## The Indoor Garden

The flower room, the conservatory, the sun porch—they are all adaptations of an indoor garden. A greenhouse, built as an integral part of the living area and opening into it, adds a special dimension to your home in the city, in the suburbs, or in the country.

This kind of a sitting room is most effective when you plan it as a place in which to relax rather than as a conventional working greenhouse. You might best display in your plant room a few flowering specimen plants set off by those with attractive foliage, a dramatic vine for winter bloom, or a cluster of fragrant orchids.

No matter where you live there are problems to overcome or problems to be avoided by proper planning. First, you must provide *moisture* for the plants without making the atmosphere uncomfortable for people. A brick floor (with properly positioned drains), a low wall partially separating the adjoining room, or a step-down into the flower room will help keep the moisture within the garden. Stay away from inlaid wood furniture and decorate only with materials suited to above-normal humidity. Even the electrical outlets should be of the waterproof variety. Next you need a source of *heat* to provide the desired temperature most efficiently and economically. The possibilities include baseboard fin radiation or under-the-floor radiant heat.

# II. Pleasurable Routines

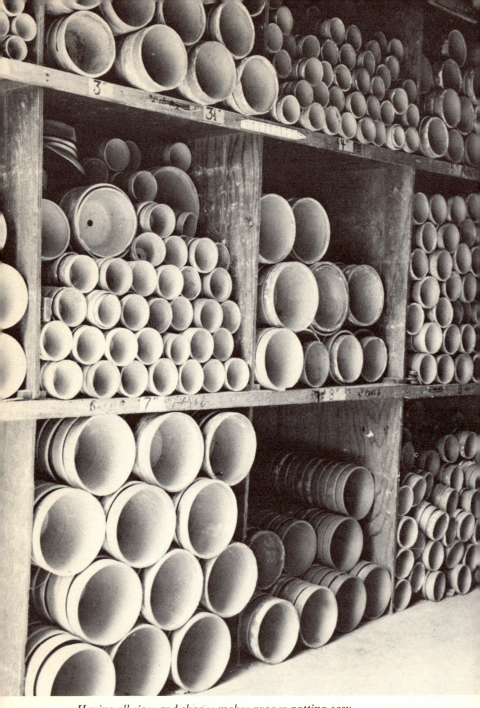

*Having all sizes and shapes makes proper potting easy.*

# 5

# Pots, Potting, and Potting Mixtures

THE MAJORITY OF greenhouse plants spend most of their productive years in pots. Therefore, the types and sizes of the pots you use, the materials of which they are made, and the techniques of potting are important.

**Types of Pots.** The size of a pot is indicated by its inside diameter, and the standard pot has an inside diameter which is equal to its depth. You will find that you can fulfill most of your needs with these standard pots. The sizes you are most likely to use will range from 2½ to 7 inches. You may need larger pots or tubs for big specimen plants.

Special containers, such as hanging baskets, boxes for display, and cachepots for the adornment of working pots, will also inevitably become part of your inventory from time to time.

Many bulbs and shallow-rooted plants do best in pots of less than standard depth. Commonly available pots include: azalea or three-quarter pots (¾ of the standard depth); bulb pans, which

*Above: Clay, peat, paper, and plastic—these are the materials. The shapes are even more varied. Below: Molded feltlike cubes make transplanting chores and ultimate planting or repotting extremely simple.*

are still shallower; and seed pans, which are approximately 3 inches deep. You can get saucers for all sizes.

Clay pots are the most common, but plastic ones are increasingly favored. A traditional clay pot has a porous wall and a hole in the bottom, both of which help to assure an adequate supply of oxygen and provide drainage and evaporation. Plastic inhibits evaporation through the walls, but it makes a far lighter pot than clay and takes less bench or shelf space. It is less fragile and is more easily stored.

Pots made of pressed peat are useful for sowing seeds and growing plants in their early stages. They are available in a great variety of sizes and shapes, including preformed egg-crate-style trays. They are the lightest and most compact of all. However, unless they are thoroughly moistened, they will compete with plant roots for water.

I am partial to the traditional clay pots, probably because they "speak to me"—through their color, weight, and even through the moss or salt deposits that grow upon them. All of this tells me about the amount of water the plant is receiving, the kind of drainage, and the quality of the water I am using.

**First Potting.** Pot size is critically important when a bulb, seedling, or rooted cutting is given its first potting. The pot must allow for the proper depth and width of soil in which the roots can perform the basic functions of anchoring the plant and gathering the optimum amounts of water, nutrition, and air. You might think that as long as a pot is big enough to hold the roots, it could scarcely be too big except for reasons of convenience, but this is *not* the case. Too big a pot may well kill the plant through excessive moisture and a consequent deficiency of oxygen—in other words, it may die by suffocation. Therefore, as a rule of thumb, select the size pot that will allow about an inch of space each side of the roots.

A seedling is ready for its first potting when it is on its own— that is, when its leaves have begun to develop and it is no longer dependent for nourishment on its cotyledons—those two halves of the seed best seen in the bean or peanut. This means its roots can now take over the gathering and distribution of food to its own system. The seedling is now ready for a 2½- or 3-inch pot. The pot

*Upper left: A rooted cutting ready for first potting.*
*Upper right: Molded plastic, a new substitute for broken crockery, to promote drainage.*
*Lower right: Firming soil with fingertips forces out air pockets and puts soil in closer contact with the roots.*

should be clean and you should soak it thoroughly in water before you use it. (If used dry, clay or peat pots will literally suck the moisture out of the soil to the detriment of the plant.)

Place a 1-inch-square piece of window screen against the hole of the pot to prevent snails, slugs, or other crawling insects from entering or nesting in the bottom. Next, put a piece or two of a broken clay pot (called *crock*) over the wire guarding the drainage hole; be certain that the bottom piece does not lie so flat that no water can pass through. You can also get molded plastic pieces to serve the same purpose as crock. Follow the crock with an inch of coarse soil. Then position the young plant in the center of the pot; hold it there with its roots spread over the little mound of soil. Now add more and finer soil—soil with similar characteristics to that of the plant's native environment. Put the soil in between, around, and over the roots; fill the pot to the rim. When you firm the soil with both thumbs, it will end up about even with the bottom of the rim, leaving a convenient reservoir for daily waterings.

*A pot that is too large or too small (left and right) will result in poor growth. Properly potted (center) the relationship of soil to water retention and adequate room for new roots will produce optimum results.*

*Above: When roots become pot-bound most plants tend to flower poorly. Right: Another alternative, the peat pot, is excellent for good root growth, if kept moist. When roots penetrate the pot wall, the plant is ready for transplanting outdoors or into a larger permanent pot for greenhouse use.*

**Repotting.** There are two reasons for repotting; one is that the plant has outgrown its container and the other is that the soil has broken down and its texture has become compacted. Soil should be a porous medium into which tender new roots can grow and absorb the needed nutrients.

Make a periodic inspection of plants to see if they are being watered properly (turn a plant out of its pot to see if there is uniform moisture throughout); or if it has proper drainage (no evidence of rotted roots, soggy soil, or a mossy surface); or if any plants are pot-bound (masses of roots filling the inside of the pot). When repotting seems advisable, choose the right size and the right shape of clean, presoaked pot. Deep-rooted plants or those having a taproot should go into standard pots, while bulbs or shallow-rooted plants do best in pans or the three-quarter pots mentioned earlier.

In general, you follow the same procedure for repotting as for the original potting, with one addition: when you repot a plant, pick away some of the old soil from the roots with a sharp stick (a label, pencil, or your fingers will do). This will enable you to place

*In repotting, allow for good drainage. The piece of screen on the bottom of the pot prevents damage from slugs and other chewing insects.*

new soil, charged with nutrients, near the roots, where they will be useful immediately. It will also help to improve the texture of the soil. If you allow the old soil ball to remain intact and add new porous soil, the difference in the two media will cause water to flow through the pot via the new soil, while that closest to the plant roots will remain dry. Eventual symptoms of starvation may come too late to give you a chance to correct the condition.

**To Repot or Not.** I have always felt that there must be a few hard and fast guidelines for deciding when to repot. Perhaps the closest I can get is to say that there are certain plants that should be continuously repotted as they outgrow their pot; there are those which resent being disturbed no matter how tight they seem to be jammed in their containers; and there are still others that resent being disturbed, but also react unfavorably to being pot-bound. To list every plant in each category seems close to impossible, but, to make your repotting easier, an indication of special potting requirements is included in the plant biographies (see Chapter 21).

## Potting Mixtures

The matter of the proper soil for greenhouse use is never simple. However, the most useful tool is an understanding of some of the basic concepts. You can then make the proper adaptations.

**The Basic Soil.** Broken-down rock and decayed matter, which form soil, provide both primary support and a source of nutrients for plants. The ratio of mineral (rock) to organic (decayed) matter is one key factor in assaying the available nutrients and the moisture-retention qualities of a particular soil. The aeration afforded by the texture of the soil particles determines, to a large extent, the degree of development (or lack of it) in a plant. Sand, as you may know, is made up of brittle mineral particles, irregularly round, that permit ready access to air and water. Clay, at the other end of the range of textures, is made up of flattened mineral particles that mass tightly together and permit little passage of either air or water. For a plant to have the various necessary nutrients delivered to it, a proper balance of pore space and solid matter is essential. Large pore spaces, from materials such as coarse builder's sand, provide little or no capillary value for the passage of water, but they do provide space for much-needed air. On the other hand, small pore spaces make capillary attraction feasible, much in the same manner that water will span the open spaces across the mesh of a fine screen. It is by capillarity that water is carried throughout the soil to the roots of the plants.

**The Theoretical Ideal.** The ideal proportions of these foregoing elements for optimum plant growth (if ever there were but one soil to choose for general greenhouse use) is ¼ noncapillary pore space, ¼ capillary pore space, and ½ solid matter. These proportions can be adjusted by raising or lowering the sand content of the soil mixture. However, if you add sand or any inert material for the purpose of varying the texture, also add a similar quantity of organic matter to offset the loss of water retention.

**That Old Devil, pH.** pH is the symbol representing the degree of acidity or alkalinity in the soil. A measurement of 7.0 indicates a neutral reading. Numbers less than 7.0, graduated down every ½ percent (6.5, 6.0, 5.5, 5.0, 4.5, etc.), reflect increasing acidity. Numbers above 7.0 show an alkaline condition; the higher the number, the greater the alkalinity.

Adjustment of the soil's acidity is often necessary, since every plant has its preference as to the kind of soil in which it grows best. So how do you test the soil? You can buy a kit from most garden stores. The kit requires you to add a liquid chemical to a

*A pH test of your soil will alert you to any necessary corrective measures.*

small sample of soil, drain off the fluid, and match its color to that on a numbered chart. This numbered color chart indicates the degree of alkalinity or acidity of your soil, or in other words, the pH.

Ground agricultural limestone will safely correct an overly acidic condition. You can also use hydrated lime, but its action is quicker and, therefore, you will have to handle it more carefully. You can add sulphur in powder form (a few ounces per bushel) to lower the pH reading in an overly alkaline soil.

**The Importance of Texture.** The kind of soil mixture in which a plant grows best is governed by the soil texture and the resultant ability to hold moisture. Any specific plant in its natural habitat

*Below: With a supply of a few basic ingredients, soil mixtures of various textures can be concocted. Right: The orderly storage of ingredients for soil mixtures, fertilizers, and insecticides is essential.*

can meet its needs by drawing upon a deeper reservoir of moist soil as evaporation takes place from the ground surface and from the plant's own leaves. However, a potted plant is exposed to almost constant evaporation from the top of the soil and from all sides of the pot as well. Therefore, you must formulate the soil to compensate for this need for daily watering.

**The Well-Textured Medium.** A good utility mixture would be composed of ½ garden loam, ¼ leaf mold, ⅛ dehydrated cow manure, and ⅛ coarse builder's sand. Turn and "fold in" the ingredients until they are well mixed, but do not break down the particles to too fine a texture.

Sand should be a medium-to-coarse washed builder's sand. It

will vary in color from one part of the country to another, but do not use the white seashore sand. It is usually too fine and contains too much salt. Sand will loosen most heavy soils and improve the drainage, but add peat moss to loosen clay soils instead of sand, since sand added to clay results in a cementlike soil.

To make a soil less porous, so that it can hold more water, add peat moss or leaf mold. This will increase the soil's acidity, so it will then be necessary for you to add a sufficient quantity of ground limestone to offset the change.

The spongy makeup of the leaf mold will provide good water retention, and the coarse sand will prevent the loam from caking and becoming an airtight mass. The manure will give the newly potted plant a nutritious start; and a few chunks of pure wood charcoal, placed at the bottom of each pot, will absorb excess acids and keep the soil sweet.

**Matching Mixture to Plant.** In a greenhouse, it is possible for you to vary the proportions of these basic ingredients to match the needs of any plant. So the first step is to learn what kind of soil your plants need. While it is certainly possible to work out specific recipes for any number of plants, your study may reveal that no more than two or three kinds of soil are really necessary. Where there is a special soil preference for the plants discussed in this book, it is found in Chapter 21.

Sometimes a clue to the best soil for a plant is found in its specific name. Thus, *Prunus maritima* is indigenous to a maritime or seaside region where the soil probably would be sandy; while *Aquilegia alpina* would do best in a mountainous, rocky soil.

**Sources of Soil.** Where do you start? You can begin with a medium garden loam as a base. Without meaning to mimic Goldilocks, I would describe a medium garden loam as a topsoil from the garden that is not too sandy, not too heavy with clay, and not too rich in humus, but just in-between. To this basic loam, add sand to increase the drainage or peat moss to decrease the drainage.

Here are recipes for preparing your potting mixtures:

The basic ingredients are:

1. *Screened garden topsoil*
2. *Peat moss*
3. *Leaf mold and/or compost*
4. *Coarse builder's sand*

To each bushel of any soil mixture add one heaping 6-inch potful of dehydrated cow manure and one heaping fistful of bone meal. These last two ingredients are available at most garden centers.

| HEAVY MIXTURE | POROUS MIXTURE | HIGHLY POROUS MIXTURE |
|---|---|---|
| ⅓ Screened garden topsoil | ½ Screened garden topsoil | ⅔ Screened garden topsoil |
| ⅓ Peat moss | ¼ Peat moss | ⅓ Coarse builder's sand |
| ⅓ Leaf mold and/or compost | ¼ Coarse builder's sand | |

ORGANIC MIXTURE
⅓ Screened garden topsoil
⅓ Peat moss
⅓ Coarse builder's sand

HIGHLY ORGANIC MIXTURE
¼ Screened garden topsoil
⅛ Peat moss
½ Leaf mold and/or compost
⅛ Coarse builder's sand

## Pasteurization of Soil

Once the texture has been established, make up a sufficient quantity of soil for your immediate needs plus a reasonable supply to keep on hand.

Any problem of disease or insects found in one flowerpot in a small greenhouse is very likely to show up throughout the house in no time at all. And, since the supply of soil is usually limited and used over a long period, it is wise to eliminate diseases, weeds, and insects at the outset by preventive control.

Soil is a living material to the degree that there is a constant interaction of various microorganisms, and the process of *pasteurization* results in only a partial sterilization and destroys only the disease-causing organisms and undesirable bacteria. Pasteurization is accomplished with temperatures not in excess of 180°, using either steam, hot water, or electricity. You can pasteurize small quantities in the oven. Use a candy thermometer to check the temperature. For larger quantities, use steam if it is already available from your heating system. In this case, a plumber can provide you with the necessary perforated pipe attached to a flexible hose so that the steam can be infused throughout a batch of soil within a box. There are also steam pasteurizers made especially for greenhouse use. Powered by regular house current, the water-filled tank generates enough steam to pasteurize 2 bushels of soil in 3 hours. The volume of soil needed will determine the worth of a pasteurizer to you.

There are chemicals with which to gas the soil, such as chloropicrin, which is sold under the trade name of Larvacide. Ninety-eight percent methyl-bromide plus 2 percent chloropicrin is also an effective fumigant. There are also drenches which will do a

*Soil can be pasteurized in small quantities.*

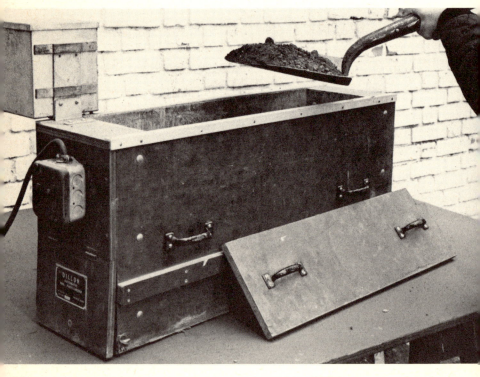

reasonably good job of disposing of many of the injurious organisms. One is formaldehyde, sold as 40 percent commercial formalin (1 part to 50 parts of water); you should apply it over the soil with a watering can at the rate of ¾ gallon per square foot. This treatment, as well as all other chemical disinfectants, should be applied outdoors and directions should be followed carefully. A paved driveway is ideal for this procedure. Spread the soil to form a layer of about 6 inches in depth and cover it with a large sheet of plastic. Seal in the chemical by mounding soil along all the edges of the plastic. Keep it covered for 48 hours and do not use the soil for potting for another 2 weeks. This allows time for fumes injurious to plants to dissipate.

Pano Drench is an easily used control for certain fungous diseases to which seeds and seedlings are susceptible. Apply it, too, with a watering can; you can use the soil 24 hours later.

## More About Soil Chemistry

As you know, many insects and diseases live and multiply in the soil and feed upon the plants growing there. Getting rid of these debilitating organisms will improve the chances of the good development of your plants. But you will also need to consider what side effects there might be from these insect and disease controls.

When heat (from pasteurization) is built up in soil, the organic materials begin to break down. In doing so they make quantities of nitrogen available. This is fine, up to a point. However, the higher the temperatures beyond the level of pasteurization, the more excessive is the nitrogen buildup. This is all right for a mature, well-established plant, but for a tender seedling it can be stifling to growth. The addition of superphosphate will offset this buildup of excessive amounts of nitrogenous compounds. In spite of such means of controlling these side effects, remember not to let temperatures exceed 180°, which is adequate to pasteurize rather than sterilize the soil.

## Soilless Mix

The term soilless mix is a relatively recent addition to our vocabulary. It refers to the combination of 2 or more inert mineral and organic derivatives to which nutrients are added. This provides a disease-free, insect-free "artificial soil." While soilless mixes are most frequently used as a medium into which you sow seeds, there are many greenhouse plantsmen who believe that the use of a soilless mixture is even more efficient than soil for growing plants to their ultimate maturity.

Another strong point in favor of the soilless mix is its extremely light weight. If you are forcing a number of daffodils planted in grape crates, they seem to weigh a ton, especially when the soil is moist at the time you have to lift the crates from underneath to the top of the bench. If you have a greenhouse on a second-floor porch or on a city rooftop where a wheelbarrow is impractical, you will welcome the convenience of these lightweight soilless mixes.

One such mixture is known as the Cornell mix and a modification of it is made of the following (for a 2-bushel quantity):

| | |
|---|---|
| 1 bushel | sphagnum peat moss |
| 1 bushel | horticultural grade vermiculite |
| | or |
| 1 bushel | perlite in place of vermiculite |
| 10 tablespoons | ground limestone |
| 5 teaspoons | superphosphate—20% powdered |
| 15 teaspoons | 5-10-5 fertilizer |

A modification of another, the California mix, is made as follows (for a 2-bushel quantity):

| | |
|---|---|
| 1 bushel | shredded sphagnum peat moss |
| 1 bushel | fine sand |
| ½ tablespoon | potassium nitrate |
| ½ tablespoon | potassium sulphate |
| 15 tablespoons | dolomitic limestone |
| 5 tablespoons | agricultural limestone |
| 5 tablespoons | superphosphate—20% powdered |
| 1 teaspoon | chelated iron |

Both of these formulas might sound like a complicated chemistry lesson, but once you buy the materials and measuring containers at a garden center, they are easy to mix and keep on hand.

To both mixtures, you will need to add nutrients every 30 days, since there is little left after that time other than the inert ingredients. The easiest way to apply this food is in the water-soluble form via the watering can or through a preportioning siphon arrangement.

**Hydroponics.** It is possible to grow any group of plants in your greenhouse without soil by feeding chemical nutrients in a solution, while the individual plants are supported in water, sand, ex- celsior, perlite, gravel, or any material that is inert or that has low fertility. This system of soilless plant culture is called *hydro- ponics*. During the 1940s there was a concentrated development of hydroponics, because it offered the promise of edible crops wherever there is water. This panacea to world food shortages has never realized its full potential, but some commercial growers in the United States are marketing vegetables grown by this form of "tray agriculture."

Here's how the system works: A supply of water and a specially formulated soluble fertilizer are maintained in a reservoir from which they are pumped up to the concrete- or plastic-lined growing bench, flooding the roots and the surrounding support medium. When the bench is filled, a float valve shuts off the pump and the enriched solution drains back into the reservoir. In this manner, the roots are never cut off from the necessary supply of oxygen and are being nourished almost constantly.

The single nutritive formula in the reservoir does not lend itself as a cultivation aid in a "mixed greenhouse"—it is for specific groups of plants (such as tomatoes, carnations, and gardenias). It is possible also to control insects through the use of liquid systemics and the entire operation can be automated. However, hydroponic cultivation is still more of a challenge to the scientifically or mechanically oriented greenhouse gardener than a popular and practical concept.

# 6

# Tools and Supplies You Will Need

When you outfit yourself with basics, consider each activity separately: watering, propagation, transplanting, plant maintenance, and greenhouse maintenance. You will need the following items.

*For watering*

    a hose or hoses with nozzles and couplers
    watering can
    hand-operated mister or fogger (if you have no automatic system)
    clogs
    plant markers (which indicate "Do Not Water" during dormancy)

*For propagation*

    a sharp knife
    a carborundum stone
    oil can
    trowel
    scrub brush and pail (for disinfecting)

measuring spoons or cups (for rooting hormones, fungicides)
stones or pegs

*For transplanting*

trowel (mentioned earlier)
dibble
a few sieves
tin-snips for cutting window screen for pots
scoops for handling large quantities of peat moss, sand, etc.

*For plant maintenance*

sprayer for insecticide
stakes
ball of twine
scissors
pruning shears
Twistems
tack gun or stapler (for attaching polyethylene)
rigid plastic containers
3-gallon galvanized pail
lump charcoal

*For greenhouse maintenance*

a ladder
hammer and nails
dustpan
paintbrush and scraper (if you apply a shading compound)

One piece of advice applies to all tools—*find the right piece of equipment for each job.* For a year I struggled with a 25-foot length of hose before I realized that, since the water outlet was in the middle of my 25-foot greenhouse, a 12½-foot hose was all that I needed to reach from one end of the house to the other. When I cut the hose in half and put on new end-fittings, I had a lighter, less cumbersome hose. This is the difference between the right and the wrong tool.

A tough pair of snub-nose scissors, good for cutting paper, string, or wire will make a good companion to a pair of pruning shears. I favor the scissor cut for pruning rather than the knife-and-anvil type. They make a cleaner cut without crushing the plant stem. A good, single-blade, carbon steel *knife* will complete the set of cutting tools you will need. But keep them sharp. Leave

*Get your hose out from underfoot.*

a carborundum stone and a small oil can in a handy location and you will be more likely to sharpen hand tools frequently.

Rigid plastic containers of various sizes and kinds will make storage of soils and their components as well as various chemicals easier. Covered plastic cans keep your mixtures dry so that they maintain a long shelf life; label them to organize your potting shed. A 3-gallon galvanized pail is often the easiest container for carrying liquids or bulk materials. Dry it after each use so that the inside will not pit and become rough. Everything pours more easily out of a smooth bucket.

Hand tools needed in the greenhouse are few. A good trowel with a stainless-steel blade is a luxury, but it will give you pleasure for a lifetime. A well-sanded dibble will make the transplanting of seedlings just a bit easier. A few sieves, a ball of soft twine, an ordinary flat scrub brush, and a soft, short-handled brush will just about complete the necessities. Oh yes, a pair of clogs will prove comfortable and warm and will insulate your feet from the damp floor during watering and extended periods of fiddling in the greenhouse.

When you grow more specialized greenhouse plants, you will find that specialized tools are necessary. Often such tools and supplies are homemade. A case in point is the orchid potting stick. The manufactured aluminum ones are well designed and certainly efficient to work with; however, I always seem to grab the one that I made out of a piece of Osage orangewood. Strings, stretched to form a grid, will support your chrysanthemums, carnations, or snapdragons but you can buy wire already shaped to do the job. But the development of your own variations on the established tools is often the best suited to your needs and, therefore, the most gratifying.

## Preventive Measures to Eliminate Crises

If you are just beginning to tend a greenhouse, no doubt you have some apprehensions: How can I be in charge of the greenhouse, instead of letting it command me? Where is the greatest trouble likely to be? What preventive steps or countermeasures might I take?

*There is no end to the available emergency heaters on the market. Having one handy is good insurance.*

*Above: Independent of the electrical system, the battery-operated temperature alarm guards your plants day and night. Below: A minimum-maximum thermometer lets you know the temperature extremes in your greenhouse since the last setting.*

Your greatest potential crisis probably is a wintertime danger: failure of the heating system, allowing your plants to freeze. (My heater acts up only on Christmas Eve or at some other time when it is impossible to get a service man to make repairs.) Hence, you will need to have a portable kerosene stove or some other self-contained unit ready on a standby basis during cold weather.

An alarm system to alert you to the impending danger is a necessary accompaniment. It must be independent of the household electrical supply. Power it with a dry-cell battery.

Burning plants with too much sunlight is another danger. This is most likely to occur after you have watered—when the leaves are still wet. Especially after a period of cloudy weather at the end of winter, you may not be aware of how much the heat and intensity of the sunlight have increased. So good greenhouse management calls for light shading at this time of year. Otherwise, a one-hour period of clear skies can kill off many of your favorite plants.

Insects and diseases are another menace. Your protection here is constant inspection of plants and greenhouse. If you leave both unobserved for long, you risk the loss of your plant collection.

The beginning greenhouse gardener tends to rely too heavily on automated controls. Although creating the proper temperature, ventilation, moisture, and light conditions are prime objectives, the maintenance of these elements in proper relationship to one another is of no less importance. So, in the beginning, I suggest you use the various controls manually in order to get the feel of the interrelationship of these crucial factors. You will then be better prepared to set the automatic controls.

*The percentage of nitrogen, soluble phosphoric acid, and available potash must be shown (in that order) on each bag of complete fertilizer.*

# 7

# Good Nutrition
# for Your Plants

THE HEALTH OF A growing plant calls for constant evaluation. It is as important to know what a normal, healthy plant looks like as it is to recognize a defective one. This norm varies with each stage of development, from seedling to ultimate flowering, and the amateur greenhouse gardener learns to recognize it through close daily observation of foliage and the plant in general.

If leaves begin to yellow, mottle, shrivel, or otherwise change, it is necessary to determine whether the problem is caused by insects, disease, nutrition, or environment. This chapter explains not only the "whys" of plant nutrition, but the need for accurate diagnosis and ways to achieve it. After that comes the actual feeding. But first, what are fertilizers and what do they do?

**Organic and Inorganic.** Organic nutrients are made up of natural plant and animal materials—manure, bones, ground fish, dried blood, cottonseed meal, etc. The inorganic fertilizers are chemical compounds, some of which are naturally mined materials while others are manufactured or are by-products of manufacture.

Organic gardeners appear to have boundless enthusiasm. Their dedication to manures and composted materials precludes the use of any processed chemicals. While I too appreciate the value of organic fertilizers, I am aware that it takes a hundred pounds of rotted manure or bone meal to do the same job that a few pounds of a processed chemical can do and do it a lot faster. Besides, everyone does not have easy access to a cow barn and not every gardener can make his own composts, so do not apologize for using chemical fertilizers occasionally or exclusively. In any event, it is doubtful if your choice makes any difference in the health of a plant—apart from the physical effect certain organic materials have when incorporated in the soil. When dissolved in water (the only state in which they can be assimilated by a plant) the actual nutritive elements are the same, whether they are of organic or inorganic origin.

When the inorganics (often called *chemical fertilizers*) first came into being, they were often used carelessly—gardeners paid too little attention to dosage. Some growers lost large numbers of plants, and the cry went up that "inorganics are dangerous." In fact, however, the inorganic fertilizers are as safe as any other product, if the directions are properly followed. Also, they are easy to store and to apply correctly. Almost every commercial greenhouse has found them to be the most efficient materials for feeding plants.

**Soil Deficiencies.** If you take a sample quantity of your garden soil, more than likely it will be deficient or contain an excess of one or more of the important chemical elements. This is not vitally important in your garden, where a plant's roots can reach out in the soil for the various necessary nutrients to feed itself adequately. However, in the greenhouse, where the plant is confined to a pot or a fairly shallow bench, you need to grow the plant in a soil that is at the highest possible level of nutrition. It is equally important to supply the nutritive ingredients in such form that they make the soil responsive to the plant's needs.

**"Complete" Fertilizer.** At the time a plant is ready for its first transplanting, it needs soil fortified with the complete spectrum of chemical nutrients. Prior to that stage, the seed had enough nutrition "built-in" to sustain the developing embryo and the newly germinated plant. You will also need to use a "complete" fertilizer at any subsequent transplanting.

A complete fertilizer presumably has *everything* necessary, but it probably does not have *enough* of everything to sustain the plant over an extended period. Such fertilizers are sold in any number of analyses and law requires the manufacturer to state the percentage of the three principal components: nitrogen, phosphorus, and potassium, in that order, on the container. I suggest that you select a fertilizer with a low analysis (20-20-20 or lower) because the higher the analysis, the more processing has been necessary. This results in diminished quantities of the valuable *trace elements* (boron, manganese, molybdenum, zinc, etc.).

**How to Change the Soil.** If you have prepared the soil properly, you are ready to reinforce it nutritionally to provide immediate stimulus to the plant as well as to meet its long-term needs. First add a nitrogenous material such as Agrinite (made up of refuse materials from packing houses), at the rate of ½ ounce per bushel of soil. This brings up the nitrogen level for the long pull. Then mix in 5 tablespoons per bushel of 20 percent superphosphate for its long-lasting protein-producing phosphoric acid. Finally, use a complete 5-10-5 fertilizer at the rate recommended on the bag. This provides the needed potash as well as trace elements. It also contains nitrogen and phosphorus (two materials you have already added), but not enough to create an excess nor in as long-lasting a form as you used initially. As your plants continue to grow within the confines of a pot or bench, daily watering eventually will wash away the necessary nutritional materials so that you will need to apply a complete fertilizer periodically— once in 2 months is usually enough. Again, the low analysis fertilizers are best (5-10-5 as opposed to 10-20-10, for example).

You will find it easiest to apply this food in liquid form. It is available as a concentrate. Dilute it with water and apply it with either a watering can or a liquid fertilizer proportioner. Do not be tempted to overfeed your plants or they will become leggy and weak—ready targets for every disease and insect that comes along.

*Plants can be fed while being watered with a hose siphon attachment that proportions a soluble fertilizer automatically.*

**What Nutrients Do for Plants.** Chemicals combine and react under the stimulus of light, heat, and water to trigger the various growth activities within a plant. Several chemicals are identified with specific activities, while others contribute in a more general way to the ultimate maturity of a plant. For example, nitrogen is responsible for the stimulation of leaf growth, and phosphorous is related to building up proteins. Potassium is tied to general vigor and influences a plant's ability to resist disease. Although trace elements are found in soils in relatively small quantities, they are no less important to plant growth than the more plentiful elements. They are responsible for a number of essential processes and characteristics.

**How to Make a Quick Check-Up.** A deficiency of any nutritional element may result in marked deformity or discoloration of leaves, stunted growth, or even death of the plant. But do not consider fertilizer a cure-all to administer promiscuously. Should a plant seem to be in less than good health, first run through your diagnostic checklist: Is insect damage present? Do the soil texture

*When boron is lacking, stunting, as on left, becomes evident.*

and the pot give proper drainage? Are the atmospheric conditions compatible with the plant's needs? Should the plant now be in an ascendant or descendant phase of its growth cycle? Only after ruling out all of the foregoing possibilities should you consider malnutrition at the root of the problem.

Even before you add nutrients to the soil, consider the soil itself, since it often holds the key to the release of the important elements that are present but in an unavailable form. An alkaline or neutral soil will usually keep these nutrients "locked in." For this reason, a soil acidity test is specially important. Testing kits are available for a few dollars in garden centers and you can use one to determine the pH (acidity) of your soil. A reading of 6 to 7, which is slightly acid, is preferred for general use. You can reach this level by adding peat moss to an alkaline soil or by adding crushed limestone to one that is over-acidic (see also Chapter 5).

Now, a test feeding is in order. Dissolve a 20-20-20 soluble fertilizer at the rate of 1 tablespoon to every 3 gallons of water; apply this moderately with a watering can. Should the symptoms of undernourishment begin to disappear in a week or so, continue feedings on your bimonthly schedule. Should the test feeding not prove helpful, do not make a second application without professional consultation. I suggest a phone call to your local county agricultural agent. You will find him listed in the telephone book under the extension service or under county government. If he cannot answer your questions, ask him to refer you to your nearest specialist in ornamental horticulture.

**Feeding the Air.** A growing plant gets nourishment from the air as well as from the soil. The small amount of carbon dioxide in the atmosphere contributes to the manufacture of sugars and starches—materials that result in plant growth. If you introduce **higher than normal levels of this essential gas into the greenhouse atmosphere, you can grow healthier and more floriferous plants.** The British greenhouse industry seems to be farthest along in this phase of scientific plant culture, at least where the home greenhouse is concerned. Nevertheless, practical devices to feed beneficial quantities of carbon dioxide into the greenhouse atmosphere are coming onto the American market and will be useful to amateurs of a scientific bent.

**When to Feed Plants.** Before you stock up on any of these fertilizers or devices for their application, you need to understand when to feed and when not to feed. If your timing is off, a plant can die of indigestion or, at best, get no benefit from the fertilizer. After an operation or illness, a person is not immediately ready to handle a sirloin steak; distressed plants are similar in this respect. Until a seedling has developed an adequate root system or until roots that were damaged in transplanting have been replaced, you should supply nutrients in minimal doses, if at all. It is equally

*Many plants which develop woody stems, such as rosemary and santolina, can be trained as standards (miniature trees) if they are well fed.*

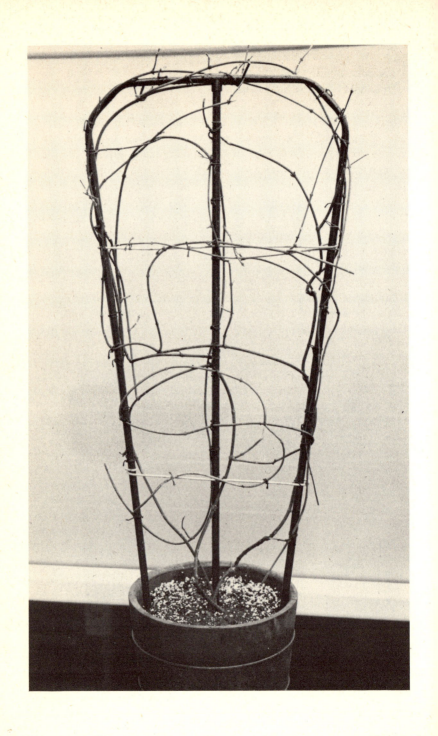

difficult for plants to utilize fertilizers when the temperature is very low or when the soil is dry. Both of these conditions usually prevail when plants are dormant; hence, plants should be in active growth with a normal level of moisture and soil warmth before "the banquet" starts.

## How to Treat Dormant Plants

The coming and going of the various seasons in the outdoor garden are perhaps mysterious, physiologically, although not visually, considering the changes in color and the dropping of leaves. However, in the greenhouse, where you may be growing plants with such diverse origins as South Africa, Japan, Brazil, England, the high Himalayas, or the desert floor of Death Valley, you might not recognize immediately which plant is resting, which is in active growth, which is completing its cycle, and which is about to start growing. In such cases of mixed seasons (if not mixed climates), knowing and recognizing the needs of each plant, and segregating and treating each accordingly are essential to successful cultivation.

The nerine produces its flowers in the fall and not until afterward do leaves appear. After active growth throughout the winter, the leaves die off and the plant becomes dormant. Normal watering during this dormant period, when there is little physical use for it, would be worse than insufficient water during the plant's reawakening. A South African veltheimia produces its leaves first; then its flower spike. This is followed by a long period of flowerless growth to replenish its strength for the next year's repeat performance.

A holding section for resting plants will prevent you from inadvertently watering them, and, in this way, you can keep valuable bulbs and other exotic plants year after year. If such segregation seems too complicated, keep a supply of wooden labels that you have dipped in bright red lacquer. Put one in the pot of each plant as it enters its dormant period. This will serve as a warning: Do not water.

*Immediately prior to commencement of new growth is the ideal time to prune, retie vines to trellis, and feed.*

*Typical deficiency symptoms as they appear in geraniums. The top row represents the upper leaves of the plant; the bottom row represents the lower leaves.* FIRST COLUMN: *These normal geranium leaves have had proper nutrition.* SECOND COLUMN: *Nitrogen deficient leaves are smaller than normal and turn progressively yellow with no specific dead areas until the entire plant is about to die.* THIRD COLUMN: *Due to phosphorus deficiency, increased purplish pigmentation makes the upper leaves look darker. Lower leaves might die as phosphorus moves upward to the newer growth.* FOURTH COLUMN: *Potassium effects move upward and downward from the middle of the plant. Leaves become crinkled and the tissue dies.* FIFTH COLUMN: *Manganese limits chlorophyll synthesis. Leaves will die starting at the bottom of the plant.*

# 8

# Controls for Diseases and Insects

IF A PLANT's normal development is curtailed in any way by anything, you can accurately consider it to be diseased. Most abnormal plants suffer not from diseases of bacterial or insect origin, but from a lack of attention to the simple everyday cultural practices.

Before looking for the miracle drug to cure your ailing plant, look at your care of the plant with a critical eye. Too little water can cause wilting; too much water results in yellowed leaves. Lack of green color can indicate an iron or magnesium deficiency. Too much sun can scorch the leaves. *Satisfy yourself that poor cultural practice is not at the root of your trouble.* Of course, a visual examination of the plant's surfaces would reveal insect presence or damage.

Should your various examinations not turn up the cause, the next logical step is to consider the bacterial, fungous, and virus diseases. There are any number of diseases: rusts, wilts, blights, spots, mildews, etc. Most of these can be treated either with a

*Above: Low fertility as evidenced by the petunia on the right can be as much a crippling factor as any specific disease. Below: Example of untreated iron deficiency in gardenia (left) and five weeks after treatment (right) with chelated iron.*

fungicide spray, or with the diseased plant kept in isolation pending recovery (with its destruction as a last resort to prevent further infestation).

Diseases in greenhouse plants are bound to occur. Some are soil-borne, others are carried by insects, and still others are a result of adding plants that are already infected. The variety of diseases is large and their diagnosis is often complex and uncertain—at least for the amateur diagnostician. However, a number of the more common plant ailments are not difficult to identify, if you will only look for them; but, better still, you can even prevent them. Certainly being on guard is easier than trying to cure an epidemic.

Diseases which are fungoid are best fought by preventive measures. Clean soil (not that reused from pots and benches) and plenty of ventilation are the first steps. Next, spray or dust your plants periodically with a fungicide. Once fungus is actually visible on even one leaf, there are a billion spores floating in the air, ready to spread the problem still further.

*A deficiency in manganese (unlike an iron deficiency) shows first in a plant's mature leaves. The loss of good green color, which is called "chlorosis" affects the areas between the major veins. Tip growth remains normal. A complete fertilizer containing manganese as a trace element will correct this condition.*

*Damping-off disease* is one of the most damaging fungus-borne infections because it attacks seedlings shortly after their germination and the stems begin to rot at soil level rather rapidly. In this way, large numbers of plants are killed off even before they actually get started. Sowing seeds too close together is one way that air circulation becomes limited and a perfect condition for the diseases is created. But, even prior to sowing the seeds, you should drench the soil with a prohibitory *damping-off solution.* As plants get older, having escaped this "infantile disease," they might be faced with a powdery mildew or one of the other fungi that thrive in dank, ill-ventilated situations. These ills will even attack a pair of old shoes left in a dark, damp closet, so why should a

*Fusarium, a fungous disease, infects the center of the flower and causes a modification in the shape of the flower in addition to the discolored area.*

tender plant be immune? Still another fungus is likely to attack the mature plant; it is called *rust*. This is sometimes found on the undersides of leaves as small brown spots. By then, the reproductive spores are formed and a good spraying of all plants is necessary (after the more seriously infected ones are removed and burned).

Virus diseases make up the next most important group. Viruses seem to be increasing in variety and their cures are not keeping up with the pace. The symptoms often include mottling and other disfigurations of leaves. Sometimes they become striped, with pale areas, and they are often distorted in a manner similar to that caused by insects.

Cure of a virus-caused infection is most difficult, if not im-

*Powdery mildew starts in a few locally infected areas and spreads rapidly.*

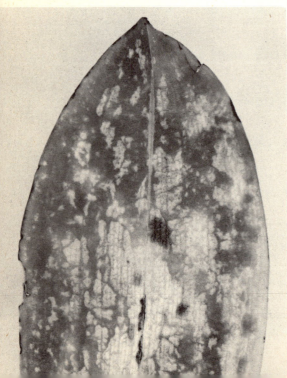

*Above: Virus (right) affects all aspects of growth but is most evident on leaves. Left: Virus symptoms in a phalaenopsis leaf.*

possible. The disease can be carried from one plant to another by insects, so this is a very good reason for keeping your greenhouse free of those insects that, otherwise, seem to be completely innocuous. If you suspect virus in any of your plants, take no chances on spreading it further by an infected knife or pruning shears. Disinfect hand tools frequently in a wide-mouth bottle filled with alcohol. Even with feeding, spraying, and general good care, plants will not grow out of the problem. Therefore, remove and destroy any virus-ridden plants to protect your entire collection.

Continuing efforts are being made to develop cures for virus diseases and a few on the market already have produced fair results in the hands of professional growers. Nevertheless, the best approach at the moment is constant surveillance and the cleanest possible growing conditions.

Most insects have their genesis in soil or on plants already in your greenhouse. They have merely been waiting for ideal conditions before they hatch.

The insects that are most dangerous to the greenhouse world are those that feed upon plants and weaken them either by chewing the leaves or sucking the plant juices. It is then, when insects begin to affect the well-being of plants, that you need to define the problem as specifically as possible and act.

Recognition is simple enough if you actually see the insect feeding upon the plant. However, in many cases, the insect is so small that it is all but invisible, or else has already done the damage and left. Many insects are so well camouflaged that, even though hundreds of them may be present, they go unseen until the plant has almost succumbed. Some greenhouse insect pests look more like specks of dust, bits of cotton, or parts of plants than like ants, houseflies, or beetles. Some spend night and day confined to the leaf axils (the point where a leaf issues from a branch) and would not be caught dead munching flowers. Still others are nocturnal feeders and, during the day, hide under the pot or along the bottom edge of the rim, making constant surveillance a necessity—or you will have an epidemic on your hands. Whenever you are watering, cutting flowers, or otherwise tending your plants, examine them carefully in order to discover any insects or traces of damage. Once the evidence points unquestionably to insects as the source of trouble, you will need to make a specific identification in order to cope (see chart on pages 132–134 for methods of control).

## How to Identify Insects

**Aphids.** These are perhaps the most prolific of all greenhouse insects. Starting as white specks of little more than dust size,

*Left: A new hatching of aphids begins to suck the plant juices. The green color of more adult aphids makes them even harder to see. Right: Mealy bugs cover themselves with a white mealy substance and cling to sheltered areas of leaves and stems while sucking plant juices.*

they quickly gorge themselves by sucking the plant juices, turn green, and grow to almost an ⅛ of an inch in a matter of a few days. They are then ready to reproduce themselves and, uncontrolled, will completely cover the plant stems and the undersides of leaves in no time. Their presence is evident by the discoloration and distortion of stems and leaves. Two sprayings, a week apart, will kill the active aphids first and then those newly hatched.

**Mealy Bugs.** These are flat, oval-shaped pests about ⅛ of an inch long. Somewhat fuzzy, they are grayish-white in color. They are mobile but move quite slowly as they suck plant juices from the undersides of leaves and from the leaf axils. They excrete a sticky liquid which soon develops a black mold over the plant's surface. When you find them in small numbers on but a few plants, you can eliminate mealy bugs by touching them with a small cotton swab stick soaked in alcohol. Treat wider infestations by spraying with a specific-control chemical.

**Nematodes.** These are particularly difficult to diagnose. The effects of these soil-borne microscopic worms are shown above the soil by a gradual die-back and yellowing of the plant in general. Below, the roots become gnarled and swollen, and soon are no longer able to function effectively. The simplest greenhouse cure is to burn the plant and be sure to do any new potting with pasteurized soil and scrubbed pots. Before destroying any plants, get your diagnosis confirmed by a professional such as the local county agricultural agent, or by a horticulturist or entomologist at a nearby university.

**Red Spider Mites.** These are among the most difficult insects for the novice to recognize, mainly because of their small size. No larger than fly specks, they cause mottled-gray areas on the tops of leaves, although the mites themselves can be found only on the undersides. In numbers, they look like specks of rust, but to make sure, hold a piece of white paper under the leaves that you suspect may be infested, tap or shake the foliage, and look at the paper carefully. If any of the minute specks begin to move, they are red spider mites. Use liquid sprays to eliminate them.

*Above: Red spiders beneath the leaves create the rusty mottled effect (left). The leaves on the right have not been attacked. Left: Scale insects are well camouflaged when young, as on these leaves. By the time adults have matured, considerable damage is usually evident.*

**Scale.** These insects are shaped like miniature flattened turtle shells. Different species vary in color from white to reddish-brown and their size ranges from $\frac{1}{16}$ to $\frac{1}{4}$ of an inch. The insects themselves, under their scalelike protection, are hard to get at and difficult to dislodge from their feeding places on the undersides and in the axils of leaves. Like aphids, they suck plant juices and cause similar damage. It is wise to make two sprayings, a week apart, to make sure of complete control.

**Slugs and Snails.** These two are much alike, the main difference being that slugs have no shell. Both move about mainly at night and enjoy damp conditions. During the day they hide in the cool shade of the floor, on the bottom edge of the pot rim, or on the very bottom of the pot. They eat all tender growth first, starting with buds and new roots, and move progressively to the less succulent plant parts. Since they are chewers, the damage they do is obvious. They can be controlled easily with a periodic selective spray or by poisoned bait put on the plant benches. Here is the newest control method: place a steep-sided dish on the plant bench and fill it to a depth of ¾ inch with beer—yes, beer! It will do the trick.

*Snails, often found with the slugs, can be controlled by the same technique.*

*Above: A slug leaves its slimy trail on its way toward the young, more tender leaves. Right: White flies make their presence known by taking wing if the plant is even slightly jostled.*

**White Flies.** These are among the most annoying of the sucking insects that attack greenhouse plants. It is not unusual to touch an infested plant and have the surrounding air virtually filled with a white cloud of flies, each less than ⅛ inch in length. Fuchsias and pelargoniums are particularly susceptible and, therefore, you should make frequent inspection of the undersides of their leaves. White flies reduce the vigor and growth of plants, and, since there is almost no such thing as a *few* white flies, a great number of plants usually are under damaging attack. Fortunately, they can be brought under control by several means—spraying, dusting, or fumigating.

**Woolly Aphids.** Each less than ⅛ inch in length, these insects are protected by a waxy secretion similar to cotton. You can find them, either singly or in groups, almost anywhere on the leaves or stems. They will cause distorted leaves and eventually a weakening of the plant from which they suck the juices. The same spray recommended for other aphids will keep them in check.

The above is by no means a complete list of plant pests, but includes only those which are most likely to cause you trouble. Others, such as leaf miners and thrips, are liable to add to your worries too; but, in this day of advanced entomological developments, the chemical companies have come up with a number of effective insecticides that control several pests.

## Insecticides

Many of the effective insecticides available today are toxic to humans, but you can use them safely if you follow the instructions carefully. It is never necessary to add an extra tablespoon of insecticide to your sprayer, and it is extremely dangerous. So the cardinal rule is to follow the manufacturer's instructions to the letter and, when called for, wear gloves and use a simple respirator that incorporates a paper or fabric air filter—one that fits over your nose and mouth.

Almost all insecticides are available in more than one form and your choice will depend upon the factors of convenience and safety. Most popular are the liquids and water-soluble powders which you dilute and apply by sprayer. The size sprayer you need is determined by the number of your plants and the size of your greenhouse.

*Systemic formulations* are those you apply to the soil; the insecticide is absorbed by the roots. The toxic material is then transmitted internally throughout the entire plant, which becomes deadly to any insect feeding upon it. The only drawback of this otherwise desirable method of control is that you must exercise great care in applying it. Your skin must be well protected.

*Store your respirator with the sprayer so one is never used without the other.*

*Fumigation by means of a smoke generator* is an effective control method, but one that is dangerous in the hands of the home greenhouse gardener due to its extremely high toxicity. Its use involves closing the vents, lighting the fuse in a one-dose can, and then leaving the greenhouse quickly and locking the door. If you attempt this, do it in the evening, keeping the heat a little higher than the usual nighttime temperature. The dense smoke carries the fumes to every part of the greenhouse and in the morning the plants are free of insects. After a thorough airing, the atmosphere is safe once again. Avoid fumigation in all but isolated locations where seepage will not reach your home. It is also important to use the proper dosage to avoid killing any greenhouse plants. But most important, if you use a smoke generator, follow all instructions to the letter and observe every precaution suggested on the label. All pesticides have their dangers and this one has more than most.

In some cases, the package label will list those plants which are particularly sensitive to a given chemical. Use first on a limited basis those products that do not reveal such information.

It is important to select the insecticide in the form best suited to your greenhouse. In cases where proximity to people or animals is a problem and you cannot fumigate, use liquid pesticides with a sprayer of the proper size for the number of plants being treated. A sprayer too large for the job can spread what might be a safe amount of chemical for one group of plants to other plants with less tolerance.

One recent innovation of special interest to owners of small greenhouses is the 1-foot strip of plastic which has been impregnated with a long-lasting insecticide (Vapona). Hung over the plant benches, it will continue over a few months to give off fumes that are toxic to insects but harmless to humans. This qualifies as an excellent preventive device.

*Smoke generators envelop every leaf with insecticide.*

*A trombone sprayer uses a bucket for a tank, making it easy for small quantities.*

*Plastic strips impregnated with insecticide (Vapona) exude their lethal fumes over several months, controlling many plant pests.*

The following chart does not set forth all of the pesticides currently sold but gives some of the best for greenhouse use. Those selected here are safe for use on the greatest number of plant varieties. However, certain plants have varying degrees of sensitivity to these chemical compounds. Therefore, be over-cautious rather than injure yourself or your plants with these toxic materials. I repeat, *all* pesticides have their dangers. Read the labels carefully, follow all directions, and use a respirator when you apply liquid sprays or dust.

*A hand duster gives thorough coverage in applying insecticides.*

| PROBLEM | REMEDY |
|---|---|
| *Aphids* | Malathion (25% wettable powder) |
| | Diazinon (50% wettable powder) |
| *Bacterial diseases* | Captan (50% wettable powder) |
| *Botrytis* | Captan (50% wettable powder) |
| *Diseases of both fungous and bacterial origin* | Bordeaux mixture (equal parts copper sulphate and hydrated lime in water) |
| | Benlate (effectiveness is broadening as tests are completed—keep informed on this material) |
| *General fungous diseases* | Zineb (65% wettable powder) |
| *Leaf spot* | Maneb (80% wettable powder) |
| *Mealy bugs* | Malathion (57% emulsifiable concentrate) |
| | Meta-Systox "R" (a systemic control) |
| | Vapona strips |
| | Thiodan (50% wettable powder) |
| *Nematodes* | There are chemical controls such as Nemagon; however, they are difficult and somewhat dangerous in the hands of an amateur; therefore, I recommend disposing of any infected plants and replacing your soil supply. |
| *Powdery mildew* | Karathane (22.5% wettable powder) |
| *Red spider mites* | Kelthane AP (Dicothol) 18½% wettable powder |
| | Meta-Systox "R" (a systemic control) |

| AMOUNT PER GALLON | SPECIAL INSTRUCTIONS |
|---|---|
| 5 tablespoons | Do not use on ferns, petunias, or crassulas. |
| 2 tablespoons | Do not use on gardenias or poinsettias. |

| | |
|---|---|
| 2 tablespoons | |
| | Follow label on commercial preparation. |
| | Follow label on commercial preparation. |

| | |
|---|---|
| 1 tablespoon | |

| | |
|---|---|
| 1½ tablespoons | |

| | |
|---|---|
| 2 teaspoons | Do not use on ferns, petunias, or crassulas. |
| 1 teaspoon | Do not use on lilies. Be sure to wear rubber gloves. |
| Hang 1 strip per 1,000 cubic feet | Replace approximately every 60 days. |
| 1 teaspoon | Do not use on geraniums. |

| | |
|---|---|
| 1½ teaspoons | |
| 2 tablespoons | |
| 1 teaspoon | Do not use on lilies. Be sure to wear rubber gloves. |

| PROBLEM | REMEDY |
|---|---|
| *Rusts* | Captan (50% wettable powder) |
| *Scale insects* | Malathion (25% wettable powder) |
| | Malathion (57% emulsifiable concentrate) |
| *Slugs and snails* | Slugit (liquid metaldehyde) |
| | Slug-Kill (15% metaldehyde dust) |
| | Snarol (metaldehyde and arsenic) |
| | Beer (Yes, beer!) |
| *White flies* | Same control as for aphids, plus the following: |
| | Cygon 2E |
| | Pyrethrum |

Read and follow carefully these dosage recommendations and also the manufacturers' special instructions given on the container.

We are in a period of continual reassessment of control methods, including those listed here, and I suggest that you check at least every six months with your county agricultural agent for the most recent recommendations.

Even if you buy your material in standard amounts, the following tables are worth copying and tacking onto the potting shed wall for future reference:

### LIQUID MEASURES
60 drops equals 1 teaspoon
3 teaspoons equals 1 tablespoon
4 tablespoons equals ¼ cup

### DRY MEASURES

| OUNCES | TABLESPOONS | CUPS |
|---|---|---|
| 1 | 4 | ¼ |
| 2 | 8 | ½ |
| 8 | 16 | 1 |

| AMOUNT PER GALLON | SPECIAL INSTRUCTIONS |
|---|---|
| 2 tablespoons | |
| 5 tablespoons | Do not use on ferns, petunias or crassulas. |
| 2 teaspoons | Same as above. |
| 2 tablespoons | |
| | Do not mix. Spread as is (½ lb. will treat 250 sq. ft.). |
| | Same as above |
| | Fill a steep-sided dish to a depth of ¾″. |
| 2 teaspoons | Follow manufacturer's suggestions as to dosage. |

### DILUTIONS OF LIQUIDS

| PERCENT SOLUTION | CUPS | TABLESPOONS PER GALLON |
|---|---|---|
| 1% (1 part to 100) | — | 2½ |
| 2% (1 part to 50) | — | 5 |
| 4% (1 part to 25) | — | 10 |
| 5% (1 part to 20) | ¾ | 12½ |
| 10% (1 part to 10) | 1½ | 25 |

### DILUTIONS OF POWDERS IN WATER

| LB. TO 50 GAL. WATER | TSP. TO 1 GAL. WATER | TBS. TO 1 GAL. WATER |
|---|---|---|
| 1½ | 2 | 1 |
| 1 | 3 | — |
| 2 | 4 | 1⅜ |

*Above: Seeds vary in size from dustlike specks produced in abundance by various orchids to these more manageable citrus seeds. Below: While many seeds float on air the coconut, largest of all, will float great distances on the water before lodging in the sand and germinating.*

# 9

# Techniques for Propagating Plants

HOWEVER SMALL YOUR GREENHOUSE may be, you can always devote a section to propagation of plants. The various techniques are best achieved at temperatures between 60° and 70° and, while this ordinarily might be difficult in a cool greenhouse, the use of a thermostatically controlled plastic- or lead-coated heating cable, stretched back and forth across the bench under the surface of the sand or other rooting medium, makes the task possible. We call this arrangement a "propagating bed" and when a section of the bench is so equipped and a glass top is added, it then becomes a "propagating frame." In a greenhouse 25′ × 10′ you could profitably use a bench section that is 6 feet long. These 6 linear feet, broken up into three 2′ × 3′ areas, with a divider nailed to the top of the bench, would allow the use of each for a different group of plants.

**Seeds.** Of the four principal methods of plant propagation practiced in the greenhouse (seeds, cuttings, layering, and divisions) the first is the most used and, by far, the least expensive. There are a few basic rules that you must follow for successful results. If it is proper to say that hygienic conditions are more important at one time than another, they are most critical during propagation. It is at this time that seeds have only a marginal ability to resist disease or insects. Therefore, be sure to scrub the wooden benches and structural framing of the greenhouse with a cresylic acid solution (1 quart to 10 quarts of water) as a disinfectant; then spray the area with a fungicide.

Use clean pots and fresh sand. If soil is used, pasteurize it or at least drench it with one of those anti-damping-off solutions, sold in most garden centers, that kill off various detrimental fungi.

Use fresh seeds of the best quality, whenever possible. The time invested and the labor expended here, on anything but the best, is poor economy. Kinds of seeds vary in shape and size—from the millions of dustlike particles produced by certain orchids to the huge palm seed, more familiarly known as the coconut.

Seeds also vary greatly in the hardness of their coatings which, in turn, governs the time necessary for germination. Some, which

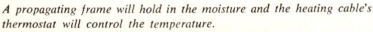

*A propagating frame will hold in the moisture and the heating cable's thermostat will control the temperature.*

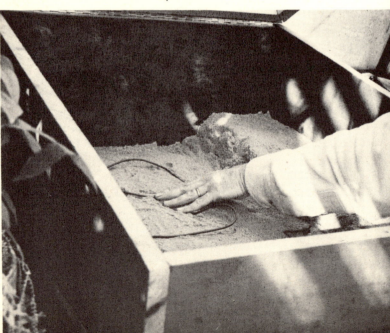

*Seeds large enough to handle individually can be started with a few to an individual pot.*

are near metal-hard, such as sweet peas, acacias, and morning glories, require filing or nicking in order to hasten the swelling, which eventually frees the seed and permits it to sprout. Still others benefit from soaking, boiling, freezing, or a mild bath in sulphuric acid. These special needs, however, are usually pointed out in the directions given by the supplier. The vast majority of seeds germinate without specially treating the seed coat. Sow by scattering them thinly on the surface of the soil or prepared medium. Traditionally, the most often-used medium has been a mixture of equal parts of screened leaf mold and sand. In recent years, however, plant researchers have found that various sterile media overcome the risk of the damping-off fungus, so deadly to seedlings, and results are usually more dependable.

Among the ingredients in popular use are vermiculite and perlite (the first is heat-expanded mica and the second an exploded

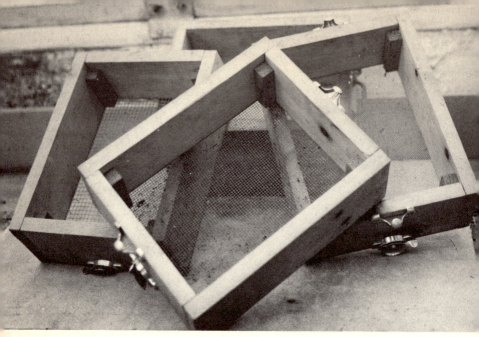

*Graduated screens, when attached together, separate coarse soil from finer grades.*

aluminum silicate). Sphagnum moss is still another useful sowing medium. All of these can be used alone or in combination with equal parts of peat moss and sand. Perhaps the most useful guide to the proper formulation is a knowledge of the natural habitat of the plant in question. A native of the tropical jungle floor is certain to germinate more successfully in a rich, heavy mixture, while many alpines and desert plants require a sandy, well-drained medium for best results.

The container you choose can be a small wooden box (12″ × 12″ × 3″) or a wide, shallow clay pot. Since seeds of different varieties take different lengths of time to germinate, use one container for each kind of seed.

First place broken crock in the bottom for drainage; then fill the pot with the potting mixture and firm it to within ¾ of an inch of the top. Scatter the seeds on the surface and cover them with a finely sifted mixture of the same medium to about 3 times the thickness of the seeds. Press down the surface to create the closest possible contact between the soil and the seed. Place the pot in a shallow pan of water so that the entire contents will be

*Left: Tamping the bed of soil helps it transmit and hold the moisture. Below: Peg board readies each planting site for large seeds or seedlings.*

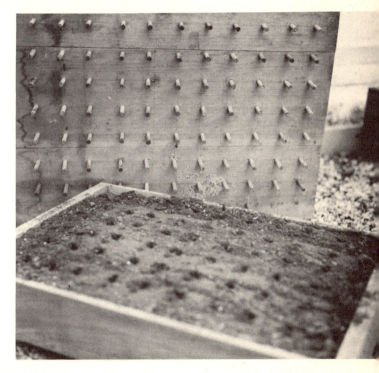

*From germination until transplanting, seedlings require constant mois-ture. Misting nozzles, hooked up to a time clock, will do the job if your daily schedule does not allow for constant supervision.*

moistened, for the first time, without disturbing the seeds and their soil covering. Whatever container is used, cover it to protect the soil from drying out until the seeds germinate. A piece of news-paper will suffice.

During this time, prior to germination, proper watering is critical. If kept too wet, seeds will rot; if kept too dry, the ex-panding new plant will fail to break through the seed coat. A constant, thorough moistness is essential.

Immediately upon the seeds' germination, remove the shading, and when the plants have grown their first set of true leaves, begin selection for transplanting. Pick out the strongest plants and re-plant them about 2 inches apart, in either a richer soil or the same medium as the seed pot, with fertilizer added. In any case, begin regular feeding at a 10-day to 2-week interval, since the roots now have grown enough to be able to absorb the nutrients. When each seedling has produced about 3 sets of leaves, pot it.

Most flowering plants require maximum sunlight to develop fully; hence, most bloom during the summer. However, with the completely artificial environment of the greenhouse, you must decide upon what approximate date you want plants in bloom; then you look up in seed catalogs the number of days necessary for each to mature and, working backward, sow the seeds at the correct time. Even the short winter days can become simulated spring if you add artificial light, regulated by an electrical timer. With such control over the seasons, you can sow seed almost any time during the year.

**Cuttings.** Propagating by vegetative means is often the quickest way to get new plants and, when no seeds are available, it is the most practical.

To propagate greenhouse plants you use *softwood stem cuttings.* (Generally speaking, trees and hardy shrubs are propagated through hardwood stem cuttings.) The stage of maturity of the stem you select will govern, to a great degree, the success in rooting.

*The first watering of transplanted seedlings gives the roots and soil the closest possible contact with one another.*

The prime requisite is a healthy, insect-free parent plant, for strength begets strength. Next, selection of the right cutting wood is of major importance. You might think that the most vigorous shoots would make the best cuttings; however, such wood has already dissipated the accumulated food reserves—or soon would do so. On the other hand, mature or woody growth will react too slowly to achieve the necessary cell division. For this reason you need to select the most typical growth for most greenhouse plants, remembering that the leaves contain the necessary food. A stem with a superabundance of flowers is undesirable because flower production creates a drain on food reserves.

A new plant of near-mature size is too likely to lose moisture (through the leaves) that cannot be replaced in sufficient quantities until roots are formed. So choose a cutting with leaves sufficient only to provide the necessary food to the rootless plant and not one with so many leaves that transpiration would prove excessive and subsequently fatal. The size of a stem cutting varies between 4

*Left: A stem cutting should not exceed 6 inches. Opposite: Leaves on the lowest 2 inches are stripped off the stem.*

and 6 inches, depending upon the spacing of the leaf nodes, the plant's branching habit, and the optimum size (including leaf area) that you can keep in a healthy and turgid condition.

To prepare the cuttings, trim each with a sharp knife to 3 to 5 sets of leaves; the cut end should be not more than ⅛ inch below the last leaf node. Remove the bottom 2 sets of leaves close to the stem. Then dip the stem into a hormone powder. Such chemicals (available in varying strengths) help to promote rooting. Now insert the cutting into the rooting medium, with its remaining sets of leaves above the surface. Place cuttings close to one another but not touching.

The section of the propagating bench devoted to cuttings will have been filled with clean, coarse builder's sand, perlite or vermiculite, mixed with a small amount of peat moss (proportions: 4 to 1). A sprinkling of ground limestone to neutralize the acidity of the peat will make this medium more acceptable to a wider range of plants. Cleanliness is more important in propagating

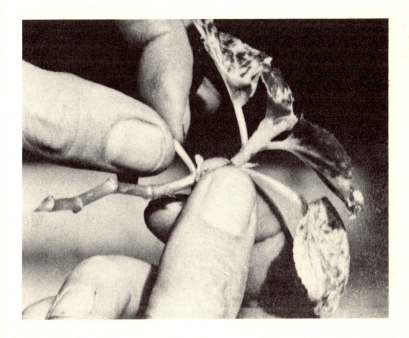

*Above: Insert cutting and
firm the coarse sand
around it before watering.
Right: Roots will form at
the leaf nodes in a few
weeks.*

than it is later on when the plants have built up reserves to fight adversity. For this reason, keep soils with their inherent microorganisms away from the delicate, unrooted cuttings.

While without roots to replace the moisture lost by evaporation through the leaves, the cuttings must have a constantly moist atmosphere. Create this either by draping a sheet of polyethylene plastic over a frame or installing one of the available misting systems. The plastic covering allows an exchange of gases, in-

*Above: Perlite, used as a rooting medium in a propagating bed, substantially eliminates soil-borne diseases. Below: If you lack room, a few assorted cuttings can be rooted in an 8-inch bulb pan. Cork the drainage hole of a 2½-inch clay pot, sink it in the center, and use it as a water reservoir for the cuttings.*

cluding oxygen, but will not permit moisture to escape. Bear in mind, however, that these same conditions are also ideal for the growth of fungi, especially since ventilation is somewhat restricted by the covering. Hence, more nearly ideal conditions (including ventilation) are possible with an automatic misting system. These electromechanical devices cause a valve to click on when water has evaporated from the surface of a contact. The resulting mist will then cause the valve to close. Since this type of mechanism depends upon evaporation, it is virtually nonoperative during the nighttime hours, thus reducing the danger of a fungus developing.

*Leaf cuttings* are advisable in the case of several plant families, especially those species whose leaves grow out from a central crown rather than from an elongated stem. Such is true of the African violet, streptocarpus, and other gesneriads as well as many species of begonias.

You can root leaf cuttings in two ways: Cut from parent plants, such as the *Begonia rex,* the rather succulent leaves with prominent veins. (The length of the leaf stem is unimportant.) With a sharp knife or razor blade, cut across each major vein on the underside of the leaf; lay the leaf flat on moistened coarse sand; and place a stone on each cut to insure its direct contact with the

*Leaves with prominent veins, such as rex begonias, may be rooted as follows: Slit the main veins. Then lay the leaf against the sand and*

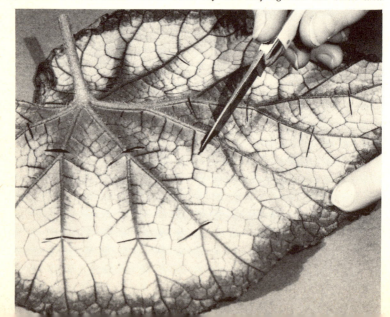

medium. After several weeks, roots will emanate from the under-side of each cut, followed by the emergence of a new leaf. When the new plantlet has developed to a recognizable form, cut it apart from the original leaf (which will have begun to wither), and pot it in the recommended soil.

The second technique is also adaptable to the begonias, as well as the previously mentioned gesneriads. Cut each leaf with 1 or 2 inches of stem. Then stick it, row upon row, in the sand of the propagating bench to the base of the leaf. A large number of new plants can be developed in this way—African violets are especially easy to root by this means.

*A cutting pot* that cares for itself automatically is a reasonable substitute for a misting system when a small amount of propagating makes the latter impractical. Place a few pieces of broken crock over the drainage hole of a 6- or 8-inch bulb pan; cover the crock with ½ inch of coarse sand. Then fit a cork in the drainage hole of a 3-inch pot and place it in the center of the larger one. Add more coarse sand to the larger pan and fill the smaller one with water; you can then insert cuttings in the sand, which will stay moist continuously for about a week, when the reservoir pot requires refilling.

*peat moss mixture. Put a stone on top of each cut to insure contact with rooting medium. When roots form, each section may be cut away and rooted individually.*

*Above: Moisture, sealed into a plastic bag, will insure rooting of stem cuttings or the germination of seeds. Below: Cuttings root quickly under a mist propagating system. When the sun evaporates the moisture on the metal screen "leaf," it raises enough to activate the misting nozzles.*

*Above: Fleshy leaves of many plants will root readily if severed and plunged into a sandy mixture. Below: When new leaflets emerge, the old leaf can be cut off at soil level. The new plant will be ready for its own pot a few weeks later.*

Another space-saving device for rooting cuttings is the "clothes-line" trick. Fill a polyethylene bag ⅓ full with a mixture of moist sand, perlite, and peat moss; it will hold 1 or 2 cuttings. Then, close the bag with a "twistem," and hang it from a cord that is out of your way in the greenhouse. You need never open the bag, thus hung, until roots are visible through the plastic—usually 2 or 3 weeks, depending upon the variety.

**Layering.** Where new growth is slow to "break," as on the woody stems of such plants as ficus (rubber plant), dracaena, ardisia, or dieffenbachia, use the *air layering method* of propagation. You accomplish this by cutting ⅓ of the way through the stem (or as many stems as you wish) with a single, slanting stroke; insert a small splinter of wood or a matchstick to keep the cut open. Dust the wound with a rooting hormone and wrap all of this with *damp* sphagnum moss. Since the moss should be kept moist, cover it with polyethylene plastic sheeting and tie at top and bottom around the plant stem. Rooting time varies with each plant species, but 6 weeks is about average. When roots begin to fill the moss, cut the plant off just below the newly rooted area and pot it in the appropriate size container and the appropriate soil mixture.

*To prepare an overgrown, lanky plant for layering, partially cut the stem, hold the wound open with a wooden matchstick, and dust the area with a rooting hormone.*

*Above: Wrap the area around the cut with damp sphagnum moss. Right: Cover moss with a sheet of polyethylene and tie the top and bottom. Below: In about one month, the newly rooted portion of the stem can be severed and potted as a new plant.*

*Left: A pot-bound plant ready to be divided. Below: After cutting apart, three plants can be potted individually.*

**Divisions.** A number of plants enlarge themselves by growing new stems around their perimeter, eventually filling their pots. Such plants consist of a clump of several stems and leaves, so you can take them out of their pots, cut them apart, and repot them as several individual plants.

You can also make divisions from those plants that produce offsets along their stems or plantlets on their leaves. Holding down the stem or leaf against damp sand with a peg or a stone will create the ideal conditions —rooting should take place in about 2 weeks. When a cluster of new roots develops to a few inches in length, separate the new plant from its parent and pot it in its own container.

*Left: Leaf margins of many kalanchoe species germinate new plantlets.*
*Below:* Begonia hispida cucullifera *is one of those interesting viviparous species, which form young plants on their leaves.*

*Above: Leaves that give rise to new leaflets may be anchored to the sand with a stone. Right: Roots will form in about 2 weeks and the new plant can then be severed.*

There are still other methods of propagation (i.e., from bulblets, root cuttings, and grafts), but the foregoing are those most often practiced in the home greenhouse. Which technique to use for the propagation of a specific plant is a decision you will have to base on various factors. *Seeds* are usually inexpensive and provide an excellent and quick source when you want a large quantity of plants. *Cuttings*, generally speaking, guarantee the progeny to be true to the parent plant (not always so with seeds). *Layering* can produce a mature plant of considerable size from a mature or woody stem in a relatively short time. *Division* will give you one or more plants immediately.

The condition of growth varies at different times of the year in different plants, making one method more desirable than another at that specific time. First consider whether a plant is an annual or a perennial. Most of the time you propagate annuals from seed, although you might use cuttings for an especially valued hybrid.

*Established in its own pot, the plant will soon start to form new stems.*

But with perennials (especially one of hybrid origin), your choice of propagation techniques increases. Many plants, which are created as a result of breeding, do not produce seeds which in turn will reproduce, and, therefore, a vegetative form of propagation has to be the choice. But which one—layering, cuttings (leaf, root, or stem), or divisions are all possibilities in specific cases—depends on the plant's characteristics. All these methods are easy to master. Plants which "break" (produce roots) readily from leaf nodes or veins and emerge from the soil as a single stem lend themselves to propagation by cuttings. Those growing as clumps or with multiple stems are easily divided by literally pulling the plant apart (each cluster of stems has its own portion of root system).

Your own facility and experience with each technique enters into the one you finally use. The skill that sets a gardener apart is knowing which particular method to use for a specific kind of plant or for a desired effect.

# III. What Will You Grow?

*The portability of clematis makes it an ideal pot plant.*

# 10

# A "Backwards" Plan to Get What You Want

AN ATTRACTIVE DISPLAY OF interesting plants almost constantly is what you want from your greenhouse. That kind of schedule takes a bit of juggling, and you may have to settle for minor pleasures several months. But those major sensations you achieve—such as a spectacular cyclamen that requires 8 months from seed to flower—will make the whole greenhouse idea seem worthwhile.

Fortunately, there are a number of relatively quick-flowering plants you can grow from seed (*Impatiens balsamina, Primula kewensis, Bellis perennis, Salvia splendens*, and *Nemesia strumosa*) and an equal number of foliage plants that you can propagate vegetatively for almost immediate effect.

As I pointed out earlier, your schedule is a "backwards" business. First, you determine just when you want a particular plant to bloom, consulting a calendar: Do you want pot plants to give for Christmas or Mother's Day? Do you want cut flowers and bulbs to brighten your home in winter? Do you want a special foliage plant for someone's birthday? Would you like a few speci-

men plants for the terrace in summer? Next, use a garden encyclopedia to estimate how much time is needed from the day a cutting
is taken or a seed is sown. It may help you to have a special
calendar or diary in which to keep the schedule for your greenhouse.

## Rescheduling a Plant's Bloom

Much of greenhouse gardening involves the "forcing" of plants into
bloom at a time other than their normal flowering period. This can
only be done if the plant has gone through its complete cycle,
which, in some cases, includes dormancy brought on either by
drought or by freezing temperatures. An important factor of the
growth cycle is that which triggers growth and, more importantly,
initiates bud formation—this factor is *light*. Many plants are
photosensitive to either short or long day lengths. Perhaps the
most familiar example is the chrysanthemum, which blooms during
the short days of the fall season. As might be suspected, this
short-day plant can be kept from blooming by artificially extending
the day length until any specific date later on. If flowering is wanted
during the summer, however, a black cloth has to be used to cover
the plants in the afternoon in order to artificially shorten the days
and stimulate earlier bud initiation. By following the schedule
recommended for a specific variety by the commercial supplier of
your chrysanthemum cuttings, flowering can be accomplished at
any specific time of the year.

Each plant species has its own growth cycle, which includes a
period of bloom, rest, leaf growth, bud initiation, dormancy, bud
development and, once again, flowering. The order in which each
segment of the cycle takes place may vary and the amount of
light necessary to start a bud into growth may also vary. The
temperatures at which other phases of growth take place will
differ even for plants originating in the same geographic area. It
is, therefore, essential to learn about each of your plants in order
to follow its own rhythm.

When does the gardening year begin under glass? It never does;
greenhouse gardening is an endless cycle with no beginning and
no end. There are plants that you can propagate at any season
(*Tolmiea menziesii, Coleus blumei, Dieffenbachia picta, Tradescantia fluminensis variegata, Zebrina pendula,* and *Senecio mikan-*

*ioides*), and great numbers that will bloom during any month without special treatment (*Saintpaulia ionantha hyb., Impatiens sultanii, Abutilon megapotamicum, Begonia semperflorens fl. pl.* 'Pink Camellia,' and *Tagetes patula* 'Spry'). Your immediate challenge is to work out a schedule of bloom, match the plants to the temperature, and then select the best method of propagation.

Do not hide your plants during any of their nonblooming periods—that is no more necessary than for a good chef to hide his copper pots, wire whisks, and canisters in the kitchen. If you keep your seed pans, empty flats, and the cutting bed in apple-pie order, they will not detract from the appearance. They are part of the total greenhouse picture and add interest to it.

### The Whys of Name Calling

The use of correct plant nomenclature is a subject interwoven with overtones of snobbery, self-consciousness, and colloquial custom. But at some point you must grab the bull by the horns and use the accepted international language of the plant world rather than all those elusive common names—and it may as well be now. There are no less than fourteen butterfly plants and, when you are discussing one or looking for one in particular, how much more accurate it is, and less exasperating, to refer to *Bauhinia monandra* and know it is *the* one under discussion.

Thanks to the Swedish botanist, Carolus Linnaeus, a system of binomial nomenclature was devised and is now accepted universally. Each plant bears two names. The first is the generic name (the singular form is *genus* and the plural, *genera*). *Rosa* is the genus of the common name, *rose*. However, since there are many kinds of roses, each kind carries a specific, or *species*, epithet (the singular and plural of the word *species* are the same). *Rosa rugosa* is a native rose of Japan. The descriptive Latin term, *rugosa*, refers to its wrinkled appearance, while *Rosa odorata* is the perfumed rose from which many hybrid tea roses are produced.

The plant genus is often named for a botanist, his patron, or a mythological figure, if not for some apparent physical feature. The species, however, more often makes reference to the plant's native habitat (*australiensis*, of Australia; or *maritimus*, of the seashore), its color (*alba, coccinea, lutea, aurea,* or *caerulea*; meaning white, red, yellow, gold, and blue, respectively), or some other physical feature.

There might be added to the genus and species a varietal name (denoting a selected, cultivated variety) or a hybrid name (the result of crossing two varieties or two other hybrids), which is indicated by single quotes. A hybrid created by crossing two species is often indicated by an "x" preceding the species epithet. Hybrid names are usually not Latinized and they seldom prove very helpful in identifying the plant.

The species is more often a definite clue. The following words are often found as the species or as part of the species epithet and, if you become familiar with them, you will be well on your way to making more sense out of a plant catalog or a plant label. These are clues that will lead to greater success in growing a wide variety of plants.

THESE WORDS SOMETIMES SIGNIFY COLOR OF A SPECIFIC PLANT PART:

albus = white
argenteus = silvery
atro = dark
aureus = golden
azureus = sky-blue, azure
candidus = white
cardinalis = cardinal (red)
carneus = flesh-colored
chrysanthus = yellow flowered
citrinus = citruslike, lemon-
   colored
coccineus = scarlet
coeruleus = dark blue
cyaneus = dark blue

discolor = of two different
   colors
flavus = yellow
fulvus =tawny orange
luteus = yellow
niger = black
purpureus = purple
roseus = rosy
ruber, rubrus = red
sanguinalis = blood-red
violaceus = violet
virens = green
xanthinus = yellow

THESE WORDS WHICH INDICATE ENVIRONMENT CLUE YOU TO THEIR
CULTURE:

agrarius (agrostis) = of the fields
alpinus = alpine
aquaticus = aquatic
arenarius = of sandy places
australis = southern
borealis = northern
campestris = of the fields or
  open country
exoticus = foreign, not native
maritimus = of the shore or sea
montanus = of mountainous
  regions

nivalis = growing in or near
  snow
occidentalis = western
oceanicus = of the sea
orientalis = eastern
riparius = of river banks
saxatilis — growing among
  rocks
silvestris (silvaticus) = of the
  woods

THESE WORDS SPECIFY SIZE OR SHAPE OF A PLANT OR SOME PART OF IT:

abbreviatus = shortened
acuminatus = long pointed;
  tapering
angustus = narrow
brevis = short
campanulatus = bell-shaped
cordatus = heart-shaped
cuneatus = wedge-shaped
digitatus = finger-form
elatus = tall
grandis = large
latus = broad

linearis = narrow
longus = long
macro = large
micro = small
minimus = very small
minor = small
nanus = small, dwarf
pachy = thick
parcus = small
planus = flat
platy = broad

THESE WORDS INDICATE SEASON OR TIME:

aestivalis = of summer
annuus = annual
autumnalis = of autumn
hibernalis, hyemalis = of winter
nocturnus = of night

perennis = perennial
praecox = very early
tardus = late
vernalis = of spring

THE FOLLOWING PREFIXES DENOTE QUANTITY:

uni = 1
bi or di = 2
tri = 3
quadri or tetra = 4
penta or quinque = 5
hexa = 6
hepta = 7
octo = 8
ennea = 9

deca = 10
centi = 100
mille = 1000
mono = one, single
multi = many
pauci = few
plenus = full, double (many-petaled flowers)
poly = many

THESE TERMS REFER TO PLANT PARTS:

andrus = stamen
anthus = flower
carpus = fruit
caulis = stem
florus = flower

folius = leaf
lobus = lobe
pedatus, podus = foot
petalus = petal
phyllus = leaf

SOME WORDS SPECIFY A SPECIAL CHARACTERISTIC:

acris = acrid, sharp
aggregatus = clustered
alatus = winged
baccatus = berried
calvus = hairless
capillaris = hairlike
caulescens = with stem
ciliaris (ciliatus) = hairy-fringed or margined
circinatus = coiled
complexus = encircled
complicatus = folded back or over
cornutus = horned
crassus = thick
crenatus = scalloped
cuspidatus = sharply or stiffly pointed
cymosus = flowers in cymes

deciduus = with parts falling (as leaves), deciduous
decumbens = reclining at base with tips upright
dendroideus = treelike
dentatus = toothed
dichotomus = forked
esculentus = edible
eximius = very unusual
ferox = very thorny
fertilis = fruitful
-ferus = bearing
filamentosus = threadlike
floribundus = flowering profusely
fruticosus = shrubby, bushy
glabrus = smooth

gracilis = slender
guttatus = spotted
hirsutus = hairy
hispidus = bristly
hortensis = of the garden
humilis = low-growing, dwarf
imbricans = overlapping
incisus = cut
inermis = without thorns or
  spines
involucratus = a group or
  whorl of small leaves or bracts
labiatus (osus) = lipped
lactatus = milky
laevis = smooth
lanatus = woolly
lanceus = lancelike, pointed
lineatus = striped, lined
lucidus = bright, shining
marginatus = with margins
mollis = soft
mucronatus = sharp-tipped
muralis = growing on walls
mutatus = changed, changeable
nudus = bare, naked
odorus = fragrant
officinalis = medicinal
-oides = like
oleraceus = of the vegetable
  garden or the kitchen
ornatus = showy, ornamental
palmatus = divided or lobed
patens = spreading
pedunculatus = stalked
pictus = variegated
pineus = of or pertaining to
  pines

pinnatus = with leaflets on the
  sides of the main leaf axis
plumosus = feathery
pulcher = handsome
pungens = sharp-pointed;
  pungent
racemosus = with flower in a
  type of elongated cluster
radicans = rooting along stem
repens = creeping
rugosus = wrinkled
sarmentosus = having runners
scandens = climbing
semper = always
serratus = saw-toothed
sessilis = stalkless
simplex = unbranched
spicatus = spiked; or with
  flower spikes
spinosus = with many spines
splendens = showy
stoloniferus = producing
  runners that take root
strepto = twisted
sub = somewhat
suffruticosus = rather shrubby
terminalis = terminal; at stem
  end
tristis = bitter, dull
-ulus = somewhat
umbellatus = with clusters of
  florets whose stems rise from
  a common point
vegetus = vigorous
viscosus = sticky
vulgaris = common
zonatus = zoned, banded

## What Limits Your Choices

Knowing what you now know about greenhouses and the plant world, what would you like to grow? Before you make your selections, answer the following three questions and keep the answers in mind as you go through the "biographical sketches" of the various candidates which follow:

1. What is the temperature range of your greenhouse? (Check one.)
    (a) cool—45° to 57°
    (b) warm—58° to 70°

2. How do you want to use your plants?
    (a) as pot plants for foliage and/or flowers
    (b) for cut flowers
    (c) for later planting in your outdoor garden

3. How many do you want and what size?
    (a) Specimen plants in 12- to 18-inch tubs *are* possible even in a moderate-size greenhouse, if the varieties you choose are used on the porch or terrace during May through October and spend most of the winter in dormancy under the greenhouse bench. They will take up bench space only during the late weeks of winter and early spring when new growth is under way.
    (b) Accent plants of moderate size for greenhouse display or indoor use, and some for planting outdoors in the summer.
    (c) Small—even miniature—specimens such as daffodil, cyclamen, gloxinia, and bellis.

## Recommended Plants for the Warm Greenhouse

Making choices of plants to grow in your warm greenhouse forms a lengthy list and a wide variety of habits of growth. Like all other plants, given the proper conditions, they will flourish—only more vigorously than most.

These are not all of the plants, but the best of all, in my opinion, for the warm greenhouse. For more information, see Chapter 21.

Acalypha hispida
Achimenes
Adiantum cuneatum

Adiantum peruvianum
Adiantum trapeziforme
Aechmea fasciata

Aechmea fulgens
Aglaonema roebelinii
Allamanda cathartica
Anthurium andreanum
Aphelandra squarrosa
Ardisia crispa
Aristolochia elegans
Asplenium bulbiferum
Asplenium nidus-avis
Asplenium viviparum

Begonia masoniana
Begonia rex
Begonia socotrana
*Begonia tuberhybrida
*Billbergia windii
*Bouvardia humboldtii
Browallia speciosa var. major
Brunfelsia calycina

Caladium candidum
*Campanula isophylla
Cibotium glaucum
**Cissus discolor**
**Citrus mitis**
Clerodendrum thomsoniae
*Clivia miniata
*Cobaea scandens
Coccoloba uvifera
Codiaeum variegatum var. pictum
Coelogyne cristata
Coleus blumei
Coleus thyrsoideus
Columnea gloriosa
Cryptanthus fosterianus

Davallia bullata
Davallia elegans
**Davallia fijeensis**
**Dieffenbachia picta**
**Dipladenia sanderi**

Echeveria gibbiflora var. metallica
Epiphyllum ackermanni
Episcia cupreata hybrids
Eucharis grandiflora
Euphorbia fulgens
Euphorbia pulcherrima

Ficus benjamina
Ficus elastica
Ficus lyrata
Ficus pumila
Fittonia verschaffeltii

**Gloriosa rothschildiana**
**Grevillea robusta**
Gynura aurantiaca
Gynura sarmentosa

Hibiscus rosa-sinensis

Ixora coccinea

Jacobinia carnea
Jasminum officinale var. grandiflorum

Kalanchöe blossfeldiana

*Manettia bicolor
Maranta leuconeura kerchoveana
Medinilla magnifica

Nelumbium nelumbo
Nidularium innocentii

Passiflora caerulea
Passiflora quadrangularis
Passiflora trifasciata
Pentas lanceolata
Peperomia caperata
Peperomia obtusifolia variegata
Peperomia ornata
Peperomia sandersii
Phoenix roebelinii
Pilea cadierei

* Adaptable to either a warm or cool greenhouse.

Platycerium grandis
*Plumbago capensis
Poinciana pulcherrima
Russelia equisetiformis
Saintpaulia ionantha
Sinningia pusilla
Sinningia speciosa
Spathiphyllum clevelandii

*Stephanotis floribunda
Strelitzia reginae

*Thunbergia alata
*Tibouchina semidecandra
Trachelospermum jasminoides
Tradescantia fluminensis variegata
Tripogandra multiflora

## PLANTS FOR HANGING BASKETS

Browallia speciosa major
*Campanula isophylla
Columnea gloriosa
Episcia cupreata hybrids

Platycerium grandis
Russelia equisetiformis
Thunbergia alata
Tradescantia multiflora

## FOLIAGE PLANTS

Adiantum cuneatum
Adiantum peruvianum
Adiantum trapeziforme
Aglaonema roebelinii
Aphelandra squarrosa
Ardisia crispa
Asplenium bulbiferum
Asplenium nidus-avis
Asplenium viviparum
Begonia masoniana
Begonia rex
Begonia socotrana
Caladium candidum
Cibotium glaucum
Coccoloba uvifera
Codiaeum variegatum var. pictum
Coleus blumei
Cryptanthus fosterianus
Davallia bullata

Davallia elegans
Davallia fijeensis
Dieffenbachia picta
Echeveria gibbiflora var. metallica
Ficus benjamina
Ficus elastica
Ficus lyrata
Fittonia verschaffeltii
Grevellia robusta
Gynura aurantiaca
Gynura sarmentosa
Maranta leuconeura kerchoveana
Medinilla magnifica
Peperomia caperata
Peperomia obtusifolia variegata
Peperomia ornata
Peperomia sandersii
Phoenix roebelinii
Pilea cadierei

* Adaptable to either a warm or cool greenhouse.

VINES

Allamanda cathartica
Aristolochia elegans
Cissus discolor
Clerodendrum thomsoniae
*Cobaea scandens
Ficus pumila
Gloriosa rothschildiana

Jasminum officinale var. grandi-
florum
*Manettia bicolor
Passiflora caerulea
Platycerium grandis
*Stephanotis floribunda
Thunbergia alata

## Recommended Plants for the Cool Greenhouse

A greenhouse is often thought of as a place where rare or exotic plants are grown and while this is often true, it can also house the commonplace, colorful, although out-of-season, flowering annuals. This is true of the cool greenhouse in particular.

Some of the most time-tested varieties of familiar petunias or marigolds put on a show of color for several months and the fact that they are easy to grow makes them even more desirable. You grow them from seed and repot them into 4-inch pots with a mixture of ⅔ garden soil, ⅓ leaf mold, and a small amount of coarse sand to insure positive drainage. Superphosphate (one 4-inch potful mixed into each bushel of the potting mixture) will provide the energy for good continuous growth. If you cut the flowers of annuals before they produce seeds, they will continue to flower over a period of a few months. Calendulas, mignonette, schizanthus, wallflowers, dwarf marigolds, sweet peas, and stock are among the most dependable and easy-to-grow annuals.

But whether they are annuals, biennials, perennials, flowering, or foliage plants, here are the ones I have found to be the most successful for the cool greenhouse:

Abutilon magapotamicum
Acacia armata
Adiantum pedatum
Agapanthus africanus
Alpines—see Alpine Plants
Aloe variegata
Arum creticum

Arum palaestinum
Azalea indica
*Begonia tuberhybrida
Bellis perennis nana
Beloperone guttata
*Billbergia windii
Bomarea kalbrayerii

* Adaptable to either a warm or cool greenhouse.

Bougainvillea glauca
Bougainvillea spectabilis
*Bouvardia humboldti
*Bromeliaceae—see Bromeliads

Calceolaria herbeohybrida
Calendula officinalis
Camellia japonica
*Campanula isophylla
Campanula pyramidalis
Cephalocereus senilis
Cestrum aurantiacum
Chlorophytum comosum var.
  variegatum
Chrysanthemum hybrids
Cissus antarctica
Clianthus dampieri
*Clivia miniata
*Cobaea scandens
Coryphantha arizonica
Crassula arborescens
Crinum powellii
Cyclamen persicum var. gigan-
  teum
Cymbidium 'Peter Pan'
Cymbidium 'Flirtation'
Cyperus alternifolius
Cyperus papyrus

Daffodils
Daphne odora var. marginata
Datura suaveolens
Dendrobium nobile
Dianthus caryophyllus
Dicentra spectabilis
Dimorphotheca ecklonis

Echinocactus grusonii
Echinocactus sarcocaulis
Exacum affine

Fatshedera lizei
Felicia amelloides

Freesia hybrida
Fuchsia hybrida

Gazania splendens
Grevillea robusta

Haemanthus coccineus
Haemanthus katherinae
Hedera helix
Heliaporous mallisonii
Heliotropium arborescens
Heliotropium rutilum
Hibiscus coeleste
Hippeastrum aulicum
Hippeastrum hybrida
Hippeastrum x johnsonii
Hippeastrum pratense
Hoya carnosa
Hyacinth

Lachenalia tricolor
Lagerstroemia indica
Lapageria rosea

*Manettia bicolor
Mimulus glutinosis
Miltonia vexillaria

Narcissus
Nemesia strumosa
Nerine sarniense
Nerium oleander
Notocactus mammulosus
Nymphaea tetragona helvola

Osmanthus fragrans
Oxalis bowiei
Oxalis cernua
Oxalis crassipes
Oxalis rubra

Pelargonium coriandrifolium
Pelargonium dasycaule
Pelargonium domesticum
Pelargonium peltatum

* Adaptable to either a warm or cool greenhouse.

Pelargonium Lady Washington
Palargonium tetragonum
Pelargonium zonale
*Plumbago capensis
Primula kewensis
Primula malacoides

Salpiglossis sinuata
Schizanthus hybrids
Schizostylis coccinea
Selaginella kraussiana
Solanum pseudo-capsicum

Soleirolia soleirolii
*Stephanotis floribunda
Streptosolen jamesonii

*Thunbergia alata
*Tibouchina semidecandra
Torenia fournieri
Trachelospermum jasminoides
Tropaeolum majus
Tropaeolum tricolor
Tulips
Zantedeschia aethiopica

PLANTS FOR HANGING BASKETS

Abutilon magapotamicum
*Begonia tuberhybrida
*Campanula isophylla
Chlorophytum comosum var.
    variegatum
Cissus antarctica
Felicia amelloides

Fuchsia hybrida
Heliaporus mallisonii
Hoya carnosa
*Manettia bicolor
Pelargonium Ivy-leaved
Streptosolen jamesonii
Tropaeolum majus

FOLIAGE PLANTS

Adiantum pedatum
Fatshedera lizei
Grevillea robusta

Hedera helix
Selaginella kraussiana

VINES

Bougainvillea spectabilis
Cissus antarctica
Cobaea scandens
Hoya carnosa
Lapageria rosea

*Manettia bicolor
*Stephanotis floribunda
Tropaeolum majus
Tropaeolum tricolor

* Adaptable to either a warm or cool greenhouse.

# 11

# A Few for Openers

THE EASIEST PLANTS to grow in your greenhouse are those for whose specific needs you have an "understanding." This is not meant to be a flip way of saying, "You can grow it if you are willing to learn about it," but rather that your horticultural pleasures, successes, and enticements will grow as your interest grows deeper. It is but a point of view, a starting point from which your horticultural abilities can develop and broaden. Begin with a handful of plants that have certain basic characteristics in common—ease of propagation, reasonable size and response to compact shaping, early flowering or maturation, and resistance to insect damage and disease. If, added together, these attributes seem to describe the perfect plant for the greenhouse gardener, then, there are a number of perfect plants.

The following group of "perfect plants" will provide all the elements that stimulate the novice—color, form, texture, and fragrance—and none is difficult to grow.

*Primula malacoides*, easily started from seeds sown in March, produce numbers of flowers in shades of rose, pink, lavender, and white over many weeks the .following winter and spring. Another species, *P. kewensis,* which also makes a good flowering plant in 4-inch pots, has a very special quality because of the white flourlike dusting over its foliage. Its color is a clear, bright yellow. Both of these primulas will do well in a cool greenhouse (50° to 55°) but will tolerate slightly warmer conditions as long as good light and ventilation are provided.

A favorite, versatile plant is *Browallia speciosa* var. *major.* Seeds sown in winter will produce summer flowers and a second sowing in July will provide winter color. While there is a good white variety, it is the vibrant blue browallia that is really striking. In addition to its use as a conventional pot plant, its clambering habit makes it an ideal subject for a hanging basket. Of course, when grown in this way it will require a little extra watering to offset any excessive evaporation.

One of the lures of greenhouse gardening is the anticipation of growing exotics—and what has a greater aura of intriguing rarity than the orchid? However, with thousands of varieties from which to choose in this largest-of-plant-families, there is little need to select only those having high heat and high humidity requirements and are, therefore, more difficult as well as more expensive to grow. One which does well in cool conditions is the cymbidium. It produces sprays of waxlike flowers and the different varieties range through many colors, from green to red and even ivory. Years ago cymbidiums required considerable space, but today the breeders have produced a strain of miniatures that have all the attributes of the genus except that they are easier to house. When in bloom a cymbidium can also be enjoyed as a living room decoration for several weeks.

Of course, it is difficult to deny the pleasure of flowering a few pots of tulips, daffodils, or crocus. However, these must be potted in the autumn and allowed to produce roots before being plunged under sand or a pile of leaves outdoors, and they must be allowed to become dormant before being forced into flower in a cool greenhouse later in the winter. However, lachenalia is a dramatic, bulbous plant that is as equally satisfying as the others and can be flowered with reasonable success without as long a dormant period. After merely a month of chilling, between potting and revival into growth, the straplike leaves will come up and are soon followed by 8-inch flower stalks. The bell-shaped flowers open soon thereafter. While red and orange varieties are available, yellow is the most striking.

The one element in the greenhouse that makes it such a special world of its own, particularly in midwinter, is that of fragrance. And very few plants can boast of any sweeter or more delicate perfume than that of the *Osmanthus fragrans*. While it can grow into a very large shrub, there is no need to let it get out of hand. One or two plants in 6- to 8-inch pots are enough to fill even a 50-foot greenhouse with its wonderful aroma. The tiny white clusters of blossoms are appreciated, therefore, even if not seen.

Another subject for the cool greenhouse is streptocarpus. Not a respiratory ailment (which it sounds like), but a most interesting native of South Africa, the streptocarpus, or Cape primrose, will flower dependably each spring and continue throwing new flower spikes above the leaves for about two months. Even when not in flower, the rich green of the crinkled leaves provides your greenhouse with a healthy looking, attractive foil for other nearby plants. Varieties are available in shades of blue, white, and rose. One of the species that is a real conversation piece is *S. wendlandii*. Easily grown from seed, it produces only one leaf, about 2½-feet long, and from its base the 1-foot flower stalk rises and produces up to thirty flowers, each 1 inch in size.

When selecting plants for your first greenhouse it seems only natural to think in terms of flowering plants. However, among those with dramatic, colorful, and fascinating form is the *Begonia rex*. Yes, it does flower, but the bloom is really secondary to the foliage. Colors range from a metallic silver to various shades of red (including bronze). Some markings swirl, others are geometric, and the surface textures range from those puckered like seersucker to those densely hairy. The shape of the leaves is equally diverse. A small collection of a dozen different varieties of *Begonia rex* will add interest to your greenhouse and provide weekly changes of plants to use in your home.

All of the foregoing plants are easy to grow. And you can flower more with equal ease, if you are not easily intimidated by "the experts." Those plants which you are told are difficult to grow are only those which have a "little something special" to watch out

for. Some seeds need their coats softened before they will germinate, other plants are especially sensitive to drafts, still others
need warmth to open the flowers but cooling-off to have them
last. Chapter 21 attempts to provide all the special information
necessary to transform each one from a "difficult plant to grow"
into another interesting subject for your greenhouse repertoire.

## For the Incurable Collector

In your career as a greenhouse gardener, it is likely that you
will become enamored with some particular plant group and
innocently begin to collect it. Shortly you will be addicted! This
is also true for cultural techniques (hydroponics and other soilless
methods). The following chapters will provide information on
some of the commonly collected groups.

*Even one pot of hyacinths is enough to perfume an entire greenhouse.*

# 12

# Bulbs, Corms, and Tubers

BESIDES REALLY BEING easy to grow, this category of plants is so varied and interesting that it never fails to stimulate the beginning gardener or satisfy even the most advanced.

There does not seem to be any easy, all-inclusive description for this classification of plants. Neither size nor shape unites them. Some bulbs and their kindred grow above ground, others below. Some produce leaves first, then flowers—others reverse the order. About the only characteristic common to all of them is their need for a rest at some time during the year, but even the time for this resting period varies from one species to another.

If there is any secret of success for getting any of them to flower, it is in following their natural sequence of growth. Each species has its own natural sequence. That is why some are planted in the fall and others in the spring. While it is possible for tulips, planted in the spring, to grow leaves at the same time as they grow roots, flowers will not follow unless the sequence provides for a good root system *first*.

*The infinite variety of bulbs, corms, and tubers is only outdone by the magnificent flowers they produce.*

Here is a quick refresher on the growth requirements of bulbs, corms, and tubers. Potting can vary from the use of a conventional pot and soil to placing a bulb in the neck of a glass and substituting water, pebbles, or even excelsior as an anchor for roots or as a growing medium. Root growth is stimulated by the addition of heat and a slight amount of moisture. The amount of heat varies from the minimum level (40° to 50°) required by hardy bulbs such as tulips, to the higher temperatures (around 70°) needed to start root action in caladiums and tuberous begonias. Root action often can be achieved without the benefit of sunlight and, for the hardy bulbs, it is even better to force them in total darkness.

**Bulbs.** The true bulb is made up of fleshy layers. The onion is probably the most familiar example and, like the onion, any bulb can be cut in half during its dormant season and the flower will be there, in the center, all ready to begin its further development when growth is rekindled. I feel that this fact is especially important to the novice grower to help him relax in the comfort of knowing that half the work is already done when he buys a bulb. Maybe this is just enough to deflate your ego, but the final result is not really guaranteed. Care still must be taken to bring the flower out from inside the bulb in the best possible condition. It is here that you will meet the true test in the technique of "forcing."

First, buy bulbs from a dealer who advertises "bulbs for forcing." The varieties might carry the same names as some offered for outdoor planting in the fall. The difference, however, is in the special preparation for early forcing which includes precooling. This is the artificial equivalent of several months of winter temperatures so that, when finally started into growth, they will be following their normal and necessary cycle. If bulbs are to be forced after January 15, it is not necessary to buy ones that have been prepared or precooled. They will get sufficient "winterizing" in the unheated garage or cold frame to make them ready for spring bloom, even though spring will be artificially created in the greenhouse.

The following "Do's and Don'ts" are guidelines for growing this group of plants:

1. *Do* pot them as soon as you get them. Bulbs, corms, and tubers tend to dry out and shrivel if allowed to sit around.
2. *Don't* use an oversized pot or the roots will tend to get dangerously dry. They have a better chance for success in a pot that is too small rather than too large.
3. *Do* force growth gradually, lest the embryo flowers are "blasted" (withered, stunted, or blighted).
4. *Do* pay attention to "finishing" the flowers. This requires slightly cooler temperatures for 4 or 5 days when bloom is achieved. Flowers will last longer with this hardening.
5. *Do* allow sufficient time for good root development, which you can determine by knocking the plant out of the pot, before forcing top growth. The temptation to shortcut here can lead to complete failure.
6. *Don't* fall for bargain bulbs. Top quality is worth the difference in price.

Now, which bulbs to plant? I face the choice of bulbs as a hungry man would approach a banquet, rubbing my hands together at the prospect of all those delicacies. I have singled out my favorites below: With hundreds to choose from, I have found certain ones (not all common ones) to be the most gratifying and reasonably easy to force successfully.

*Daffodils, like tulips, should be potted as closely to each other as possible.*

**Tulips, Daffodils, and Hyacinths.** Bulbs of tulips, daffodils, and hyacinths should be potted as soon as they are delivered to you (from late September to early November). Use pans or three-quarter pots, since the root structure does not run very deep. Be certain to soak the pots thoroughly before using them or they will absorb water from the soil and allow the new roots to get dry and "burn up." Use a rather heavy soil (one not too rich in organic compost or peat), since its compact composition helps to hold the bulbs erect without trouble of extra staking. Actually, the soil's make-up is not very critical since the bulbs are virtually self-sufficient at this stage. The soil, nevertheless, should have the capacity to hold water, since dryness will interrupt the development of flowers and even thwart their maturity.

I like to put in as many bulbs as a pot will hold—to the point of their almost touching one another. The neck of the bulb should be barely covered. Actually it will become more exposed as it develops, and daily watering washes the soil down into the pot. Now, give each pot a good soaking, place them in a large wooden box in an unheated garage, and cover them with coarse dry sand.

*The first watering after planting is crucial.*

The ideal temperature for the development of roots, prior to early forcing, is 50°. If flowering is not necessary until mid or late winter, the pots can be stored under sand, which is covered with salt hay, in a cold frame. Further watering should not be necessary until the pots are brought into the greenhouse for forcing.

Tulips and daffodils are forced into flower in a similar manner. However, before starting the forcing procedure, uncover a pot and tap out the bulbs with the soil intact to inspect them. If bulbs are in flats, dig out one bulb. There should be a heavy root system and foliage showing an inch or so above the soil. If both of these conditions are not present, it is too soon to force them and doing so will only result in very weak, stunted, and deformed flowers at best. When roots and slight top growth are evident, bring in a few containers at a time (weekly intervals will help stretch out your "crop") to the coolest part of your greenhouse.

*Above: Covering bulbs with coarse sand allows root growth prior to their dormant period. Below: The layer of salt hay protects the bulbs from a premature thaw.*

Keep them watered and, in a few days, position them where the temperature can be maintained fairly consistently at 60°. When flowers are almost fully opened, move them, if possible, to a cooler spot. This "hardening off" process helps the lasting quality of the flowers.

Hyacinths can be forced in much the same way. However, top growth is not a prerequisite as with tulips and narcissus. The pots should be forced immediately at 60°. Three or four weeks will be necessary before hardening off the flowers.

Of the following, some are rare, some are common; some are bulbs, a few are corms, and others are tubers. But each has something special about it that makes it worth growing.

*Bring a flat or a few pots of daffodils into the greenhouse each week to have a steady supply coming into bloom.*

**Achimenes (Gesneriaceae).** This member of the Gesneriaceae has tiny rhizomes that look like catkins from a birch tree. Plant five or six in a shallow 6-inch pot and keep warm (60° to 65°), slightly moist, and shaded until germination. Continue in a shaded location but increase watering and feed with liquid fertilizer through the period of flowering. Then reduce water and gradually dry off top growth before you store the pot. Do not repot until the third year.

**Agapanthus africanus (Liliaceae).** Commonly called lily of the Nile, it is a bit large for a small greenhouse; however, it is worth the room if a few square feet are available. Since it usually flowers in midsummer, it is best as a tubbed plant on the terrace—kept outdoors from May to October. Clumps of bright blue trumpetlike flowers are held above the leaves on 2½-foot stems.

Plant the tuberous roots in late winter with tops above a heavily organic soil. Water and feed lavishly until after flowering, then slack off in the fall. Rest under a bench in a cool greenhouse until you are ready to force it again the following March or April.

While agapanthus flowers best after becoming pot-bound, the bulbs will eventually raise themselves almost out of the pot due to overcrowding. At that time, divide the plant and repot. Do not leave excessive room around the clump of bulbs.

**Apios americana (Leguminosae).** This plant is more of an interesting oddity than a real beauty. Its purplish-brown flowers are pealike and hang in clusters from the vining stems. Grow it on wire or bamboo stakes. Three or four tubers should be planted in a 5-inch pot.

**Arum creticum (Araceae).** A native of Crete, blooming in the spring, this tuberous plant grows to 1 foot in height and has a creamy-yellow flower up to 6 inches long on a 10-inch stem. Leaves are arrow-shaped, up to 5 inches long. It needs a rest during the winter, when watering is kept to a minimum. In the late winter start it growing with a little warmth and water. Propagate it by seed or division of tubers in a rich organic soil mixture; it requires warm, moist conditions in spring and 40° minimum temperature during the winter.

**Babiana sambucina (Iridaceae).** This small-scale plant does well indoors after it has been brought into flower in a *cool greenhouse*. The thin stems are only 6 inches high and during February and March they hold clusters of bluish-purple flowers with centers brightened by their yellow anthers. Plant 1 dozen corms in a 5-inch bulb pan using a highly porous soil mixture.

**Begonia tuberhybrida (Begoniaceae)—Tuberous Begonia.** These complex and recent hybrids were started by crossing Andean and Bolivian species and, therefore, do well under the conditions of a cool greenhouse, although a warm greenhouse often has a cool spot that suits them. Color and flowers for decorative accent were the hybridizers' goals, and the double form proved to be the most dramatic of all. To get large flowers, pinch out the first buds. When the second set of buds develops, pinch out the two male flower buds which appear on both sides of the central female bud. This is the female flower that

*Tuberous begonia (camellia type)*

will become large and decorative. Although plentiful watering is required when the plants are well rooted and in flower, once flowering is over, water should be gradually withheld and the plants allowed to rest in the winter and remain dry at about 45° to 50°.

Propagate plants by seed or dormant tubers; however, since most varieties in cultivation are the result of intensive hybridization, the gardener would be wise to purchase his supply of tubers from the hybridizer and not attempt their propagation. Start tubers in March in boxes of moist peat at 65° and pot them up in a light mixture as soon as growth appears. As the sun becomes stronger, provide shade and a humid atmosphere. Continue to repot in larger containers as the plant grows. Once in its final pot, the plant can be fed. Since the flowers are heavy, staking will be required.

**Caladium candidum (Araceae).** These colorful foliage plants from South America add a bright touch when many other plants are not in full flower. They grow up to 2 feet high with heart-shaped leaves which are nearly white in this hybrid, but offer combinations of red and orange, green and white in other species. They are propagated by the division of tubers in the spring and when growth begins they should be potted in rich soil, at temperatures of 65° to 70° and with moist conditions. Give them shade from strong sunshine, ample light at other times. When leaves are well developed and have a heavier texture, they will stand cooler conditions. Lay the pots on their sides to rest during the winter and keep them dry at a temperature no lower than 55°. When plants are fully dormant, remove the tubers from the pot and dust them with sulphur to prevent fungus before storing them in peat moss in a cool, dry place.

**Crinum powellii (Amaryllidaceae)—Crinum Lily.** Here is a hybrid of two South African varieties of this bulbous genus. How often one can say that a plant is "one of the most beautiful" and still be believed, I'm not quite sure, but it is true in the case of this crinum. The delicate pink trumpet-shaped flowers, held above the narrow straplike leaves, are especially rewarding, considering the ease with which the plant grows. Potted in the spring in an 8- to 10-inch pot, using a mixture of ⅓ peat, ⅓ sand, and ⅓ garden soil, it will grow steadily throughout the summer, begin flowering in October, and last until December. Over the winter watering should be withheld and the pots stored in a cool but frost-free location. Growth can be started again in May. Every 3 or 4 years, offsets can be separated from the parent bulb and potted individually. Fortunately, crinum lilies can be enjoyed by all greenhouse owners since they will thrive in a cool or a warm situation.

**Curcuma roscoeana (Zingiberaceae).** This plant produces a 1-inch spike of brilliant colors in a warm greenhouse. A Burmese native, this tuber likes a moist atmosphere at about 75° and should be potted (1 tuber to a 7-inch pot) in a highly organic soil mixture.

**Cyclamen persicum var. 'giganteum' (Primulaceae).** This giant form from the eastern Mediterranean was introduced here in the latter part of the nineteenth century. Its flowers, which are large, in colors of red, pink, salmon, purple, or white, appear in winter and early spring. The leaves are kidney-shaped, dark green and sometimes marbled. The plant likes cool, airy conditions with a winter temperature of 45° to 50° and a summer one not above 70°. Sow seeds thinly during August; they will germinate at a temperature of 60° to 65°. When rooted, seedlings can be potted in 2-inch pots. Keep them at 55° in a slightly moist atmosphere until the weather becomes colder, when you should reduce the moisture. Pot in good compost, being sure to shade them from the bright sunshine; feed with a liquid fertilizer during the summer. Bring plants into the cool greenhouse in September at about 50° to 55° and water them sparingly. They will flower the following winter.

**Cypella plumbea platensis (Iridaceae).** This plant is a South American bulb akin to the iris. Its blue flowers are held on 2-foot stems and can be forced at moderate temperatures in either a cool or warm greenhouse.

**Daffodils (Narcissus) (Amaryllidaceae).** Daffodils are so familiar that it almost seems unnecessary to discuss them. However, I suggest that you try some of the miniature species and hybrids rather than the more common giants, such as Fortune, King Alfred, and Mt. Hood. It is true that the large flowered varieties are easily grown in wooden boxes, planted bulb to bulb in the fall. Kept in the cold in the beginning of winter and brought into the greenhouse in midwinter, they flower in 4 to 5 weeks. They can be cut by the dozen and used indoors. But, try a few 5-inch pans of the hybrid 'Tête-à-tête.'

The pure colors, fresh apple-green leaves, and erect form give them many times the stature indicated by their actual size. Nevertheless, they are flowered in the same manner as the more common varieties.

Allow 4 to 5 weeks from the time of potting in the fall until the ground freezes outdoors. By then, a root system has been established. Then put the pot in a cold frame and cover over with a few inches of sand. Keep it there in a frozen, dormant state until midwinter or later. The bulbs are made ready to force into flower by bringing them into the gradually increased warmth of the greenhouse. Here, they are first kept under the bench until growth is an inch or two high. Once they are placed on the plant bench, growth will increase as a result of more heat and more light. Any well-drained, porous soil will suit their needs.

**Eucharis grandiflora (Amaryllidaceae)—Amazon Lily.** One of the finest bulbs for a warm greenhouse, this is a great favorite wherever grown. It is frequently used for forcing, with several bulbs placed in a large pot, producing clusters of snow-white, fragrant flowers on 12- to 18-inch stems. The ovate leaves are large and attractive. They need frequent watering while growing at a temperature of 65° to 70°. One pot of eucharis will fill a 30-foot greenhouse with its fragrance.

**Freesia hybrida (Iridaceae).** Most of the freesias of today are from the species, *F. refracta*, which came from South Africa and has much smaller, creamy-white flowers. There are now many colors ranging from snow white through yellow to crimson, and some blue and mauve forms. All of the current hybrids bear larger flowers than their parents. The flowers are very fragrant, appearing in early spring. They can be propagated from corms in a utility mixture of moderate fertility but good drainage; place 6 or 7 bulbs in a 5-inch pot. Plunge the pot in sand in a cold frame for 6 weeks until growth starts. Water sparingly until strong growth develops. Decrease the watering of freesias after flowering since the leaves turn yellow and die off. Keep pots quite dry from June to September. Freesias can also be grown from seed sown in the spring.

**Gloriosa rothschildiana (Liliaceae)—Glory Lily.** The "glory lily" is a Kenyan climbing plant with swept-back, wavy-petalled orange, red, and yellow flowers of great beauty. Its leaves are narrow and lengthen into graceful tendrils. Its long stem (3 to 6 feet) may require support. The tuberous root should be grown in good compost of 3 parts loam, 2 parts peat, and some coarse sand. The greenhouse should be warm—about 60°.

Remove offsets from old tubers in the fall. The dormant tubers should be placed in pots on their sides and be kept warm and dry over the winter. Repot them in February or March and start at 75°, one tuber per 6-inch pot, or 3 tubers per 8-inch pot. Give plenty of water during the growing season. Gradually decrease water after the lily blooms until the soil and leaves dry off, when you store them again for winter. Examine plants periodically for scale, bulb mites, and aphids.

**Hippeastrum aulicum (Amaryllidaceae)—Amaryllis.** These exotic plants, often incorrectly referred to as "amaryllis," come from Brazil. The lilylike flower appears in the winter before the leaves begin to grow and has a crimson-colored trumpet about 6 inches long on an 18-inch stem. Its subsequent leaves are broad and straplike. The large bulbs are buried only halfway down in a rich soil mixture, closely potted. You can plan a succession of blooms with bulbs started into growth in January and coming into flower in March. A cool greenhouse will maintain the flowers once they have developed, but to start early growth keep pots in a warm atmosphere of about 70°. Watering should be continued, with feeding after flowering until growth is complete—around the end of August. Then gradually withhold watering until November so that the bulbs can rest. Plants should need repotting only every three years. Propagation is from offsets or seeds, which take at least three years to become a flowering-size plant.

**Hippeastrum hybrida (Amaryllidaceae).** This plant has large and very conspicuous flowers, ranging in dark red, scarlet, pink, or white that bloom from winter through spring with 2 to 4 on a stem.

**Hippeastrum x johnsonii (Amaryllidaceae).** This is one of the earliest hybrids of H. reginae x H. vittatum, a flower of dark red with white stripes that blooms in spring.

**Hippeastrum pratense (Amaryllidaceae).** This plant has bright scarlet flowers with a yellow base up to 3 inches across, with 2 to 3 flowers on a 1-foot stem. It blooms in late spring.

**Lachenalia tricolor (Liliaceae)—Cape Cowslip.** The Cape Cowslip has tubular, rich flowers of yellow and red on long, 10- to 20-inch spikes. The leaves are broad and strap-shaped, sometimes spotted purple. As its common name implies, it originated at the Cape of Good Hope.

It should be planted in rich, loose, fibrous loam, such as composted sod and manure. It should also have up to ⅕ coarse sand for drainage. When propagated, this plant should be kept at 50°.

To start, propagate by offsets. These will multiply and most will flower the following year. Seeds sown in the fall will germinate in about 2 weeks and flower in late winter. But, easiest of all is to tear off a number of leaves and bury the bottom inch of each leaf in sand. Firm the sand and keep it slightly damp. In time a new bulb will form at the base of each leaf. Potted individually, bulbs will flower the following year.

Pot in 5-inch bulb pans or wire baskets. The wire baskets should be lined with an inch of sphagnum moss.

After planting, water to settle the soil. Then water sparingly until growth starts. Do not try to force bulbs with high temperatures until the flower scape appears. Then they can be forced gently, at 55° to 60°. Lots of sunshine and seasonal fresh air are beneficial.

Watch for aphids especially.

**Nelumbium nelumbo (Nymphaeaceae)—Lotus.** The East Indian lotus has been prized since the beginning of history, as is evidenced by the use of its form in both Egyptian and Greek art and architecture. However, it is seldom grown in greenhouses because of one misconception or another. First, you do not need a pond or a pool, but merely a tub will suffice. And second, the tub need not be terribly wide (14 inches is enough), because both the leaves and the flowers are held high above the surface of the water. A sunny location in a warm greenhouse will supply its needs. In March, fill half the tub with an organic soil mixture. Then add enough water to make a slurry. Place the lotus plant a few inches under the surface and then fill the rest of the tub with water to within an inch or two of the top. While the delicate pink flowers are spectacular in June, July, and August, the leaves are an attraction at other times. Feed heavily and regularly for best results. When the seed pods have formed and dried, allow the water to evaporate slowly until the tub is no longer wet but only slightly moist. If kept this way for the winter, the plant will be ready to start into growth again after a six-month rest.

**Nerine sarniense (Amaryllidaceae)—Guernsey Lily.** This South African plant is both colorful and showy. Its dark-salmon flowers grow on leafless stems, 1 to 2 feet high. They have recurved, long stamens. Leaves open after the flowers have faded and develop as long straps. They can be grown at 45° to 50° in full sunlight in a loose, fibrous soil with peat moss, leaf mold, and sand added to keep it light and well drained. Keep the soil dry until growth appears; increase the water through the growing season. After the plant flowers, be sure to keep it in full light in order to rejuvenate it for the next season. When the leaves turn yellow, let the soil dry out.

Propagate plants by offsets after several years of growth and separate the bulblets while the plants are dormant. Plant bulbs in 4-inch pots; top dress soil in August. Aphids and red spiders are pests to watch for especially.

**Nymphaea tetragona helvola (Nymphaeaceae)—Pygmy Water-Lily.** Found in Idaho as well as in northern areas of the Orient, this water-lily is perfectly suited to the cool greenhouse. Most water-lilies are too large for the average home greenhouse, but this and hybrids of it are easily grown in a small pool or a 12-inch tub. With leaves only 3 or 4 inches across and its small, yellow, afternoon-blooming flowers, it will add a new dimension to a corner otherwise too cool to be made attractive.

Kept in a container with a highly organic soil mixture, it will often reproduce by self-sown seeds if the water level is brought to the top of the soil level during the winter months.

When growth begins again in March, add more water and feed by putting a half cup of dehydrated manure into a square of cheesecloth, tying the diagonal corners, and shoving this "tea bag" under the surface of the soil.

**Oxalis (Oxalidaceae)—Bermuda Buttercup.** These bulbous or tuberous rooted plants come in many different colors and, depending on the species, flower at different times of the year. The *O. cernua* from South Africa (though called the "Bermuda buttercup") has bright yellow flowers in the spring. The *O. bowiei* is stemless and blooms on foot-long stalks topped by a cluster of large rosy flowers in summer and fall. The *O. crassipes* or *O. rubra* bloom all year-round, with rosy flowers that have red veins.

All should be grown in an acid soil consisting of ½ peat moss or leaf mold and ½ light compost and sand. Dormant tubers should not be watered heavily until growth starts. Give them plenty of sunshine or the flowers will not open fully. Oxalis can tolerate a wide range of temperature, from 45° to 60°.

To propagate, divide tubers or grow from offsets. Early oxalis should be divided and planted in August or September. Year-round bloomers like the *O. rubra* do best if divided in January or February, although any month is acceptable. Seeds should be placed in light soil at 60° for best germination. Plants should be placed in 8-inch wire baskets lined with an inch of sphagnum moss and filled with soil. The baskets should each hold 4 to 6 tubers an inch below the surface of the soil. Or, the tubers can be placed in pots, one per 4-inch pot, or three per 5-inch pan. They should have fresh soil each season. Beware of the green fly; he will wreck your oxalis if he can get a good foothold.

**Schizostylis coccinea (Iridaceae)—Kafir-Lily.** This South African tuber is not a lily as its common name implies, but is a member of the Iris family. Its red or pink star-shaped flowers are excellent for cutting and they form loosely upon irislike leaves starting in late summer and continuing well into the fall. Like many South African plants it enjoys strong, unfiltered light. However, rather nontypically, it will only thrive if constantly supplied with plenty of water.

The plants should be dried off gradually when the leaves have begun to yellow, a month or so after flowering. The tubers should then be taken out of the pots, the soil cleaned away, and each clump of tubers separated to make new plants for the following year. Then, store them in a cool, dry location in peat moss or even in crumpled newspaper until they are ready to be repotted in March.

**Sinningia speciosa (Gesneriaceae)—Gloxinia.** The form and color of this tuberous plant recommend it to every gardener with a warm greenhouse. While it originated in Brazil, today's hybrids are all but unrecognizable as progeny of the species. The trumpet is longer and wider and some are either ruffled or scalloped. The colors range from a dark electric blue or brilliant red to delicately brushed-on pastel. Having achieved the ultimate in shape and color the hybridizers' latest efforts are being concentrated on fragrance.

Tubers should be started in February on a bed of peat moss at a temperature of about 70°. As soon as top growth starts, begin watering the peat moss gradually. When leaves are an inch or so long, pot each tuber individually in 3-inch pots, moving them eventually into 6-inch pots. An organic soil with sand added will suit their needs. They will flower in June and July. After flowering, the tempo of growth will slow down. At that time watering should be lessened. When all the leaves have died down, watering can stop and the pot should be placed under the bench to rest until the following February. The top layer of soil can then be teased away and the pot top dressed with a highly nutritious mixture. It is then ready to commence a new cycle of growth. However, in order to reproduce especially choice hybrids faithfully, leaf cuttings should be used.

**Tropaeolum tricolor (Tropaeolaceae).** This is a Chilean species grown from a small tuber in the cool greenhouse. The entire plant ranges only a foot or two during its summer growing season, so grow it on a form arranged in a 5-inch pot. This is a miniature in both foliage and bloom. As the name indicates, the flowers have three zones of yellow and orange and black at the tip. Start the tubers into growth at the end of the summer and they will be ready to flower by late winter and will continue flowering into June. After flowering, watering should be reduced. When the foliage dies down, it is time to remove the tuber and store it in a dry, cool location until repotted and started into growth again in August or September.

**Vallota speciosa (Amaryllidaceae).** Best known as the Scarborough-lily, this plant produces a spike with several scarlet trumpetlike flowers. Rich green straplike leaves surround the base. Pot the bulbs singly in 5-inch pots with a porous soil mixture. Keep them in the warm section of a cool greenhouse and, when they bloom, harden the flowers under cooler conditions for 4 or 5 days to give them better substance and lasting power.

**Veltheimia viridifolia (Liliaceae).** This plant is a winter-blooming bulb of special beauty. Its clusters of small tubular flowers are neatly arranged on top of an 18-inch stem, which is surrounded at its base by wavy-edged green leaves. The flower itself is greenish-yellow, with some of the hybrids available in orange tones. Pot singly in a porous mixture with the bulb half exposed. Grow in a cool greenhouse.

**Zantedeschia aethiopica (Araceae)—Calla-Lily.** The calla-lily from South Africa can be grown in greenhouses that have a nighttime temperature of 55°. These large, funnellike flowers, 8 to 10 inches long, are particularly glorious when they arrive in late winter and spring. Good, loamy soil and plenty of water are needed to produce the first good bloom. After the plants bloom, take them outdoors in May and give them very little water. After four months, they will have died down; then repot them in 6- to 10-inch pots, where they will shortly start growth once again.

FORCING DATA ON A FEW FAVORITES

| | DEPTH OF CONTAINER | SPACING OF BULBS | INCHES BELOW SURFACE | TEMPERATURE IN STORAGE | EARLIEST DATE OF FORCING PREPARED BULBS*** | EARLIEST DATE OF FORCING UNPREPARED BULBS | TEMPERATURE FOR FORCING | TIME NEEDED TO FLOWER |
|---|---|---|---|---|---|---|---|---|
| Tulips | 3½" to 5" | Almost touching | ½" | 50° | Dec. 1st | Jan. 1st | 60° to 70° | 4 to 5 weeks |
| Narcissus | 4" to 6" | Almost touching | 1" | 50° | Dec. 1st | Dec. 10th | 55° to 60° | 5 to 6 weeks |
| Hyacinths | 4" to 5" | ½" to 1" apart | ½" | 50° | Nov. 26th | Dec. 15th | 60° | 3 to 4 weeks |
| Iris* | 4" to 6" | 3" apart | 1" | 50° | Nov. 15th | Feb. 1st | 54° for 3 weeks; then 58° to 60° | 6 to 8 weeks |
| Lilies** | 5" to 7" | 6" apart | 1" | Order for delivery when you need them for forcing | Dec. 1st | — | 60° | Approx. 4 mos. |

* Iris: Water thoroughly. Do not place bulbs closer than 1" apart or lack of light will result in failure to flower.
** Lilies: To speed up flowering: Light a 100-watt bulb 4' above every 12 pots from 4 P.M. until 9 or 10 P.M. each night after growth begins. Syringe once a day with lukewarm water.
*** You "prepare" a bulb by refrigerating it artificially to complete its period of dormancy. This can be achieved in a shorter time than that required for natural dormancy.

# 13

# Cacti and Other Succulents

THE DEVELOPMENT OF this exotic group of plants started so many millions of years ago that neither the geography nor the climate of the world were as they are today. During that Eocene epoch, plant growth everywhere was lush and vigorous, reacting favorably to a humid, warm atmosphere. But, gradually, all that changed. The earth's surface heaved and shifted in some places and, in others, volcanic action formed new terrain. Rainfall patterns changed drastically and the heretofore unknown phenomenon of seasons, with great extremes in temperature, developed.

Some plants died, never to reappear again. Others struggled for survival and even altered their physical makeup. Broad leaves, which used to evaporate great quantities of water into the air, gradually became smaller. In time they appeared narrower, even as needles, and eventually certain species developed a hairlike covering to insulate their water-retentive parts. These survivors accomplished what the dinosaur, dodo bird, and the giant horsetail rush could not. They triumphed over every possible adversity and

*The variety of form and texture in cacti must be seen to be believed.*

continued to thrive and reproduce themselves in a still-changing world. These were the cacti.

While all cacti are succulents, all succulents are not cacti. Succulent plants are those with fleshy leaves or stems that have the facility for storing water and subsequently drawing upon it slowly. There are a number of plant families which have succulent members. And, strangely enough, more of these historically indestructible plants have been killed by kindness in cultivation than by adverse natural conditions. Although they slowly adjusted their physiology over the millennia in order to endure drought, malnutrition, scorching heat, and even marauders, they are not equal to the sudden "ideal" conditions of our greenhouses. Under such circumstances, they are likely to drown or die of indigestion if we are not cautious.

All these plants need not be well watered any more than all cacti can do with almost no water. Each species has its own requirements. Meet these requirements and the plants will thrive and provide you with magnificent flowers as well as with unique forms that will keep you engrossed.

Cacti are almost exclusively of American origin. Even the prickly pear (the fruit of the opuntia), now found in abundance throughout the Mediterranean and Middle Eastern areas, once was indigenous only to the Americas. So, a collection of cacti is a form of Americana.

Some of my favorite genera in the cactus family are representa-

*A notocactus dispels the concept that cacti are not decorative.*

tive of the various distinct shapes. Mammillaria, commonly known as the pincushion cactus, is widely enjoyed both for its round and its cylindrical forms, and is clothed with orderly spaced clumps of tiny spines. The bright flowers usually are produced in abun-

*A cactus garden of over a dozen species need not occupy over 6 square feet.*

dance, especially in *Mammillaria fragilis* and *M. elongata*. These two can be grown for relatively long periods in the greenhouse without outgrowing their allotted areas. The genus Opuntia is far less symmetrical in its habit of growth. Rather than producing a solitary elongated or round stem which gets bigger and bigger, its stems continually send out new stems at all angles. In *O. microdasys*, these flat pads are dotted with soft tufts of golden hairlike growth. The *O. erinacea*, on the other hand, is almost completely covered with off-white masses of long spines. *Astrophytum myriostigma* is a ribbed species which develops the exact form of the bishop's hat (its common name). It is a nice, dignified-looking plant until it comes into flower. Then a bright daisylike bloom, erupting from the center of the converging ribs, gives it a comedic appearance—a wonderful example of nature's versatility.

All of these cacti will thrive in a potting medium made up of equal parts of coarse sand, average garden soil (not too clayey), and leaf mold. The physical act of potting is really no different than for other plants; select the width and depth of a container to provide for a small amount of additional growth and for drainage crockery under the network of rangy roots. After potting and

*A paper collar makes a sticky job a lot more comfortable.*

before a plant has developed a strong network of roots, you should exercise care to provide only the minimum amount of water and nutrition. Once the cactus is established, provide small amounts of bone meal every 6 months (about 1 tablespoon to each quart of soil). Water thoroughly after each complete drying during the spring and summer growing period. Fall and winter is the rest period for most cacti of arid origin; at that time provide only minimum amounts of water.

Another group of cacti includes species which grow in a jungle environment and in areas other than the desert so often associated with these prickly plants. The most striking members here are the epiphyllum and schlumbergera. *Epiphyllum oxypetalum,* known as the night-blooming cereus for its powerfully perfumed flowers, open for one night in a burst of glory. It is a toss-up as to which is more dramatic—the *E. oxypetalum* or its close relation, *Selenicereus grandiflorus.* The *Schlumbergera gaertnerii* is much like the better-known zygocactus (Christmas cactus) but its funnel-shaped flowers are fringed and therefore showier. Most of the jungle cacti are rampant growers and, in their native haunts, clamber over the ground; some climb trees and still others hang from cliffs. It is not unusual to find a plant that is 20 or 30 feet long. So you see, these are not for the small greenhouse, unless you make new plants from cuttings every few years.

Anyone starting a collection of cacti sooner or later comes across the fascinating "stone mimicry" and plants "with windows." While they are not cacti, they *are* succulents and are closely related insofar as their environment, cultural requirements, and flowers are concerned. Now assigned to various genera of the Aizoaceae family, they all were formerly grouped under one broad genus, *Mesembryanthemum.* Two that look most like stones are *Lithops bella* and *Pleiospilos nelii.* When they grow in a pot filled with soil that is top-dressed with gravel, it is not until the two very fleshy leaves of these varieties split wide open and their daisy-like flowers emerge that they can be distinguished easily from the rocky surface. *Lapidaria margaretae, Conophytum minutum,* and *Titanopsis calcarea* are three good representatives of additional genera of stone-mimicking plants.

It may seem unlikely, but it is a fact that there are plants that have small windows incorporated into their leaf tips. Species such as *Fenestraria aurantiaca, F. rhopalophylla, Ophthalmophyllum lydiae,* and *O. verrucosum* get all but buried by wind-blown sands in their native desert. Their tiny windows admit light within these plants, so the food manufacturing process is able to continue at full speed.

Bear in mind in growing these succulents, and cacti too, that they really do not grow in deep, pure sand. Usually there is considerable organic matter mixed in with the sand, and the soil layers become richer as they go deeper. But, even the sand has a high mineral content and certainly cannot be considered as inert or lacking in nutritional value. The deserts where cacti grow are not the consistently torrid areas you might imagine. While the days are hot, with bright, clear skies, the nights are quite cold and temperatures often drop into the mid-forties. Most of the low nighttime temperatures occur during the dry season of winter, when the

*Left: Easily grown along with cactus,* Lithops gulielmii *(Aizoaceae) is almost impossible to distinguish from the stones that surround it. Below:* Fenestraria aurantiaca *captures sunlight through stem-tip windows.*

plant's outer skin is at its toughest and is best able to provide insulation. So, you see, a cool greenhouse is ideal for these succulents, and virtually no shading is necessary.

The commercial sources for these "bits of jewelry," either in the form of seeds or of young plants, are not numerous, but they offer a broad variety. Also, swapping among amateurs is common.

Additional succulents (including cacti) that do particularly well under greenhouse cultivation are the following:

**Cephalocereus senilis (Cactaceae)—Old Man Cactus.** This wooly-headed column attracts many cool greenhouse owners who find that it is fairly easy to grow. It is necessary to keep its long white hairs clean from dust. Pot it in a gritty compost with good drainage. Keep it dry in winter at a temperature of 40° and water it freely in spring and summer. To propagate, sow seeds in sandy soil in March, provide bottom heat, and place in pans within a propagating frame or plunge cuttings into a sand compost. This plant rarely flowers when cultivated and is grown solely for its interesting form and surface texture. However, should it flower for you, it will do so at night, producing pink blooms which seem to pop right out of the plant.

**Coryphantha arizonica (Cactaceae).** This cactus from Arizona grows in a clump and prospers in a cool environment. It has large pink flowers and globular stems covered with tubercles and long spines. It needs a gritty, well-drained compost and you must water it freely in spring, with little watering during the other months. Propagate it by division.

**Crassula arborescens (Crassulaceae)—Jade Plant.** This succulent herb from South Africa grows into a shrub 3 feet high. Its leaves are small, round, and gray-green with red margins and red dots. The flowers are white and held in panicles, but you rarely see them in cultivation, although they are showy. The plant needs gritty soil, full light, and a minimum temperature of 45°. Keep it on the dry side in winter; however, water it enough to keep it from shriveling. Increase the volume of water as warm weather arrives and continue to water well throughout the summer. Propagate it by seeds or by stem or leaf cuttings taken in summer. Insert cuttings in the compost only after they are allowed to dry in the air for a few hours. The callus formed in this way is necessary to prepare the tissue for rooting.

**Crassula sarcocaulis (Crassulaceae).** Also from South Africa, this plant grows up to 1 foot and flowers in the summer. Its small pink flowers are held in cymes above small, pointed green leaves.

**Echeveria gibbiflora var. metallica (Crassulaceae).** Like many other Mexican succulents, this one blooms during the summer and rests in the winter, so be sure to apply less water when it is in a semidormant state. The metallic-blue foliage of this variety contrasts with its bright red flowers. Give this attractive pot plant plenty of sunshine in a warm greenhouse or it will become leggy and far exceed its usual 8 to 10 inches. You can root stem cuttings in sand during the spring.

**Echinocactus grusonii (Cactaceae)—Golden Barrel.** This is one of my favorite cactus plants from Mexico. It is a deeply ribbed, bright green globe with very long, stiff yellow spines that give it the name "Golden Barrel." It is a slow grower and, while it rarely flowers in cultivation, it will grow eventually to considerable size and make a fine specimen. It should be potted in a porous mixture, watered moderately in the spring, freely in the summer, and kept dry during autumn and winter. It should be kept out of strong sunshine to keep from scorching. The best winter temperature is 40°. Propagation can be made by seed or by cuttings inserted in sand in the summer.

**Epiphyllum ackermanni (Cactaceae).** This is a very tough-looking plant to produce such a lovely ornamental flower. Epiphytic in nature, it can be found in Brazil clambering up the trunks of trees. From flat stems with few spines, a large exotic crimson flower blooms in summer. There are many hybrids in a wide range of colors, some of which flower at night. They need a rather richer soil than the desert varieties of cactus and a minimum temperature of 50°. They should be kept on the dry side in the winter, but syringed from time to time. If they shrivel during their dry period, they will plump up again when you resume watering in the spring. To propagate, insert cuttings made at the joints into sand.

**Kalanchoë blossfeldiana (Crassulaceae).** This succulent plant, native to Central and South Africa, is well suited to a cool greenhouse. It provides brilliant red flowers in late winter, and grows up to 10 inches tall. Seeds can be sown in spring, with the temperature kept at 60°. When the seedling can be handled, prick out and repot, continuing to repot in a well-drained soil as the plants develop. In winter, keep the soil almost dry; good ventilation is important.

**Notocactus mammulosus (Cactaceae).** This very spiny cactus is from Brazil and Argentina. It is a small plant, growing about 3 feet high, with beautiful, showy, and fragrant yellow flowers. Its globe-shaped surface is covered with well-guarded ribs. It does well in an organic soil mixture to which sand has been added for porosity. Water it moderately during the winter and even less during the spring, summer, and fall. It should be kept at a minimum winter temperature of 45°. To propagate, cut offsets away from the parent plant in the spring and root them in sand.

Still others include:

*Astrophytum capricorne* is a low, tough-skinned, fissured mound with tufts of wooly, white hairs.

*Echinocereus rigidissimus* is, like many cactus forms, unbelievable. Its short, barrel-shaped stem is covered with row upon row of stiff spines, each cluster radiating from a center seam, like hundreds of frilly sequins appliqued white on green.

*Gymnocalycium saglione* is a globe that appears to have been partially deflated. Its gray-green surface erupts with miniature clusters of curved spines.

*Lophocereus schottii monstrosus* is a waxy, smooth cylinder with protrusions extending in an alternating arrangement along the entire surface.

*Lemaireocereus thurberi*, like all other members of this genus, is a ribbed column with evenly spaced clusters of spines along the ridges.

*Mammillaria candida* is so perfectly round and completely covered with radiating white spines that it resembles a tennis ball. Most other species are equally round but vary as to the overall size of the plant and the texture of spines.

*Opuntia pachypus* is a small candelabrum of thumb-thick branches—a good pot plant.

*Rebutia senilis cristata* is a creeping cluster of hairy stems.

# 14

# Bromeliads

I AM ALWAYS WARY of the phrases "ever-bearing," "trouble-free," or "perpetual-blooming." Because of my awareness of the pitfalls in these phrases fulfilling their claims, I hesitate to say that any plant is "fool-proof." However, if any plants should fit into such a category, it would probably be the members of the Bromeliaceae, or pineapple family. Most of these striking plants are lacking in common names so you might just as well get used to the Latin right from the start. This large group (over 1,800 species) of tropical and subtropical plants fits loosely into the category of succulents, not because they have the ability to store water within their leaves or roots but because they store water in the vaselike center of the rosette formed by their leaves and, since the "bromeliads" (the common epithet for the entire family) are natives of the rain forests and swamp regions of Central and South America, their perpetuation is well assured. The roots, even of the terrestrial species, are less important as water gatherers than the built-in vase.

*Cork bark filled with sphagnum moss supports a hanging display of tropical aechmeas.*

The epiphytic species, living upon trees and nourishing themselves on water and bits of decaying leaves blown their way, include some of the most colorful varieties of plants and lend themselves to easy culture in the home greenhouse. Those of you with a cool greenhouse need not despair for bromeliads can be grown with reasonable success if you choose the warmest corner and a sunnier location than is necessary in a warmer house.

I used to grow my bromeliads on pieces of cork bark attached to the greenhouse interior supports. Then I found that I could not move the plants when they came into bloom. Now, in order to enjoy them more fully, I employ a portable "bromeliad tree." A small, contorted branch rising from the center of a 7-inch flowerpot (wedged in place with chunks of osmunda or sphagnum moss) forms the support for five or six specimens. The plants are attached to the branch with thin pieces of copper wire. The end result is a portable, colorful, easily maintained plant collection.

With over 1,800 species falling into more than a dozen genera, there is obviously a problem of selection. Perhaps the most popular and colorful are the *Aechmea caudata variegata, A. fulgens discolor,* and *A. fasciata* (all very desirable species) with flowers ranging from golden yellow through rose and blue to red and violet arranged on equally colorful panicles. Other favorites are the *Vriesia splendens* or *V. barilletii*, which bloom with a flat, broad, swordlike golden inflorescence. While these vriesias are normally terrestrial, they can be incorporated, with the epiphytes, in the aforementioned planting with substantially normal growth for extended periods. Additional varieties to add to your collection are

*Various bromeliads planted in a bench display will lend splashes of color over a long period.*

*Billbergia saundersi, Cryptanthus zonatus zebrinus,* and *Guzmania musaica.* Now, to add a tropical atmosphere to the planting, hang a few "strands" of *Tillandsia usneoides* from the branches. This is the Spanish moss which, while neither Spanish nor a moss, is a bromeliad of the southern United States and South America. I might interject at this point that all members of the Bromeliaceae family are American. True, they can now be found in other parts of the world, but they were originally introduced from the Americas as were cacti and anthuriums.

Even when not in flower, most of these varieties have sufficient interest in the striation of their leaves to put on quite a show and they do not require that premium position in full sun. I have seldom found insects to be a problem with bromeliads, other than an occasional outbreak of scale. Detect them early. Control is easily effected by a spraying of Malathion. If you keep them healthy, provide a dappled light, and keep their natural "vases" filled, they will certainly flower. Some of the best species for you to try follow.

**Aechmea fasciata.** Closely related to the pineapple, it grows in its native Brazil as a tough, leathery rosette of green and gray horizontally striped leaves. The flower rises atop a stiff stem like the plume of a drum major's hat in bright pink and blue. It grows best in a warm greenhouse and can be propagated by cutting offsets from the parent plant. Pot them in a richly organic soil, with peat moss or fir bark added.

**Aechmea fulgens.** Purple flowers emerge from scarlet berrylike bracts that hold their brilliance for 2 months. Smaller than *A. fasciata,* this rosette of leaves grows up to 10 inches high and the flower scape up to 20 inches. Its leaves are banded in olive green and purple. Culture and propagation are the same as for *A. fasciata.*

**Billbergia windii.** From Brazil, this makes a unique house plant and an attractive addition to a cool greenhouse. The plant is about 1 foot high, with bell-shaped flowers that hang in greenish spikes out of pink bracts. The leaves are swordlike, about 9 inches long. This particular billbergia is the result of crossing *B. nutans* with *B. decora.*

You can propagate it by division, severing the suckers at the base of an established plant in spring. Pot in coarse, well-drained soil and water it well during the spring and summer. In late September withhold water gradually until the soil is almost dry. Water slightly during the winter and maintain a temperature of 50°.

**Cryptanthus fosterianus 'Foster's Hybrid.'** These low-growing bromeliads have long been popular for their fascinating variation in foliage. Their leaves form a rosette, are wavy-edged, stiff, and about 6 inches long and 1½ inches wide, in colors of grayish-green, purplish-brown, or red toward the base. They are banded with brown. Flowers are inconspicuous. You can grow these best with osmunda as the potting medium or wired to a section of tree trunk. They need lots of sunshine and a warm, moist climate in the summer. In the winter, hold back the moisture. You can increase the plants easily by offsets or division in the spring.

**Nidularium innocentii.** This Brazilian plant is known for its beautiful leaves, which are 10 to 12 inches long and 2 inches wide. The upper side is dark green and the underside is reddish-purple. Leaves grow out of a central whorl, where small, white, nearly unnoticeable flowers appear.

Pot the plant in a compost of osmunda fiber, peat, and sand and also a little decayed leaf mold. Nidularium makes a good house plant in a cool room with some sunshine. Temperature should be about 60°; give shade during the summer.

# 15

# Orchids

FEW PLANT FAMILIES have the infinite variety, the wonderful lasting qualities when in bloom, and the exotic aura attached to orchids. In addition, many species of orchids have the unusual characteristic of mimicking other plants—not in appearance, but in fragrance. There was a time when orchids were grown only by the wealthy. But orchid societies, through their fine publications, have provided to a broader public the clear, simple, factual information, which has exploded some of the myths and mysteries formerly associated with orchids and given new courage to the amateur. The common misconception that most orchids bloom only once every seven years is a distortion of the fact that certain species require about seven years from seed until their first flowering. However, even this is no longer true, since, with today's judicious hybridization and specialized methods of propagation, the time required for maturity has been cut down to four years.

Until recent years, the commercial orchids familiar to most were those Cattleyas grown in the warm greenhouse. The excessive

*Left:* Dendrobium nobile

cost of providing the necessary heat (especially in the northern states) helped to perpetuate the myth that *all* orchids are costly to grow. The truth is that coolhouse orchid varieties number in the hundreds and many hothouse varieties have been bred to tolerate intermediate temperatures and are consequently of moderate cost today.

Success in growing orchids depends, to a great extent, on having a "feeling" for the basic needs of each variety. Some orchids are native to the northern United States, some are from the steaming jungles of New Guinea, while still others are indigenous to the high slopes of the Andes and the lowlands of the Malayan archipelago. Each is subject to its own special conditions of temperature, light, and humidity.

We are usually familiar with the terminology when discussing most plants. Roots, stems, buds, etc., are commonplace words and well understood. However, orchids have their own very special vernacular attached to them. Here are a few of the most useful terms.

*Eye*—the bud from which new growth emanates, located at the base of the pseudobulb.

*Pseudobulb*—an enlarged upright stem, which is that special structure for the storage of food and water.

*Back bulbs*—those pseudobulbs of an orchid plant farthest from the point of new growth. They can be with or without leaves. Their main purpose is to supply food to the more actively growing parts of the plant. When the two or three oldest back bulbs are severed from the plant and left on the bench they will often sprout new growth from dormant buds.

*Peat*—in modern-day orchid culture, refers to the osmunda fiber (root of the osmunda fern), used as a potting medium instead of peat moss, which was once used for this purpose.

*Sheath*—that protective envelope in which the flower bud develops just prior to blooming.

*Blind plant*—one that does not flower due to a cultural deficiency, although it is of sufficient maturity to do so.

*Potting stick*—a hardwood or aluminum ramming tool about 12 inches long, used to wedge osmunda around plants during repotting or for forming the roots in whatever potting medium is being used.

*Pot hanger*—wire especially formed so that one end can clip onto the
   rim of a pot and the other end can be hung from a greenhouse
   rafter.

Unlike most plant families, orchids have an additional dimension which must be considered before their entire habitat is understood. Some are terrestrial in habit, having fibrous roots in the
soil similar to our more familiar garden plants. They grow well
potted in a garden loam to which peat and sand have been added.
There are other orchids, considered semiterrestrial, which have
fleshy roots and require a porous growing medium. Paphiopedilum
and cymbidium fall into this category. They establish good roots
in a mixture of equal parts of leaf mold, peat, and osmunda. The
third group of orchids is made up of the epiphytes. These are
plants which attach themselves to trees and rocks by aerial roots.
They do not absorb any food through roots anchored in soil,
and their aerial roots obtain no benefit from the host plant; their
only source of nutrition comes from the air and that decaying
matter which accumulates around the tangle of roots and slowly
breaks down into usable organic matter. Therefore, the potting
medium for epiphytic orchids acts almost solely as a support for
the plant.

*Paphiopedilum hybrid*

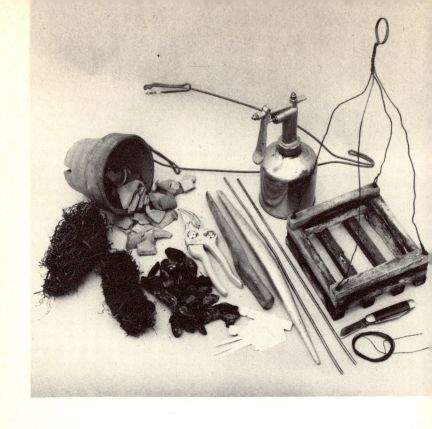

*Above: With a supply of wire stakes, containers, potting media, hangers, and miscellaneous tools, you can repot any orchids. Left: An orchid literally walks out of its pot.*

## Repotting

Most orchid plants are sold in pots and, therefore, the amateur's first experience with potting an orchid is actually in *re*potting.

When the pseudobulbs of epiphytic species grow over the side of the pot, it is time for a larger pot. Immediately after the plant has flowered, it will rest briefly for a period, which varies with the different species. Repotting should be done at this time so that, when growth does begin, the new roots will take hold in the fresh medium and there will be little or no setback to the plant.

Since orchids are, basically, shallow-rooted plants, deep pots are not necessary and can even be injurious by requiring too much bulky potting medium that can easily become soggy and cause root tips to die back. Remove the plant and, if the next larger pot proves too cumbersome, the plant should be reduced in size by cutting off and discarding all pseudobulbs farther back than the third or fourth from the lead bulb (the one made in the last growing period). Some plants will have several leads and each of these can be severed (with a minimum of 3 back bulbs) to produce several new plants.

Remove loose pieces of the old potting medium from around the roots of the plants. Select a newly cleaned pot and hold the trimmed plant in it at the normal level for potting.

With the oldest bulb about ¾ of an inch from the side of the pot, the lead bulb should be in about the center of the pot to allow for the ensuing growth. Different species vary considerably as to their vigor and, therefore, one mature plant can properly be repotted into a 5-inch pot while another of comparable age would require an 8-inch size.

Once the correct pot size is selected, place a small piece of aluminum screening (fine mesh) inside, to cover the drain hole to prevent the entrance of snails, slugs, and other pests. Next, add an inch or two of broken crock to provide drainage, and, finally, anchor the plant in place.

Just as there are supporters for both the plastic and clay pots, there are those who are now advocating the new potting media for epiphytes. For fifty years, osmunda (chunks or shredded pieces of the root of the osmunda fern) has been the accepted and highly successful medium for potting orchids. It does not break down readily and it provides sufficient porosity for good drainage and aeration. It does require some effort to wedge it in place around the plant but, once firmly set, no further attention is needed for a few years.

Requiring less effort, and having their share of proponents, shredded fir or redwood bark are equally good potting materials. Used by first placing a small amount under the roots and then adding some around the roots, it is tamped in place until the pot is full to within an inch of the rim and the plant is firmly in place. Regardless of which material is used, the eye, from which the new pseudobulb will emerge, should be level with the surface when the potting is finally completed. Other potting materials in vogue at present are shredded coconut hulls, ground tree fern, and even foam plastic impregnated with nutrients. Each has its advantages as well as shortcomings and while osmunda is the accepted, conservative material, with fir bark steadily increasing in popularity, each of the others should be explored too.

Those orchids without pseudobulbs, such as the vanda, angraecum, aerides, and phalaenopsis, will need periodic attention by adding osmunda, but actual repotting after the plant reaches a mature size will seldom be required.

The terrestrial varieties are potted in the same manner as most garden plants, using 2 parts fibrous loam, 2 parts peat moss, and 1 part oak leaves (crumbly but not decayed) to which one 4-inch potful of crushed wood charcoal and one of sand should be added for each ½ bushel of total ingredients. Top dress these plants annually, using more of the same potting mixture in order to maintain a nutritious growing medium. '

The correct watering of any particular orchid plant is perhaps the most important single cultural requirement and depends upon an understanding of the plant's habit of growth.

Aerides, cymbidium, masdevallia, vanda, disa, paphiopedilum and most other orchids with no pseudobulbs or those having fleshy roots fall into a group which has no dormant period and, therefore, grow continuously throughout the year. They should be watered thoroughly, be allowed to drain, and not be rewatered until the potting medium is dry again. These waterings will vary from daily to weekly, depending upon the amount of heat and the kind of container in which the orchid is grown.

*Above: Separate groups of 3 or 4 pseudobulbs, each having a growing "eye," and trim back the roots. Left: Chunks of osmunda fern root are compacted around the orchid roots. Below: When newly potted, the plant should be firmly held in the pot.*

There are also species which have a short period of dormancy. This group includes the cattleyas, many dendrobiums, and odonto-glossums. Watering of these should be reduced after they have finished flowering, but the pseudobulbs must not be allowed to shrivel.

Still others, such as the thunias and the deciduous forms of calanthes, need a definite dormant period. During this time all watering should be withheld. The water should be reduced when the leaves start to yellow and when flowering is over and all leaves have dropped, the plants should be allowed to become completely dry. This is the period of rest that is absolutely essential to the proper development of the next crop of flowers.

In the case of dormant and semidormant varieties, it is necessary to observe the plants constantly, since watering must gradually be increased when the first sign of new growth appears.

The use of a water-breaker is necessary in order to apply sufficient water without disturbing the potting medium or breaking off any delicate buds.

Segregation of plants according to the foregoing degrees of dormancy is essential. It is equally practical to segregate all plants in heavy bud, for it is at this time that the need for heavy watering has reached its peak and the trend toward moderation begins. Care must also be given not to wet the open flowers as they will spot and not last as long as when kept dry.

The temperature and the humidity in the greenhouse will affect the speed of evaporation from each pot and, therefore, the intervals between waterings. One method of maintaining a satisfactory balance is to wet down the walks, under-bench areas, and the bench surface between the pots each day. However, do not add moisture to the air in this manner or directly to the pots unless there is a rising temperature. For example, in Massachusetts the temperature begins to fall at about 3 P.M. during July, while the peak is not reached in Washington, D.C., until 5 P.M. Such precautions will prevent plants from going into the nighttime hours with any surface moisture that might cause disease or rotting.

If ever in doubt as to whether a plant should be watered or not, let it go until the next time. Many more plants are killed from overwatering than from drought.

## Ventilation

Many orchids, being tropical in origin, will not tolerate gusts of cold air falling upon them from top vents open during the winter. Where air cannot be warmed by passing over the heat pipes as it enters the under-bench vents, a mechanical ventilator can be employed. These small electrical devices (with a blower and movable louvers) should be installed overhead at either end of the house, over the walk. Placed in this location, the device allows a minimum of direct air flow to hit the plants. It will provide a periodic replacement of the air and supply a stimulus to its movement. The mechanism is easily controlled by a thermostat or an electric timer.

## Orchids for the Cool Greenhouse

These require a minimum nighttime temperature of 50° to 55° and are grown at approximately 60° during the day. Of course, this temperature cannot be maintained easily during the summer months without some method of artificial cooling. In southern states the coolhouse orchids are as much of a luxury as are the warm-growing varieties in the north.

A wide number of plants which do well under cool conditions include some of the most beautiful species. The cymbidium, native to the Himalayas, is grown for its long spikes of waxlike flowers in soft pastel shades. Japanese hybrids of the miniature varieties make them more practical to grow than the large standard-size cymbidium. Odontoglossums are among the finest for cut flower purposes. While native to subtropical countries, they are always found in mountainous terrain and, unlike most other orchids that require a dry, dormant period, this genus profits from cool, moist conditions all year-round.

The paphiopedilum (lady's slipper) is another easy-to-grow favorite, but only the varieties with plain green leaves will tolerate cool greenhouse conditions. The species with mottled leaves are more tropical and require temperatures in excess of 65°. Hybrids of the species *Paphiopedilum insigne* produce large flowers, some with striking colorations, and all remain in full flower, either on the plant or as a cut flower, for several weeks. Paphiopedilums are also found in catalogs under the older name of cypripedium.

*Paphiopedilum, from seed flasks to community pot, through repottings to flowering—about a 4-year process.*

Consider the following recommendations for a broader selection.

*Cochlioda rosea* is a Peruvian epiphyte flowering during winter on short racemes.

*Cymbidium Alexanderi* 'Westonbirt' is one of the best, with large pink and white flowers for late winter. It is epiphytic.

*Cymbidium* Flirtation, a miniature, is winter flowering.

*Cymbidum* Madonna has 4-inch flowers on large plant during February.

*Cymbidium* Panwelsii is one of the oldest and best heavy-bearing hybrids. It has large, bronze flowers.

*Cymbidium* Peter Pan is a semiminiature with prolific spikes bearing green flowers in spring.

*Dendrobium nobile* is a popular epiphyte and produces fragrant white flowers with purple tips. It blooms in January and often flowers again in June.

*Epidendrum radicans* is a strange-looking terrestrial species whose reedlike stems produce roots at the nodes. Its flowers bloom in the spring. They are brilliant orange-red with a yellow lip.

*Laelia anceps* is a Mexican epiphyte whose clusters of delicate lavender-pink, 3-inch flowers bloom in the winter months.

*Odontoglossum grande* is a dependable epiphytic species that blooms in midwinter with several large gold and lustrous brown-striped flowers.

*Odontoglossum pulchellum* is an early spring flowerer. Its very fragrant white blooms resemble lily-of-the-valley. It is a Guatemalan epiphyte.

*Paphiopedilum* Bromfield is a hybrid with outstanding large green and tan flowers which bloom between Thanksgiving and Christmas.

*Odontoglossum hybrids are ideal orchids for the cool greenhouse.*

*Paphiopedilum insigne* is a winter-blooming species. Its flowers are apple-green, with purple spots and white edging. It is striking in appearance and remains in good condition for over a month.

*Sophronitis grandiflora* is a Brazilian epiphytic native. It is a small plant with brilliant scarlet flowers lasting several weeks in midwinter.

*Zygopetalum mackayi* has deep purplish-blue markings and a dramatically veined lip which make it one of the most striking of all. It is epiphytic and a native of Brazil.

## Intermediate Orchids

The following species can be adapted to the warm section of a cool greenhouse or the coolest part of a warm greenhouse. Through this elastic kind of thinking, a collection can soon become quite extensive. These particular orchids require a minimum night temperature of 60° and include the largest number of orchid species. There are many others that fit into this category. However, the following are a few recommended for their ease of cultivation.

Making up this group are cattleyas, with their tremendous number of beautiful hybrids, those cypripedium having mottled leaves, and many of the dendrobiums. The miltonia, one of the most beautiful genera with pansylike flowers of large size and deep colors, is represented here, as is *Brassavola digbyana*, one of the most striking of all orchids with its deeply fringed lip, chartreuse color and heady perfume. Some additional species and selected hybrids are:

*Angraecum veitchii* has large sprays of white star-shaped flowers in the winter. All angraecums are epiphytes.

*Brassavola nodosa* is fragrant at night when clusters of greenish-white flowers are open in the fall.

*Brassia lawrenceana var. longissima* is an epiphyte with sprays of chartreuse and brown flowers which are outstanding for their inordinately long sepals. It blooms in the fall.

*Cattleya* Bow Bells is one of the finest white flowers of good size, shape, and texture. It is a fall-blooming epiphyte.

*Cattleya guttata* is a leathery-leaved epiphytic species with spray of unusually marked flowers with rose-purple lip and green-spotted petals and sepals. It blooms in the fall.

*Laeliacattleya* Grand Gate is an unusually colored peach and yellow-green flower that blooms in late summer. It is another epiphyte.

*Miltonia* Clown Mask is white with bright red markings. Blooming occurs in the fall. It is an epiphyte.

*Miltonia* Feuerwerke is a fine red.

*Miltonia* Wasserfalle is another of the German-made red crosses.

*Paphiopedilum* Maudiae 'Magnificum' is the green and white lady's slipper which flowers in spring and fall.

*Pleurothallis roezlii* is a small epiphytic plant which bears an unusual deep-purple flower.

## Orchids for the Warm Greenhouse

Those orchids which do best with a minimum nighttime temperature of 65° and a daytime average of 75° include some of the very dramatic species. The phalaenopsis (both species and hybrids) must be grown under the conditions of high heat and ample humidity of a warm greenhouse. The compromise of an intermediate house cannot carry these tropical varieties through to successful flowering on anything but a sporadic basis. *Phalaenopsis* Dos Pueblos 'Santa Cruz' has a good, large (5-inch) white flower that blooms twice each year on arching spikes. *Phalaenopsis* Cast Iron Monarch is one of the hybrids in recent years producing the delicate form of phaelenopsis with a heavy substance that results in a long-lasting flower, on the plant or for cutting. Phalaenopsis hybrids such as *P. luddemanniana* add a special quality to any collection with their bright purple flowers.

Another important warm house orchid is the vanda. Its unusual, straplike leaves are of a leathery texture. From the stem between the leaves, a flower spike emerges and, in the case of *Vanda bicolor*, a cluster of several deep purple and white flowers come into bloom and remain in perfect condition for well over a month. The hybrids produce considerably larger flowers, such as *V.* Roths-

*Cymbidium hybrid*

childiana, with a good blue and *V*. Nellie Morely, a fine rasp-berry. The vandas, grown in osmunda, or fir bark, and given strong light, frequent watering and a periodic feeding will respond well and flower heavily, often both winter and summer.

There are other species that do best in the warm house, such as *Cattleya violacea*, the rose and purple flower of Brazilian origin. The yellow-orange waxlike flowers of *Stanhopea wardii* would be desirable for its perfume alone. Additional species well worth the effort of growing are *Oncidium splendidum, Catasetum macro-carpum, Dendrobium phalaenopsis*, and *Angraecum sesquipedale*.

Other species you may wish to grow include:

**Coelogyne cristata.** This deliciously fragrant plant has pendulous clusters of white flowers tinged with yellow. It comes from northeast India in the Himalayan region. Its pseudobulbs have a gooseberry shape from which the flower spike emerges in the spring. It will grow well along with cattleya in a warm greenhouse during the summer; how-ever, cooler temperatures are best for it during the winter. For propa-gation, place a few separated back bulbs on a slightly moist surface to induce the growth of an "eye." Once this new growth appears, the plant can be placed in a pot and a root growth supported by fir bark. Grow to maturity in a warm greenhouse.

**Cymbidium hybrids.** Flowers of this terrestrial orchid are produced in the spring on arching spikes and their beauty lies not only in their delicate shades of pink, green, yellow, and ivory, but in their waxen texture. It is not unusual for flowers to last 1 or 2 months.

The species from which the very involved hybridizations have been bred come mainly from Burma and Assam. The miniature hybrids have gained in favor tremendously in recent years, with *C*. Peter Pan and *C*. Flirtation among the most popular. They like a cool green-house in winter, 45° to 50°, and higher temperatures during the summer when humidity and shading are necessary on new growth to prevent sun scorch. A fairly rich mixture of compost, including crumbling oak leaves, is best for potting. Propagation is by separating back bulbs and inducing dormant buds to break.

**Dendrobium nobile.** These epiphytic orchids are found over a wide range from India to China. The species, *D. nobile*, is deciduous, flowering on the growth made during the previous year. The 2- to 3-inch flowers come from the upper nodes of the jointed pseudobulbs in pendulous groups of 2 or 3. They are velvety, with rounded sepals and petals. The petals are white tinged with purple and have a round lip that is purple bordered with white. Growth is rapid during the spring, so plants need generous watering and high temperatures with good light. Once the pseudobulbs have matured, hold the water back; the leaves then yellow and drop. Winter plants over in full light and a cool atmosphere of 50°. This is the parent of many hybrids such as 'Montrose,' 'Stella,' 'Hallmark,' and 'Virginale.'

**Miltonia vexillaria—Pansy Orchid.** This South American orchid has been the subject of hybridizers' attention for several years, and now the pansylike flowers are produced in a great variety of colors. *Miltonia Ketha, M. Liberte,* and *M. Strom* are excellent examples of the new dramatic hybrids. They should be cultivated in a cool, moist and shady atmosphere in summer, and in winter the temperature should not go below 55°. Repotting is best done in spring, when new growth is taking place. Compost should consist of ⅔ fine osmunda fiber and ⅓ fresh sphagnum moss. Pots need not be large—a 4- or 5-inch size is usually sufficient—but good drainage is required, so place plenty of broken crock in the bottom of the pot or several chunks of charcoal. This will not only provide the necessary drainage but will keep the growing medium from becoming "sour."

## Selecting Plants

In selecting representative plants of different species to start an orchid collection, choose those plants which not only have temperature requirements similar to one another but are suited to that which the greenhouse can provide. Reputable sources can be found in the bulletin of the American Orchid Society and, while seedling plants are offered at attractive prices, it is best to choose those of flowering age. Learn to recognize the rhythm of each plant's cycle, since its needs are different during each stage of growth. Records should be kept of each plant's date of bloom and number of flowers, and a capsule appraisal of its quality (size, texture, form, and color). Such information will serve as a guide for future purchases with a view toward an improvement of these traits as well as to obtain plants which will flower during all the seasons.

# 16

# Ferns

AMONG THE MOST graceful and useful greenhouse plants are the ferns. Diverse in form, texture, and shading, they have sufficient merit to stand on their own or to be used as lush background for colorful flowering plants. While they can be grouped into coolhouse and warmhouse varieties, most ferns appreciate a moist atmosphere and some protection from direct sunlight. This latter requirement makes certain greenhouses better suited than others to fern culture. A northern exposure, which is not best for most flowering plants, is ideal for ferns.

Among the tropical ferns are the davallias. Species such as *Davallia bullata, D. fijeensis, D. solida,* and *D. elegans* can be grown in pots or with their hairy rhizomes trained to cling to a hanging basket. If you start a davallia from scratch, giving it moisture and periodic feedings, in a few months you will have a basket covered with the hairy rhizomes referred to as "squirrel's feet."

*Davallia canariensis* is well adapted to the coolhouse, so no greenhouse gardener need be deprived of growing and enjoying this member of the Polypodiaceae family. Davallias propagate easily from spores scattered on sieved sphagnum moss if they are kept well watered and shaded. Rooted pieces of rhizomes can also be potted to start new plants.

Maidenhair ferns rival the davallias for their beauty. Unlike most ferns, their fronds are often curved, with each frond made up of separated leaflets on the stem so that the general effect is that of informal delicacy. The South American species, such as *Adiantum peruvianum* and *A. trapeziforme*, are ideally grown in temperatures of 55° and higher; *A. pedatum* and *A. cuneatum* thrive under cooler conditions. *A. pedatum* is the deciduous species native to North America and will do best in the cool greenhouse; *A. cuneatum*, of Brazilian origin, is best satisfied by the 55° to 60° temperatures of the intermediate greenhouse.

When ferns are mentioned, it is only natural for us to think of the hayscented fern (*Dryopteris aemula*), the Christmas fern (*Polystichum acrostichoides*), and the lady fern (*Athyrium filix-femina*), all northern ferns. However, greenhouse gardeners have the world from which to choose their subjects. Such varied and exotic forms as the stag-horn fern (*Platycerium grande*), the Hawaiian tree fern (*Cibotium glaucum*) and the bird's nest fern (*Asplenium nidus-avis*) are all important members of this striking group.

Some are terrestrial (growing on the ground), and some are epiphytic (living off the ground, using another plant, such as a tree, for support). Still others are of a climbing habit and are especially useful in a permanent greenhouse planting. Among the more interesting forms are the ferns that sprout forth new plantlets at the tips of their fronds and propagate themselves freely in this manner. *Asplenium bulbiferum* and *A. viviparum* are two such species.

Shading, moisture, and good ventilation are important for healthy ferns; keep the air stirring, as they will not thrive in dark stagnant bogs. The terrestrial varieties grow down where the temperature is a few degrees cooler than the higher surrounding atmosphere. The epiphytes are found up on trees where they are more apt to catch a breeze while remaining shaded. As nature seems to compensate for location and exposure, we would be wise to follow suit in the greenhouse culture of ferns.

Syringing the leaves of most ferns is beneficial, but is not a substitute for thoroughly watering the roots. This should be done on a regular basis, allowing them to nearly dry out between waterings. Repotting all ferns is best done as their new growth commences. Dividing large plants with a knife will prevent the severe setback that would result from tearing apart the root system. Water well after potting in order to eliminate excessive air pockets and insure good contact of soil particles with the delicate roots.

**Asplenium nidus-avis (Polypodiaceae)—Bird's Nest Fern.** It is found throughout the tropics and has lance-shaped fronds up to 4 feet long and 8 inches broad, growing from a nestlike rosette. It grows best in a very moist, shady atmosphere at a winter temperature of 55° to 60°. Keep water out of the crown, and sponge off the fronds from time to time to keep them clean.

This fern can be propagated by spores sown on top of a pot of fibrous loam with peat and coarse sand mixed in. Later, pot it in a mixture of sphagnum and peat moss.

**Davallia fijeensis (Polypodiaceae)—Squirrel's Foot Fern.** Both this species and *D. bullata* are from the area of the Fiji Islands and Java. They are highly decorative when grown as hanging baskets. Their tendency is to envelop the entire surface of the basket with their furry rhizomes and, before long, a ball of fronds has developed. A warm greenhouse with high humidity is necessary. Davallias are easily propagated by snipping off pieces of rhizomes and attaching them with wire staples (even large hairpins will do) against a basket filled with sphagnum moss.

Scale might develop, but a mild dose of Malathion will control it. A full dose might set back the plant as well as the insects, so do not use the full amount usually indicated.

*A collection of some of the smaller, slow-growing alpines can be grouped in a single pot.*

# 17

# Alpine Plants

THE TERM *alpine* refers not only to those plants which grow in the European Alps, but to those grown in any high mountainous region of the world. There are many botanical families which are circumboreal, that is, they find a favorable growing site in a number of widely separated northern locations around the world. So it is not unusual to find one species of a plant growing in the Alps, a relative in the Himalayas, and still another species high in the Rockies.

Alpine plants have much to commend them to the amateur greenhouse gardener. First, the plants themselves are diverse and fascinating in form and color. Most are low growing, so they are easily housed in a small structure. In addition, they grow at a cool temperature, needing only enough heat to keep out the frost. This makes heating inexpensive and requires a minimum of above-ground structure.

If your property includes sloping land, you can easily build an alpine house with the center walk and most of the wall area below grade. The extra insulation of the surrounding soil against the walls keeps the house warm in winter and cool in summer.

Until recent years, the cultivation of alpines was restricted largely to botanical gardens and professional specialists. However, the inquiring amateur soon sifted through the technicalities, gleaned the necessary information, discarded that which was too involved, and came up with an abbreviated, though successful, method of cultivation.

The greenhouse gardener should have a mental picture of these high regions: full sun part of the day, unfiltered by trees but tempered by fog that often does not burn off until the day's strongest sun has passed. The night air becomes cool at sundown because of the high altitude. The surface, usually rocky, can absorb the daytime heat and gradually release it at night, tempering that area of microclimate immediately around the plants. The plant is more often watered by morning fog and evening condensation than by actual rainfall; the daily quantity of water seldom varies greatly, although in some areas there are prolonged dry seasons, as well as prolonged periods of snow cover.

Good drainage of moisture is due to the rocky soil and sloping ground. Less apparent is the *air drainage*, which is often the pitfall of the grower of alpines. The hillsides create perpetual air movement. Constant exposure to the elements, with a minimum of protection, has a leveling influence on temperature.

Now, how do you re-create the environment in which these durable, yet delicate, plants will be asked to survive? The ideal alpine greenhouse is positioned north and south to take advantage of the greatest number of sunlit hours with the minimum of self-created shade. A low, even-span roof is traditional, but a slightly higher pitch than usual (about 100°) will help keep condensed moisture from dripping off the glass onto the plants. With this type of roof, the plant benches can be about 1 foot closer to the glass than in conventional greenhouses. Put your center path at a level that will give you the most convenient access to the plants.

Also make provisions for partially shading the glass on very hot sunny days—either with roller shades or a sprayed-on compound—however, a high light intensity at most times will benefit the majority of alpines. Most alpine plants grow best in pans, which are no more than shallow clay flowerpots. Good drainage is a prime requisite. A soil made up of ⅓ leaf mold, ⅓ coarse sand,

and ⅓ garden loam usually will provide the ideal conditions. Crushed limestone or slag serves well as a top dressing, and, in cases where even greater drainage proves necessary, mix in the limestone. When you add water to the pot, the excess should drain through the hole in the bottom (true of all greenhouse plants). If water pools on the surface for more than a minute or two, the soil mixture needs the addition of one of the coarser materials. A daily morning watering of alpines will suffice in all but the hottest periods when an evening watering also would be advisable.

Alpines are more than just plants you will want to grow. They coax you to look into books for their background. You may even find yourself studying paintings and photographs whose original subject was not of a botanical nature in order to spot clues on the culture of plants which seem only incidental to the landscape.

## Plant Selection

I commend my selection of alpine plants to you as representative of various groups that are diverse in every aspect of their growth—

*An alpine greenhouse does not require as much headroom as one for most other plants.*

shape, texture, color of foliage, form, and season of bloom. In many catalogs the term "starter group," "beginner's selection," or some similar expression often is used. In alpines, however, there is no such category. While certain ones *are* temperamental, most will thrive and flower if their needs are met.

Among the more familiar plant genera, which have alpine species worth growing, are the following: *Primula, Sedum, Potentilla, Linum, Dianthus, Phlox, Rhododendron, Geranium, Achillea, Gentian,* and *Saxifraga.*

Other alpines which are not too difficult to obtain or to flower include the following: *Anemone alpina,* which can be started from

*Alpines grow well in cool conditions with well-drained soil.*

seed in July or from tubers in March. The sparkling purple and white flowers will show in May. *Geranium napuligerum* produces a deep rose summer flower while *Viola cucullata*'s blue blossoms continue from early April into May. A wide variety of saxifragas fall into the alpine category and you will, no doubt, start with *S. cotyledon pyramidalis* and add *S. granulata, S. cochlearis,* and *S. aizoon.* These three represent areas extending from the Arctic to the Maritime Alps. *Gypsophila repens* is another alpine whose delicate bloom lasts over many weeks.

Our own country is not without its alpine aristocrats, and the lewisia is a fine example. Both *Lewisia brachycalyx* and *L. howellii* have been hybridized, producing attractive plants with jewellike flowers. *Shortia galacifolia* is eye-catching even when it is not in flower. The dainty *Cyclamen vernum* represents the rocky, arid slopes of Iran, while *Primula nutans* is a high-altitude native of China's Yunnan Province. *Primula farinosa* and *P. hirsuta* are additional candidates for interesting color and texture in the alpine house.

Synonymous with the European Alps is the edelweiss (*Leontopodium alpinum*), which can be flowered successfully in a well-drained soil.

From the varied conditions to be found within the alpine terrain, it is obviously difficult to generalize in discussing potting media. However, certain basic ingredients can be gathered, to be added or omitted depending upon the plant's affinity for or tolerance of a location with good drainage and a high limestone base. Leaf mold, a rich garden soil, and coarse builder's sand can be mixed to make a "base" for either a well-drained or a heavy soil. Crushed limestone gravel or pebbles (from $\frac{1}{8}$- to $\frac{1}{2}$-inch) are useful for both mixing and top dressing. Pans (flowerpots which are wider than they are tall) are best for potting since their shallower depth makes thorough watering easier and insures good drainage. And for this category of plants, I recommend clay rather than plastic containers. Remember that most alpines are spring and summer flowering and they rest during the winter. Ample watering is required during periods of most active growth. During dormancy, provide only enough water to sustain a minimum metabolism (about once a week). Waterings of manure water, made by steeping dehydrated manure for several hours, will provide the necessary mild stimulus at the time of bud development.

# 18

# Chrysanthemums

CHRYSANTHEMUMS ARE NO LONGER merely the fall flower seen at football games. As soon as researchers recognized the photosensitive qualities of the plant, they made one innovation after another to reach today's achievements whereby "mums" can not only be flowered at any season of the year, but can even be scheduled for a specific *day*. This is good reason why many a home greenhouse gardener depends on chrysanthemums for cut flowers and pot plants.

There are some varieties (pompons) that branch readily and have a small- or medium-sized flower. These are utilized for pot plants. There is an equally long list of varieties that includes large flowers that grow on tall, straight, strong stems that are ideal for cutting. Basically, both kinds are grown in the same way, with the exception of the pinching of tip growth of the pompons to stimulate branching. But, more about that a little later.

Purchase your rooted cuttings of chrysanthemums from a specialist, since he will only propagate "clean" stock and will offer a choice of varieties to suit your timing needs and your taste for certain colors and forms.

While the length of day remains long, as it does during the summer months, only vegetative growth will be created. However, as soon as days become shorter, as is the case in late summer, bud initiation is triggered, and once these buds are firmly established and are the size of peas, the length of day is no longer of critical importance. The foregoing is the natural response of the chrysanthemum to day length. Although I might be oversimplifying the process, the exciting aspect of growing mums in the greenhouse is the fact that you can create your own seasons and even control the length of day. Shortening the length of day is done by covering your plants with a black cloth stretched over a wire framework; daylight can thus be excluded every afternoon from 4 P.M. until 7 A.M., when the cloth is removed.

While the garden varieties of mums are referred to as early, mid-season, and late varieties, they are all, nevertheless, fall-blooming plants. Greenhouse varieties, however, are referred to by their responsiveness to "short-day treatment." An "eight-week mum" means that it will bloom eight weeks after we have begun to create artificially shortened days. Do not, however, shade your mums until they have grown naturally for six weeks.

These artificially shortened days will even stimulate bud formation in the middle of the summer, when no normal, self-respecting chrysanthemum would do anything but grow leaves. If this works (and I assure you, it does), the formation of buds can be held back by the creation of artificially lengthened days during the fall and winter. The use of artificial light ( 1½ watts per square foot) will continue the illusion of summer until buds are wanted. The easiest way to accomplish this additional lighting is by stretching the wires 2 to 3 feet above the plants, with a 60-watt bulb every 4 feet. Connect these lights to a time clock and set it to go on daily for 3 hours at 10 P.M. for a 1-month period. Then, with extended lighting discontinued, the normal effects of the fall season will take over with the ensuing bud formation. This process is dependable and practical, even for the amateur greenhouse gardener.

If you have wintered over a few favorite varieties that are unavailable from commercial sources, they can be rooted easily from cuttings provided that the parent plant is a healthy one. Strip off the leaves from the bottom half and dust the stem with a rooting hormone. The cuttings, if shoved into coarse sand and kept damp, will root in 2 weeks. Plants should be moved into successively larger pots as they develop; water should be applied daily and a liquid fertilizer applied every 2 weeks. Do not wait for fungous and insect problems: spray with a mixture of Captan and Malathion for prevention and control.

Potted plant varieties should be potted with one cutting to a 4-inch pot or 3 cuttings to a 6-inch pot. Growing tips should be pinched out a week to 10 days after potting. This will promote branching and, when each of the new shoots has grown 3 to 4 inches, their tips should also be pinched out. The subsequent 4 or more stems will form the framework to support a great number of flowers.

Chrysanthemums, grown for use as cut flowers, can either be potted with 1 rooted cutting to a pot or planted directly in the bench. The growing tips of these varieties should *not* be pinched, since long, straight stems are desired for cutting purposes. However, after buds have formed and are the size of peas, snip off the axillary buds, leaving the one central terminal bud, allowing it to receive the total amount of available energy and develop to its full potential.

# 19

# Pelargoniums

OF THE MANY plants grown by greenhouse gardeners, few enjoy the popularity of the pelargoniums. Their need for a cool environment makes them inexpensive because a minimum of heat is used. And their requirement of full sun makes them easy to grow—at least insofar as lack of shading is concerned. It is not unusual to see an entire greenhouse devoted to various pelargoniums, since the varied features of their diverse species consumes the interest of the beginner as well as that of the advanced amateur. While all the genera treated here are pelargoniums, they are often referred to as geraniums in plant catalogs.

The genus, Pelargonium, can be separated into four groups for the practical purposes of the collector. The most common is that of the zonale geranium, known botanically as *Pelargonium x hortorum* (the "x" indicating a natural hybrid). Members of this group are most often used for outdoor bedding and winter potted plants. Bred in white and shades of pink to brilliant red, they can be rooted at any season of the year. Strip lower leaves from cuttings taken from the topmost 4 or 5 inches of robust stems. Dust cuttings with a rooting hormone and shove them into coarse sand to a depth of 2 inches. Kept moderately moist and shaded, the cuttings will root in about 3 weeks. When roots are 1½ to 2 inches long, pot singly, starting with a 3-inch pot and transplanting eventually to 5 inches, as necessitated by growth. Keep the plants cool (50° night temperature) and maintain a dry atmosphere. Water daily, but be sure the soil mixture drains sufficiently so that the roots are never wet for long. Varieties you might try include those with sharply defined zoned markings on the foliage. I suggest *Pelargonium x hortorum* var. 'Mrs. Pollock,' *P. x hortorum* var. 'Mrs. Henry Cox,' and *P. x hortorum* var. 'Beckwith's Pride.'

The second group within the genus is that of *Pelargonium domesticum*. These regal varieties are often found in catalogs under the heading of "Lady Washington" pelargoniums. Their large-petaled flowers come into bloom from mid-spring to early summer. Unlike the zonale geraniums, which are best grown anew from cuttings each year, these plants can be held over year after year, making show specimens from the second year on. Take cuttings about a month after flowering (when the stems have begun to harden up a bit). They root easily in a mixture of ½ sand and ½ peat. Pot and repot them successively in larger containers until you reach the 6-inch size. After you have used the "mother plant" to render cuttings, cut it back hard and syringe it daily to encourage new growth. During this period, do little direct pot watering. When new top growth has begun, knock the plant out of its pot, root prune it, and repot it into the same size pot (6-inch) with a mixture of 2 parts garden loam, 1 part peat, and 1 part coarse sand. Add a 5-inch potful of bone meal to each bushel of soil. This annual treatment will insure a spectacular display for 4 or 5 years. New plants will be developing at the same time, of course.

The Lady Washington pelargoniums are coveted by white flies, so be on the lookout for them. Make certain that your initial cuttings are clean (no flies or eggs) and check the undersides of the leaves periodically, spraying with Malathion either upon first sighting of white flies or on a preventive schedule every 10 days.

The combinations of delicate shades of pinks, purples, and reds

*Fancy-leaved geraniums are as decorative as those bred for their flowers.*

are endless. My favorites are 'Ruth Eleanore,' a pink and dark crimson;'Black Lace,' almost pure black; and 'Earliana,' which is a small, compact "pansy-flowering" type.

The ivy-leaved pelargoniums form the third group. By the time you have added a few varieties of this type, it will be quite clear that pelargoniums are certainly worth more space—possibly even a house of their own! The versatile ivy-leaf is ideal as a hanging basket. Three or four plants in a 12-inch wire basket, lined with sheet moss or sphagnum and filled with soil, can be grown on the bench until the tips drape themselves over the basket's sides. Then, after you suspend it from an overhead support, the plant soon will be completely furnished with leaves. Since any hanging basket has a tendency to dry out quickly, put less sand than usual in the

soil mixture. Most varieties of ivy-leaves lend themselves to training as standards. Keep the plant to a single stem, supported by a
bamboo pole. Do not pinch out the tip until the desired height of
the head is reached. Then do periodic pinching to round out the
crown which will cover itself with blooms for many months at a
time. Among the most popular of this type is L'Elegante, the sunset
ivy geranium. Its variegated green and white leaves become tinted
pink when allowed to grow dry in the full sun. 'Mexican Beauty' is
as good a red as 'Jean Roseleur' is pink.

Propagated like the zonale types, the ivy-leaves root readily and
grow rapidly. You can train them upon a trellis to make a striking
wall covering in a lean-to greenhouse. Kept cool and not too
moist, they will provide a long flowering period with few problems
of insects or disease.

The last major group of pelargoniums includes the many fragrant and fancy leafed varieties, which are available from a number of commercial specialists. The variety is enough to awe even a
veteran plant collector. The scented varieties never fail to amuse
and amaze. Besides those with unspecific but pleasant pungent
odors, there are those whose bruised leaves have a definite scent
of rose, pine, peppermint, lemon, nutmeg, coconut, orange, ginger,
apple, or strawberry. In form, there are such species as *P. dasycaule,* a succulent plant with fleshy leaves; and *P. coriandrifolium,*
a fern-leafed plant with a trailing habit; or the clambering *P.
tetragonum*, with jointed stems. The list goes on, with each species
unique in one respect or another.

Within this group the fancy-leaved varieties are included. Most
are small, compact plants, and the variegation of the foliage would
be reason enough to grow them even if they did not flower (which
they do). 'Crystal Palace,' 'Gem,' 'Pistachio' and 'Happy Thought'
are good examples of this decorative type. These, too, may be
treated like the zonale geraniums in all respects.

A point to remember in cultivating all of these forms of pelargoniums is the desirability of re-creating their native environment.
Found growing on the slopes of the Cape Province in South Africa,
they benefit from a long day of bright sun—unfiltered by smog.
When night comes, the temperature drops 20° or 30° into the
50's. The rocky soil drains off the sparse rainfall during the
growing season—November through March.

# 20

# Vegetables and Fruit

UNLESS YOUR GREENHOUSE is a means of supplementing your income, there will probably be no logic in what you decide to grow. The Gilbert and Sullivan line, "I want what I want when I want it," may be as close to reason as you will get. And what's wrong with that? The fact that only eight tomatoes were harvested from six square feet of greenhouse space in no way lessens the enthusiasm of the grower who has just served them to a group of admiring guests.

The idea that greenhouse crops cannot be as delicious as those grown outdoors is bunk. However, two ingredients must be present to produce texture and good taste: maximum tolerable sunshine and adequate nutrition. Both of these will result in quick growth and high sugar content. The botanical names of these common fruits and vegetables are only included to provide those clues which might be helpful in their cultivation.

The varieties of vegetables you can grow under glass are those which mature in the shortest time, have the most compact growth, and basically are not root crops (with the exception of small, round radishes). The crops which can be grown most successfully are cucumbers, lettuce, tomatoes, peas, beans, and radishes—all "out of season" if you follow certain rules. Let us take the cucumbers first.

**Cucumis sativus (Cucurbitaceae)—Cucumbers.** For the sake of space, grow them vertically upon a wooden trellis or wire supports.

First, construct an unpainted box of pine, cedar, or redwood with inside dimensions of 14 inches wide, 20 inches long, and 10 inches deep; drill several drainage holes in the bottom. The soil should contain ⅓ leaf mold and ⅔ garden loam. Start seedlings in 2- or 3-inch pots. When they have 2 sets of leaves, transplant two or three of the strongest looking to the box. Water them upon planting and daily thereafter with plain tap water. Once a week add a liquid fertilizer to the water. The vine will soon reach the support; tie it loosely to the trellis with soft, heavy twine. Pinch off tendrils from the main stem of the vine, allowing only tendrils on the lateral growth to remain.

Now for the secret of good taste in cucumbers. There are both male and female flowers on each plant. You can easily identify the female by the bulge of the embryo fruit immediately under the flower. Leave

*Bibb matures as open heads, making an outstanding midwinter gourmet lettuce.*

this one to grow and pinch off all the male flowers, since pollination will result only in bitter taste, hard seeds, and swollen fruit.

All of this requires daily attention, but it takes little more than a minute or two to do the pruning and watering and to give the leaves a syringing.

**Lactuca sativa (Compositae)—Lettuce.** This is undoubtedly one of the most rewarding greenhouse vegetables and, for my money, Bibb is the one to grow. Each cluster of crisp leaves will make a salad for two, and you can grow heads directly in the bench or in a wooden flat that is 4 inches deep. Since lettuce is a cool-weather crop, grow it anytime except during midsummer. Space seedlings 8 inches apart in a rich soil mixture to which you have added limestone. Take care to transplant them so that no part of the leaves is below the soil level.

**Lycopersicon esculentum (Solanaceae)—Tomatoes.** Here again, choose a medium-sized variety such as Burpee's 'Gloriana' or 'Globemaster Hybrid' in order to harvest a crop during the period when sufficient light is available. One stout seedling planted in each of six 8-inch pots (or any other deep containers) will provide enough tomatoes for normal home use.

Here are a few tricks that can pay off in exceptional results. First, train each plant with its single stem against a stake, or, better still, to an upright wire attached 5 feet above the pot to any supporting component of the greenhouse. You can grow the plant on top of the bench or directly in the ground. The latter method will produce the best fruit, especially if the bottom of the pot is broken out to allow the roots full depth to explore for water. The growing tip of each lateral should be stopped, or pinched out, at the third set of leaves so that the plant has the general appearance of a column. Also pinch out secondary growth in the axils of the leaves.

Since there might be too few insects in the greenhouse to insure the pollination for setting fruit, I suggest that you daub the flowers with a small, soft camel's-hair brush.

After a cluster has formed and fruits begin to swell, thin out the leaves which surround them. They will need additional sunlight for proper ripening.

**Pisum sativum (Leguminosae)—Peas.** The house wall of a south-facing lean-to is particularly suitable to growing peas, since they need considerable light for fast growth. A trellis is necessary. When the crop is finished, install in its place a more decorative plant, which you have started in a pot elsewhere in the greenhouse.

*Grapes can be trained on the flat wall of a cool lean-to greenhouse.*

**Phaseolus vulgaris (Leguminosae)—Beans.** These are also easy to grow under glass. I suggest you stick to the snap or bush varieties rather than plant pole beans, which need too much room for the average greenhouse.

**Vitis vinifera (Vitaceae)—Grapes.** Growing in the greenhouse, grapes offer the ultimate in luxury, both for eating and sheer decoration. Since the grape vine is naturally a clambering, climbing, multibranching, vigorous plant, I do not suggest that you grow it in ground beds unless you can devote an entire greenhouse to its culture. However, tending one or two pot-grown vines is an experience you should not miss. The fruit can be outstandingly delicious, and the beauty of a well-laden vine on the terrace in early summer is spectacular.

Where to start? First, the variety you grow should be "worth the trouble." The outstanding greenhouse grape for early forcing is the black 'Hamburg.' Its fruit has a thin skin, is juicy, and is very sweet. It is not easy to come by, but you can track it down. It will root easily from stem cuttings—or even a bud with a small piece of "heel" will root and develop quickly. 'Schuyler' (black) and 'Seneca' (white) are also good candidates for the greenhouse. Use soil composed of approximately 25 percent organic matter and the remainder made up of a light garden loam to which you have added sufficient limestone to make the entire mixture slightly alkaline (pH over 7). When your cuttings have developed sufficient roots to fill a 4-inch pot, transplant them—one plant to a 12-inch tub or in an equally large terra-cotta pot.

Now is the time to insert a strong stake deep into the pot, extending 4 feet from ground level. Train the new vine as a single stem against this support, rubbing off any side buds. When growth reaches the top of the stake, attach crossbars with raffia or wire. Then wire or tie a circular support of split bamboo to the perimeter. The growing tip of the vine is now ready to be pinched out to promote branching and the creation of a crown of new growth. Remove all tendrils as they develop, since they will only lead to a tangle difficult to undo. Tie the vine to the "wheel" with soft string or raffia, rather than depend upon the tendrils to anchor it. This training can be completed the first summer.

After a two- or three-month period of freezing weather outdoors, bring the potted vine into the garage for gradual vernalization. Such an artificial spring will begin to swell the growth buds. At this point, a cool greenhouse will carry forward the growth process.

When flowers open, dust them lightly with a camel's-hair brush. Pollinated in this way, in the absence of the usual insects, the grapes will form and gradually swell. Cut out any fruit that is too crowded, since it will not develop properly and will keep other clusters from attaining full size. Keep the vine well watered and provide continuous warmth and full sunshine until the fruit matures.

Almost any fruit can grow under glass, but many are not practical because of the sparse yield per square foot. However, I have found some, such as grapes, to be worth the trouble for their decorative value and for the pleasure of watching their steady development from the swelling of buds to the unfolding of leaves, and from the formation of each flower to the ripening of fruit.

**Cucumis melo (Cucurbitaceae)—Melons.** In the same category of "worthwhile impracticalities" as the grape is the melon. Melons grow best with one or two plants to a deep pot or bench filled with rich soil. Train the vine on wires attached close to the glass. Use light shading to keep tender leaves from burning. Pollinate flowers by hand with a camel's-hair brush and, as the fruit develops, support each melon with a net sling. Varieties of cantaloupe that bear small fruit are best, since the melons can be supported easily until fully ripe.

Do not confuse growing fruits and vegetables to maturity under glass with starting them for the outdoor garden. You can properly schedule and easily carry out the starting process to provide well-advanced, strong plants for planting outside after the danger of frost has passed and the soil has warmed enough to avoid any checking of growth.

The full cycle of the growth of food crops under glass has not been practiced or developed in this country because of the luxury of the many climates which occur simultaneously within our borders. Few European countries enjoy such varied latitude and they produce, on a large commercial scale (even for export) greenhouse fruits and vegetables which we grow as a pleasant diversion.

# 21

## Additional Plant Biographies

**Abutilon megapotamicum (Malvaceae)—Flowering-Maple.** Although known as the "flowering-maple," this plant is not a maple at all, but a mallow of tropical Asian origin. Its leaves are maplelike, and its bloom is distinctive, having numerous pendulous bell-like flowers. Colors vary from yellow through orange to red. Plants will flower in 3- to 4-inch pots. You can keep them year after year and they will not get out of hand if you prune them in the spring as new growth begins to form.

**Acacia armata (Leguminosae)—Kangaroo Thorn.** In Australia this shrub grows 10 feet tall, although it does not grow very wide. Since it does not have a particularly attractive form, it must make up for the space it takes by its beauty when in flower—and that it does! In spring, it is a cloud of soft yellow bloom. You can overcome its tendency to get too tall by keeping it pruned back after flowering. When you can hold it down no longer, replace it with a younger specimen. It is good to have a few plants coming along at all times. They can be grown easily from seed. The only trick is to get the seeds to germinate, which you can do by placing them in boiling water for a minute or two. Nicking the hard shell with a nail file will also help toward quicker germination.

**Acalypha hispida (Euphorbiaceae)—Chenille Plant.** This is an unusual ornamental from New Guinea, with flowers in the summer that look like drooping red tails 12 to 20 inches long, extending from axils of heart-shaped evergreen leaves. With very moist organic soil mixture in a moderate to warm greenhouse at 55° to 65°, it will grow up to 10 feet, so this shrub has to be pruned to keep it under control. Propagate it by cuttings taken from mature growth at any time of the year. Pot firmly in 4-inch pots, using peat moss with rich compost and loam, then provide heat of 70° to 75° to give it a good start. Water freely and give it shade on bright spring and summer days; in the fall and winter, water moderately and give it all the sunshine possible. Watch out for red spiders and mealy bugs.

**Achimenes (Gesneriaceae).** See Chapter 12.

**Aechmea fasciata (Bromeliaceae).** See Chapter 14.

**Aechmea fulgens (Bromeliaceae).** See Chapter 14.

**Agapanthus africanus (Liliaceae).** See Chapter 12.

**Aglaonema roebelinii (Araceae)—Silver Queen.** This small pot plant from central Malaya makes a fine room decoration. Its silver leaves, variegated with bright green markings along the main veins, are oblong-lanceolate and grow up to 10 inches long and 5 inches across. When mature, it produces white flowers in the summer, which are followed by red berries. This plant likes warmth (55° to 65°), moisture, and shade with a well-drained organic soil mixture. You must water it freely during its growing season. When *A. roebelinii* is in flower or is brought into the house, water it sparingly or syringe the leaves once a day. Propagate by seeds, cuttings, or division of roots almost any time.

**Allamanda cathartica (Apocynaceae).** A vine from Guiana and Brazil, this plant is a showy climber that has funnel-shaped yellow flowers in summer. Spectacular when trained under the roof of a warm greenhouse, it can also be grown in bush form in a tub.

This vine is easily grown in an organic soil mixture with a minimum winter temperature of 55°. During its active growth, give it plenty of water and sunshine. After it flowers, let the plant rest and water it only enough to keep the season's young growth from shriveling. Shading is not necessary except lightly during the warmest months. In mid-January, before growth starts, cut the plant back to ripe wood. You can use these prunings as cuttings. As soon as they are rooted, pot them and, as growth continues, move each cutting into a larger container. Once the plant is in the size of container you want for its ultimate use, let it become root-bound in the pot. It will flower best in this condition.

**Aloe variegata (Liliaceae).** A South African native, this succulent plant is most desired in a coolhouse collection for its attractive leaves. Their rosette form and partridgelike markings outweigh lack of drama in the blooms—small red flowers that hang loosely on a tubular stem. The thick, succulent leaves, which store water during the long South African dry season, are closely packed and beautifully chevroned in green and white. Do not overwater them or they will rot at the base. They like a well-drained, gritty soil mixture and adapt well to varying

*The species and varieties of aglaonema run the gamut of green and white variegation.*

conditions of temperature. In both summer and winter you may give them full sun. They are best propagated by division, kept dry in winter, and given normal watering, spring through fall.

**Angraecum veitchii (Orchidaceae).** See Chapter 15.

**Anthurium andreanum (Araceae).** Native of tropical America, this exotic, winter-blooming pot plant begins flowering while it is small. The flower consists of a waxy coral-red spathe with a drooping, yellow-tipped, white spadix. Its dark-green leaves also make the anthurium useful as a foliage plant throughout the year.

It needs to be well shaded in a warm, moist atmosphere and requires a rich organic soil. In these conditions the plant will grow 2 feet tall in the course of a year.

Flowers often will last a few months and will set viable seed upon maturity. Sow the seed on the surface of damp sphagnum moss and keep them warm. They can be potted a few weeks after germination.

**Aphelandra squarrosa (Acanthaceae).** This tropical plant, South American in origin, produces striking yellow flowers in autumn or winter and is beautifully marked at all times by its equally striking leaves, which grow 1 foot high. It requires similar conditions to those of its natural habitat, that is, a warm and moist tropical climate.

You may grow the plants from seeds or from cuttings taken in the spring. Take cuttings with a heel of the old wood and plant them in a compost of moist sand and peat; the soil should be well drained. Its organic content should provide enough food to insure a well-developed plant. Keep warm and moist until rooted, and then transplant cuttings into 3-inch pots and then into 5- or 6-inch pots as the roots become restricted. After flowering, the plants can be partially rested, but they should always be kept in a fairly warm greenhouse.

**Apios tuberosa (Leguminosae).** See Chapter 12.

**Ardisia crispa (Myrsinaceae)—Coral Ardisia.** From the East Indies, this is a compact shrub, also known as Acrenulata, which grows up to 4 feet tall in an organic soil mixture. It has brilliant, drooping clusters of red berries that last against its shiny foliage for 6 months. A temperature of 65° is needed for good growth in spring and summer and 55° is needed to carry it over the winter. When flowers appear in April, provide more ventilation; it is necessary for pollination and fertilization. Do not feed the plants after the flowers appear, since new growth at this stage will prevent the setting of berries. Never let the soil dry out after the berries are formed.

Propagate ardisia in February by seeds or cuttings, the latter method being quicker, in a warm, moist greenhouse (or in a closed propagating frame at 70°) in rich compost. At this time, you should also prune older plants hard, including cuttings rooted in the previous year, and repot.

**Aristolochia elegans (Aristolochiaceae)—Calico Flower.** This dramatic plant is a close relative of our hardy, outdoor "Dutchman's pipe." For a well-covered roof in a warm greenhouse, this graceful climber from Brazil has no peer. It also produces fantastic blooms in the summer. Its leaves are kidney-shaped, 2 to 3 inches long on pendulous branches that you should train on wire. The flowers are a curious yellow-green tube, veined purple and white outside; the wide-mouthed cup is purple and brown inside. They grow vigorously in any porous soil at a minimum temperature of 60°. In the summer, water them freely and keep them lightly shaded. Propagate by seed sown in spring or by firm cuttings taken in the summer and rooted in sandy soil at 70°.

**Arum creticum (Araceae).** See Chapter 12.

**Asplenium nidus-avis (Polypodiaceae).** See Chapter 16.

**Astrophytum capricorne (Cactaceae).** See Chapter 13.

**Babiana sambucina (Iridaceae).** See Chapter 12.

**Begonia masoniana (Begoniaceae)—Iron Cross.** This plant is probably from Indochina. While greenish-white flower clusters are produced in spring, its year-long interest is its round, crinkled leaf, which is gray-green in color with a purple cross in its center. An overlay of silver and a hairy surface add to its unusual appearance. Propagate it by seeds or leaf cuttings, plant it in a light soil of leaf mold and sand with some loam, and keep it moist and shady at 55°.

**Begonia rex (Begoniaceae)—Fancy Leaf Begonia.** This native of Assam was a striking foliage plant in its original form, yet the hundreds of hybrids produced since the mid-nineteenth century have become progressively more dramatic. Ones like *B. rex* 'Countess Louise Erdody' with a distinct whorl in the center of each leaf or *B. rex* 'Mikado,' a combination of purple, silver, and lavender, lead you to wonder where the next step will take this showy species.

It prospers in a warm atmosphere (65° to 80°) with a slightly acidic, organic soil. Do not keep the pot wet, but keep it moderately moist. The sunlight should be somewhat filtered to prevent the leaves from burning. Of critical importance in creating the proper environment is provision of adequate ventilation at all times. Propagation is simple since four or five plants can be produced from each leaf.

**Begonia socotrana hybrids (Begoniaceae).** Flowers are red, pink, or white in mid-autumn to early winter, with large leaves up to 10 inches across. The succulent stems and the heavy-textured leaves produce a lush and effective pot plant. *B. socotrana* is a native of the Socotra Island in the Indian Ocean. Cuttings can be taken in spring and grown in warm, airy shade. The parent plant is usually discarded. Keep compost moist, but you can spray the plants in hot weather. This caution—large flowered plants are susceptible to mildew. Among the most popular are 'Emita' (red) and 'Glorie de Lorraine' (rosy pink).

**Begonia tuberhybrida (Begoniaceae).** See Chapter 12.

**Bellis perennis nana (Compositae)—Dwarf English Daisy.** This is the cultivated and hybridized form of the English daisy, a common lawn weed in western Europe. While there are much larger varieties, this miniature is outstanding. The multipetaled flowers are about the size of a dime and the seed packets of mixed colors include a wonderful assortment of soft pinks, whites, and reds. A 3- or 4-inch pot with one plant is as beautiful as any plant ten times its size. While it is actually a biennial, bellis can be grown as an annual. Seeds germinate very readily and, if you separate, transplant, and feed them with soluble fertilizer, they will bloom in a few months. They do well in a cool greenhouse and will even tolerate warmer conditions.

**Beloperone guttata (Acanthaceae)—Shrimp Plant.** This attractive plant is a recent introduction from Mexico. The whitish flower is concealed in shrimp-pink bracts which give the plant its beauty from spring to autumn. It grows as a shrub up to 18 inches high in cultivation and does best with almost full light in a cool greenhouse. Water it thoroughly, but do not allow it to remain wet.

Propagate by cuttings of firm new shoots which you nip off in the summer and insert in a sandy compost. Keep in a propagating frame, providing shade and bottom heat until new roots appear. Place in 3-inch pots and pinch out new growth to insure a bushy shape. Staking of the main shoots is advisable as the plant develops, since the stems are relatively weak.

**Billbergia windii (Bromeliaceae).** See Chapter 14.

**Bomarea kalbrayerii (Amaryllidaceae)—Climbing Peruvian Lily.** From Colombia, this twining herbaceous perennial makes a rich greenhouse plant when you plant it directly in a ground bed. The flower is red and orange in terminal umbels with 2½-inch oblong acuminate leaves which are deciduous. The twining stems of the tuberous plant can reach 10 feet. Bomarea is best propagated by seed, although division of roots is also possible. It needs a fairly rich soil mixture and a minimum winter temperature of 40°; little watering is necessary at this time.

**Bougainvillea glabra (Nyctaginaceae).** This plant is less spectacular in flower than *B. spectabilis*, but it is also less rampant in growth. After you have had the thrill of growing *B. spectabilis*, you might settle down with this one for a less tumultuous future.

**Bougainvillea spectabilis (Nyctaginaceae).** A native of Brazil, this vine is a tall (30 feet or more) rampant grower that has to be cut back periodically to keep it in bounds. Its showy crimson bracts literally cover the new growth in late winter. It can be grown in a ground bed or in a large pot trained upon a trellis or wall. Use a potting mixture of ⅓ sand, ⅓ loam, and ⅓ peat moss or leaf mold to which has been added a cup of dried manure and a cup of bone meal. Then, given a little heat to start it off, it will need no further encouragement. New plants can be produced by rooting stem cuttings in sand.

**Bouvardia humboldtii (Rubiaceae).** The bouvardia, an evergreen shrub from Mexico, requires an intermediate greenhouse temperature never falling below 50°. This strong-stemmed, small-leafed plant bears clusters of sweetly scented, trumpet-shaped flowers in various colors.

To have these much-welcomed flowers during late fall and throughout winter, cut the growth back hard after blooming is finished. Keep newly appearing shoots pinched back until the beginning of August, then leave them alone.

Pruning after flowering will keep the plant to a foot or two in height, and a small tub or 8-inch pot is a large enough container.

To propagate, take cuttings from new shoots in the spring. Wait until these are 2 inches long before nipping them off. Insert in a 6-inch pot of sandy soil and keep at a temperature of 65°. Pot separately into 3-inch pots when roots appear and, as top growth occurs, pinch out the growing tips to insure well-shaped plants.

Rest plants after their flowering by allowing soil to dry out occasionally. Water sparsely in winter. Start them into growth again in spring by lightly spraying the plants daily and gradually increasing the water supply.

**Brassavola nodosa (Orchidaceae).** See Chapter 15.

**Brassia lawrenceana var. longissima (Orchidaceae).** See Chapter 15.

**Browallia speciosa var. major (Solanaceae)—Amethyst Flower.** From Colombia, this makes an ideal hanging basket with a profusion of glowing, 2-inch blooms in gentian blue. The plant has a shrublike habit and grows about 18 inches high. You can make sowings in March, May, and June. By sowing at various times, the greenhouse gardener can have plants in flower over a period of 2 months or more. The seedlings should be pricked out quickly and transplanted 3 or 4 to a pot. Keep them warm (55° to 60°) and in a light position, watering and feeding them moderately. Staking will become helpful as they grow. Also see Chapter 11.

**Brunfelsia calycina var. macrantha (Solanaceae)—Lady of the Night.** This shrub is known for its intense fragrance at night and its luxuriant foliage which shows off the blooms to fine advantage. The flowers, which have a silky sheen, are violet with a white eye and bloom in clusters intermittently all year. The shrub will grow 3 feet high in a tub filled with rich, loose compost at 55°. Give it normal watering and feed it every 2 weeks during its growing season. The flowers will last for several weeks if kept cool. Propagate by cuttings in the spring or fall. Water only enough during the winter to keep the soil from drying out.

**Caladium candidum (Araceae).** See Chapter 12.

**Calceolaria herbeohybrida (Scrophulariaceae)—Pocketbook Plant.** This has become a favorite greenhouse subject, and rightfully so, because of its unusual form and the striking display presented by even a few well-grown plants. The rich colors of yellow, brown, and red are often found all together in the single flower. Hybridizers have bred the best selections so that a plant in a 4-inch pot is a mass of pouchlike blooms, with only enough leaves to set it off like a well-filled bouquet. Early summer is the best time to start new plants. Sow seeds thinly in a well-drained seed mixture (½ sand, ¼ peat, and ¼ screened soil) and cover them very lightly. Keep seedlings at 70° until transplanted to 4-inch pots. Then a temperature of 48° to 50° will suit them. Feed the transplanted seedlings monthly with a liquid fertilizer. They should have enough space on the bench to allow good air circulation. Without sufficient air, red spiders will move in quickly. Protect them from direct sun at all times. Flowering should begin in the spring. It is best to treat the plants as annuals, but you can propagate them from cuttings very easily to perpetuate any of special merit.

**Calendula officinalis (Compositae)—Pot Marigold.** A native of southern Europe, the flowers of this plant look somewhat like a many-petaled daisy. However, the colors, ranging from soft-yellow through shades of orange to rust, set off against broad, heavy-textured lanceolate leaves of bright apple-green are most distinctive. The species grows about a foot high, but the newer hybrid developments are of larger proportions—each flower is 3 to 4 inches across and the stems are up to 2 feet high.

Sow seeds in January and then pot in a medium-textured soil mixture. Flowering will start as the days become longer in March and it will continue into October. Keep cutting off the faded flowers or, better still, use blooms as they open for cut flowers. As an annual for the cool greenhouse calendula has few equals.

**Camellia japonica (Theaceae).** This camellia is one of the most gratifying of all plants for the cool greenhouse. Although it grows over 20 feet high outdoors in mild climates, it is not difficult to keep a plant confined to a 12-inch pot or tub if you prune it annually so that it does not exceed 5 feet. A shrub with heavy-textured, glossy leaves and multipetaled flowers of great delicacy, the camellia is a very gratifying plant. It can be grown in the greenhouse and used, when it blooms, on the porch or indoors. Or, you can cut and float blossoms as a table decoration.

Obtain plants from southern nurseries by mail in the spring; they will provide years of pleasure. Soil should be acidic and should include leaf mold, sand, and peat (⅓ of each). Do not be too quick to give a root-bound plant more room. Flowering is most dependable if the pot is not too roomy. Flowers are white, red, or pink; may be solid colors or flecked; and are either double-petaled, semidouble, or single. Blooms average 3 to 4 inches across, although there are a few very attractive miniature flowers about 2 inches in size. Late spring is the usual blooming period, although each variety has its own timing. A little extra heat will hurry along the flowering if you wish.

**Campanula isophylla (Campanulaceae).** Of Italian origin, the campanula is one of the most popular plants in Europe for use in window boxes or hanging baskets. The trailing stems, covered with small bell-like flowers, provide color over a period of several months. Suited to either the cool or warm greenhouse, the plants can be potted or grown to trail over the edge of the greenhouse benches. This summer-flowering plant is not at all temperamental and will perform well even if the soil is not the best. Water it well and, if it is cut back after flowering and not overwatered in the winter, it will produce a wealth of flowers for several years. While the natural color is blue and can be grown from seed with ease, the white form is a sport that can only be reproduced from cuttings. During propagation keep it lightly shaded and water it carefully, keeping moisture off the foliage to prevent damp-off.

**Campanula pyramidalis (Campanulaceae).** Of southern European origin, this biennial has often been hybridized and varieties of noble proportions are now available. We all like to show off our skill now and again, and what better subject to use than this spectacular plant. One single-stemmed plant in an 8-inch pot can reach 4 to 5 feet in height and be literally covered with pale-blue bell-shaped flowers from top to bottom. It is a *tour de force* for the cool greenhouse gardener.

Seeds should be sown in July and kept as cool as possible during the heat of the summer. As they grow, the plants should be shifted to larger pots in a richly organic, well-fertilized soil mixture. Grow them steadily throughout the winter and in the spring. If your greenhouse becomes cramped for space, put them outdoors in an open cold frame with each stem staked. Bring them inside once again in midsummer and feed them weekly with a solution made from steeping a cupful of dehydrated manure in a few gallons of water. This is a plant you will certainly want to grow—at least once.

**Cattleya Bow Bells (Orchidaceae).** See Chapter 15.

**Cattleya guttata (Orchidaceae).** See Chapter 15.

**Cephalocereus senilis (Cactaceae).** See Chapter 13.

**Cestrum aurantiacum (Solanaceae).** This is a climbing shrub. Well, not truly a climber—it has more of a clambering habit. It gets tall enough (4 to 5 feet) for its beautiful clusters of orange flowers to be seen from anywhere in the greenhouse. It does well in cool temperatures (45° to 50°), and you can grow one in an 8-inch tub or plant it directly in a ground bed. The more pruning that is done, the better shaped the plant and, eventually, the more flowers will be produced on the terminal growth. Cuttings taken from the current year's growth will root easily enough if extra heat is provided. A lead-covered heating cable in the propagating frame is especially helpful. This high temperature (65°) is necessary only until the plant is on its own roots. Once in a rich growing medium in a 4-inch pot, it will enjoy a cooler climate.

**Chlorophytum comosum var. variegatum (Liliaceae)—Spider Plant.** This is a fascinating striped plant from South Africa, which can grow to 4 feet long and makes an effective hanging basket. It produces tufts of young plantlets on the end of its flower scapes; if you pin down these tufts into rich compost, they will root readily. Use small pots. Keep the plants lightly shaded and well watered in summer; winter temperature should be above 45°.

**Cissus antarctica (Vitaceae)—Kangaroo Vine.** This is a strong, long-stemmed vine from Australia that will withstand low temperatures (down to 40°) and partial shade. The shiny, oval-shaped leaves are 4 inches long, coarsely toothed, and leathery. They are shiny green on reddish stalks, which need support. Keep them graceful with careful pruning and training; water when needed. Pinching out the tip growth will promote branching and develop a dense plant with a graceful trailing habit. All but the softest new growth will root easily if you insert 6-inch sections in coarse, damp sand.

**Cissus discolor (Vitaceae).** A Javanese native, this climbing plant is ideally suited to a warm, moist situation. Given these conditions it will grow vigorously and take on its full range of color. It is a vine that only requires its foliage to put on a beautiful display, since the leaves are dark green with marbling of pink, rose, and white. The undersides of the leaves are solid purple. Cissus can be propagated by putting cuttings of any part of the vine (except the soft 5 or 6 inches at the tip) in coarse sand. Kept moist and warm, cuttings will root in a few weeks. Watch carefully for mealy bugs, as you must for many vines.

**Citrus mitis (Rutaceae)—Calamondin Orange.** This is a decorative pot plant from the Philippines. Even if it never fruits, its foliage and fragrant, star-shaped white flowers are worth space in your greenhouse. Leaves are evergreen, shiny, and oval. The fruits are actually miniature oranges, about 2 inches in diameter. The plant grows up to about 2 feet in height and requires an 8-inch pot in order to give its roots plenty of room. A slightly moist atmosphere and a minimum temperature of 45° are necessary during the winter and, when it flowers, it needs ample air. After *Citrus mitis* fruits, prune it back somewhat and place it in full sun to ripen the new wood. Water freely during the summer and hold back in the winter, but do not allow the soil to dry out at any time. A rich compost with a high proportion of loam as a base is required. Propagate it by cuttings.

**Clerodendron thomsoniae (Verbenaceae)—Glory-bower.** This vine cannot be praised too highly. It steals the show whenever it is in flower. A native of West Africa, it grows vigorously in a warm greenhouse and produces a number of bright red flowers, each surrounded by a pure white calyx. While it is a vine, it cannot cling or twine and, therefore, it is necessary to tie it to a support set in the pot or tub. Grow the plant actively all summer, after its May and June blooming period. In late summer cut down on the daily watering and allow the plant to defoliate. During the winter it needs only a 50° temperature, very little light, and a minimum amount of water. In March it is gradually started into active growth again by increasing the light, temperature, and water.

It is propagated best by cuttings taken in February and placed in the highly humid atmosphere of a propagating frame with coarse sand as the medium. A month at 70° should be enough to start the growth of new roots. Then keep repotting into successively larger containers until it is in a 12-inch tub. The soil should be highly organic, with sand added for drainage and a monthly feeding provided to insure vigor from February to September.

**Clianthus dampieri (Leguminosae)—Glory Pea.** This is an interesting curiosity. Its brilliant red color, birdlike form, and waxen texture draw you to it. The plant can be grown from seeds either in a moderately cool greenhouse (50° to 55°) or in a warm greenhouse, provided that proper precautions are taken during its seedling stage. Each seed should be sowed in an individual peat pot and, when it is time for a larger container, do not disturb the roots but merely plant pot and all into a larger pot. If the roots are disturbed, success is very doubtful. However, once over this adolescent stage, if kept watered, continued growth and flowering are reasonably assured. While not a strong climber, its habit is that of a vine and some manner of support is necessary to keep it in bounds.

**Clivia miniata (Amaryllidaceae)—Kafir Lily.** The striking blooms of this native of South Africa appear in spring, dominating a wealth of rich, evergreen, 2-foot long, straplike leaves. The plant grows 2 feet tall. The trumpet-shaped flowers are borne in yellow-orange clusters and stand just above the leaves on strong stems. Its seeds develop inside small, berrylike fruits. This plant does best in a warm temperature of about 60° and rests during the early winter at 45°. It is best to leave it firm in its pot and top dress it with fresh soil each spring, so as not to disturb the roots. Older plants will require a 10- or 12-inch tub. You can propagate by seeds, but the quickest method is to separate offsets from 4- or 5-year-old plants. Pot the fleshy roots firmly but carefully and allow the new plant to remain undisturbed in its rich, fibrous compost for several years. Feed it annually with a slow-acting fertilizer. Place in a shady spot, except in midwinter, to prevent the foliage from being sunburned.

**Cobaea scandens (Polemoniaceae)—Cup and Saucer Vine.** This South American climber produces a wealth of green leaves and a number of brilliant purple flowers. Each cuplike blossom is surrounded by a bright green calyx, which forms the "saucer." It grows luxuriantly in either a cool or warm greenhouse. Any soil suits it and it grows easily from seeds sown in February. By early summer it will be ready to perform. Cobaea often continues as a perennial in the greenhouse for several years. If your conditions are not completely to its liking, it will be merely a successful annual.

**Coccoloba uvifera (Polygonaceae)—Sea-grape.** You will rarely see this 3-foot shrub in greenhouse cultivation, although it is most attractive and useful. It grows up to 20 feet in its native tropical American environment, which shows how out-of-hand it could get in the greenhouse if not pot-bound. Its white flowers are fragrant and are carried in racemes 6 inches long. Its shiny evergreen leaves are nearly circular (5 inches long and 7 inches wide). The plant enjoys a rich compost with extra sand mixed in and will thrive in a winter temperature of 60°. Propagate it by cuttings of young wood in early summer.

**Cochlioda rosea (Orchidaceae).** See Chapter 15.

**Codiaeum variegatum var. pictum (Euphorbiaceae)—Croton.** This native of Malaysia makes a highly ornamental foliage plant. The leaves are brilliantly colored, from near-black through red, orange, pink, cream, or any combination of these. The leaf shape varies—some are lanceolate, some are lobed, and others are linear. Flowers are whitish and inconspicuous. Plants need a minimum winter temperature of 60°, a humid atmosphere, and ample light to bring out the leaf colors. Crotons must not be placed in a draft and, when you bring them into cooler rooms, do so in easy stages, placing them in a slightly cooler location each day, since sudden temperature changes cause leaf drop.

Propagate them by stem cuttings taken in spring or summer and provide bottom heat in a close, moist atmosphere. Once fully developed, a croton should be well watered in the summer and fed with a liquid fertilizer about every 2 weeks.

**Coelogyne cristata (Orchidaceae).** See Chapter 15.

**Coleus blumei (Labiatae).** This Japanese native has very decorative foliage and is a sure-fire success in either a warm or cool greenhouse. It is easily grown as a pot plant. The great variety of leaf coloration makes coleus a popular subject for collecting—15 to 20 distinct varieties are worthy of consideration. The leaves are velvety in texture, are ovate, have toothed margins, and are up to 3 inches long and 1½ inches across. The plant produces insignificant flowers of blue and white. Remove these flower spikes (unless you want seeds) to promote further branching. A rich fibrous loam is best for potting. Water plants frequently during the growing season. Coleus requires a warm, light place; pinch it frequently to avoid legginess. An 18-inch plant can be contained in a 6-inch pot; however, with a larger container and regular feedings, you can develop a speciment shrub 3 feet high and 3 feet across.

While coleus is an annual and can be grown from seeds, you can also root it from stem cuttings every month in order to have good-sized plants maturing during each season. Rooting will occur in a week to 10 days in sand, or in a combination of peat moss and sand.

**Coleus thyrsoideus (Labiatae).** This plant is without especially decorative leaves but you should grow it for its dark electric-blue flowers. Cuttings of this species, started in spring, will provide your greenhouse with a splash of unusual color by midwinter. Like *Coleus blumei*, it needs a winter temperature of 55° to 60°.

You can propagate it from seed sown during February and March. Keep seedlings at 60° to 65°, although you can root stem cuttings more easily during the spring or summer.

**Columnea gloriosa (Gesneriaceae).** This pendulous plant from Costa Rica makes a fine hanging basket. Large, tubular, scarlet flowers with yellow throats are borne along the trailing stems in May and June. This plant likes a compost with good drainage and a minimum temperature of 50°. Water plentifully during the summer, but from late October to early March give only enough water to keep the plants from drying out. Propagate by seeds in February or March or by cuttings taken during March from ripened stems. In either case, seeds or cuttings should be kept at 65°.

**Cordyline terminalis (syn. Dracaena terminalis) (Liliaceae).** This native of tropical Asia has bright foliage in a wide range of colors. Its leaves are oval, up to 1 foot long and 4 inches wide, and come in bright reds and pinks with streaks of green on both sides of the midrib. The plant does best in a rich soil with a temperature of 60° and a moist atmosphere during the growing period. In the winter it should be kept rather dry at a minimum temperature of 50°. It takes a few years to produce a usable size plant from seed, so I recommend rooting cuttings in March. Cuttings of 1 inch can be taken from the main stem and inserted horizontally to half their thickness in a sandy compost. They will probably need bottom heat to maintain a 65° to 70° temperature. A well-drained, rich compost is needed for potting after roots are 1 inch to 2 inches long.

**Coryphantha arizonica (Cactaceae).** See Chapter 13.

**Crassula arborescens (Crassulaceae).** See Chapter 13.

**Crassula sarcocaulis (Crassulaceae).** See Chapter 13.

**Crinum powellii (Amaryllidaceae).** See Chapter 12.

**Cryptanthus fosterianus 'Foster's Hybrid' (Bromeliaceae).** See Chapter 14.

**Cucumis sativus (Cucurbitaceae).** See Chapter 20.

**Curcuma roscoeana (Zingiberaceae).** See Chapter 12.

**Cyclamen persicum var. 'giganteum' (Primulaceae).** See Chapter 12.

**Cymbidium Alexanderi 'Westonbirt' (Orchidaceae).** See Chapter 15.

**Cymbidium Flirtation (Orchidaceae).** See Chapter 15.

**Cymbidium Madonna (Orchidaceae).** See Chapter 15.

**Cymbidium Panwelsii (Orchidaceae).** See Chapter 15.

**Cymbidium Peter Pan (Orchidaceae).** See Chapter 15.

**Cypella plumbea platensis (Iridaceae).** See Chapter 12.

**Cyperus alternifolius (Cyperaceae)—Umbrella Plant.** This attractive foliage plant from Madagascar belongs to the sedge family. It is semiaquatic and valuable as an edging for indoor pools. Its solitary stems, varying in height between 18 and 24 inches, have ribbonlike leaves spreading out on the top like the ribs of an umbrella. It is easy to cultivate in a warm greenhouse at a minimum temperature of 55°. The compost should be rich. It must be kept very moist; keep it from drying out by using a saucer of water under the pot. You can propagate by sowing seed in the spring, but it is best to divide the rootstock.

**Cyperus papyrus (Cyperaceae).** This plant comes from Egypt and is the largest of the genus. It is known as the "Egyptian paper reed," since papyrus was made from the stems of this species. A warm greenhouse suits it best, but it will tolerate slightly lower temperatures. It should be tubbed because its stems grow up to 10 feet high and it will spread out-of-hand if planted in a ground bed inside your greenhouse. You can keep it lower by constant pruning, which will encourage new growth.

**Cytisus canariensis (Leguminosae)—Yellow Broom.** In late winter, the cool greenhouse often needs a splash of color and one of the best plants for the purpose is the yellow broom. Small, narrow leaves are borne along its stems and fragrant pealike flowers virtually cover each stem for several weeks. Best grown in cool conditions, the plant should be pruned back to the height of a few inches after flowering. Shrubby plants like this one can only be kept to a reasonable size by drastic pruning. Cuttings root readily in coarse sand.

**Daffodils (Narcissus) (Amaryllidaceae).** See Chapter 12.

**Daphne odora var. marginata (Thymelaeaceae).** This daphne is desirable on several counts. The heavy-textured green leaves bordered with yellow are beautiful in their own right. When its pink flowers bloom in late winter it is even more appreciated and its perfume fills the greenhouse, which gives it a secure place on any plant bench. It will tolerate warmth but it is happier in a cold environment. Usually small, this daphne makes an excellent pot plant and can be propagated from cuttings in early spring.

**Datura suaveolens (Solanaceae)—Angel's Trumpet.** This plant has a tendency to be too large for the small greenhouse. It is 4 feet in height and almost 3 feet wide when small—but what a plant! It might well be worth the room to grow one every four or five years and discard it after flowering, although it can be pruned back hard and kept within bounds for a while. The green leaves form a perfect foil for the numerous large white, drooping, trumpetlike flowers. The fragrance exuded is a wonderful bonus. Seeds are viable but save the months of establishing a new plant by buying or begging a rooted cutting in the spring. If you root your own, make certain that the cutting has a "heel" (piece of the stem attached) and root it at about 60°.

Although a native of Brazil, *D. suaveolens* is from the colder, high altitudes and is best suited to the cool greenhouse.

**Davallia fijeensis (Polypodiaceae).** See Chapter 16.

**Dendrobium nobile (Orchidaceae).** See Chapter 15.

**Dianthus caryophyllus (Caryophyllaceae)—Carnation.** Carnations have been so important to the commercial florists that considerable research has been devoted to producing strong, healthy, colorful, dependable strains. With these assets also available to the home greenhouse gardener, a few carnations *must* be included in your repertoire. Do not start from seeds; buy rooted cuttings from a carnation specialist. Pot the plants when you get them or put them directly into the growing bench. Check the soil since it probably will require some lime to insure that it is slightly alkaline. Mix in plenty of organic material too. As soon as the cuttings are acclimated (after a week), pinch out the growing tip to promote branching. While the greenhouse temperature need not exceed 50° to 55°, do not apply insecticides when the air is too cold. Spray for green fly and red spider about every 3 weeks on a warm day. Good ventilation is an essential safeguard against these infestations.

Colors now available are astounding; pure yellow, dark red, pink, white, and bicolors are among the best. The spicy perfume has been a deliberate consideration of the hybridizer, as have the strong stems that make carnations so ideal as a cut flower.

**Dicentra spectabilis (Fumariaceae)—Bleeding-heart.** This plant is a native of Japan and is closely related to the native American wild flower, *D. eximia*. Its fernlike leaves act as a perfect foil for the gracefully arching stems which hold the pink heart-shaped flowers. This plant can be kept buried outdoors or in an unheated garage until February. Then, with a gradual increase in temperature followed by a slight increase in the daily amount of water, it can be forced into bloom in March. Bring in one pot at a time at short intervals to provide flowers constantly from mid-March to late April.

At the end of the summer, divide each plant and repot in a porous, organic soil.

**Dieffenbachia picta (Araceae)—Dumb Cane.** This Brazilian foliage plant is most useful since it is not at all temperamental. Although it will grow to 8 or 10 feet tall, it can be cut back at any time and the pruned-off stems, stripped of their leaves, laid on sand in the propagating frame, where they will root and thus perpetuate a supply of young plants. Like many plants that grow in a warm, moist atmosphere, new plants can also be made by air layering. Its leaves are about 10 inches long, with blotches of green, white, and chartreuse. While we are often warned that dieffenbachia is poisonous, it is no more likely that you will eat one than that you will go out in the garden and chew on a barberry or hemlock. A soil mixture high in organic material is ideal, but make up ¼ of its volume with coarse sand to provide adequate drainage.

**Dimorphotheca ecklonis (Compositae)—Cape Marigold.** All members of the composite family have daisylike flowers and this is no exception. White rays with a blue center disk make this one striking. Like many plants of the South African region, the flowers close at night, so they are a failure as cut flowers for any but daytime use. Propagation is easiest from seed and a cool greenhouse is ideal. Plants are about 2 feet high at flowering.

**Dipladenia sanderi (Apocynaceae).** A warm greenhouse subject originating in tropical South America, *D. sanderi* is a small shrub with funnel-shaped flowers of a most delicate pink. Other varieties (ranging from light yellow to crimson) are also available, but the pink form is the most beautiful to my eye. Once blooming starts in the summer, flowers will keep coming for 2 or 3 months. New plants can be started easily from stem cuttings taken in February. Coarse sand is the best medium, and, if kept moist and at a temperature of approximately 70°, root growth will be sufficient for transplanting in 3 or 4 weeks.

**Echeveria gibbiflora var. metallica (Crassulaceae).** See Chapter 13.

**Echinocactus grusonii (Cactaceae).** See Chapter 13.

**Echinocereus rigidissimus (Cactaceae).** See Chapter 13.

**Epidendrum radicans (Orchidaceae).** See Chapter 15.

**Epiphyllum ackermannii (Cactaceae).** See Chapter 13.

**Episcia cupreata hybrids (Gesneriaceae).** These Nicaraguan creepers started with the attractive habit and leaf texture of the species and through the skill of the breeders have now evolved into a wide group of dramatic greenhouse plants. The brown and silver of 'Chocolate Soldier' and the metallic illusion created by 'Silver Sheen' are but two examples of the commercially available hybrids of merit. Most are readily adaptable as hanging basket subjects; however, when suspended close to the glass, shading must be applied to prevent burning. The name "episcia" is derived from the Greek word for shade—further evidence of the value of botanical terms. The flowers are usually small but brightly colored (orange and yellow, or red). Use a highly organic soil and water well, but do not allow a soggy condition to develop. Stem cuttings will root easily at most times of the year. Prevent any sudden chill to which these plants are extremely susceptible.

**Eucharis grandiflora (Amaryllidaceae).** See Chapter 12.

**Euphorbia fulgens (Euphorbiaceae)—Scarlet Plume.** This plant serves my greenhouse in December and January as a pleasant relief from its overworked and commonplace cousin, the poinsettia. It, too, is a native of Mexico and enjoys temperatures around 60° or 65°. If you pinch the growing tips shortly after you pot two or three rooted cuttings in a 6-inch container (with a richly organic soil), they will develop arching branches about 2 feet high. Clusters of crimson flowers will form at the end of each branch over a period of several weeks. The plant should be cut back after flowering and kept alive over the winter with moderate watering. Root new growth as stem cuttings during the summer and keep a few old plants growing as well. By its second year, the well-branched structure becomes heavily flowered. Use one or two of the older plants as gifts to make room for the new ones coming along.

**Euphorbia pulcherrima (Euphorbiaceae)—Poinsettia.** This needs no description—it is so closely associated with the Christmas season—but here are a few facts about its culture. It is very sensitive to light, so switching on the greenhouse light at night for a few minutes will trip the mechanism that starts bud development. Since this early bud initiation will also result in early flowering, a record during your first year of growing poinsettias will help you to adjust your planting in subsequent years. The white-flowered variety will stay in good condition much longer than the red—and do not overlook growing the pink. A good source of stem cuttings for your own use is from a gift plant of especially good quality. Root cuttings in a combination of sand and peat moss during the summer and put three cuttings in a 6-inch pot with well-drained soil. Pinch once and even twice if growth permits, until Labor Day. This promotes branching. Then, grow at 60° (with no drafts of cold air) until flowering.

**Exacum affine (Gentianaceae).** One word seems to describe this plant: "neat." Its regular ovate leaves always seem to be a healthy rich green and atop each stem is a star-shaped bluish flower with a bright golden eye. Seeds of this annual should be sown in midwinter in the warmest part of your cool greenhouse. Once beyond infancy, it will take lower temperatures in its stride. When growth quickens, around May, stem cuttings can be rooted in sand (with a heating cable providing constant warmth), so that by late summer (when flowering begins) a good supply of plants will be on hand. *Exacum affine* is rather exclusive in its heritage since it is only found as a native on the island of Socotra in the Indian Ocean.

**Fatshedera lizei (Araliaceae).** A bigeneric hybrid from *Fatsia japonica* var. *moseri* and *Hedera hibernica,* this plant was developed by Lizé Frères in Nantes, France. It is a decorative evergreen shrub that has greenish-white flowers on large spikes in late autumn. It needs to be protected from temperatures below 40° and it likes some shade. Propagate it by stem cuttings only. It is a very satisfactory foliage plant.

**Felicia amelloides (Compositae)—Blue Daisy.** This plant has sky-blue, daisylike flowers with yellow centers, narrow hairy leaves, and long stiff stems.

It should be planted in slightly acidic soil and always kept moist. The temperature of the greenhouse should be 50° to 55°. If cuttings are taken in May or June, you can expect flowers the following winter. The first bloom may be disappointing; the second will not be, if kept free from frost.

Place cuttings in 4-inch pots. Increase the size of the pots as the plant grows or put the plants into hanging baskets. The clambering habit makes them ideal for this treatment. Plenty of water and light shade in summer should make this half-hardy annual very lush. The plant is mildly subject to mealy bugs, aphids, and thrips.

**Ficus benjamina (Moraceae)—Fig Tree.** This species is but one useful member of a very useful and varied genus. A graceful tree, it lends a tropical effect to the warm greenhouse and you can bring it indoors for a week at a time as a dramatic house plant. It looks best when it is 6 to 8 feet high, so cut it back periodically to keep it a practical size (it will exceed 50 feet in its native India or in the ground bed of a large conservatory). Although it is an evergreen and will benefit from moist summer conditions, it requires only a little water during the winter. You can root stem cuttings best in a warm propagating bed—one with an electric heating cable.

**Ficus lyrata (Fiddleleaf Fig) and F. elastica (Moraceae) Indian Rubber Plant.** These are two of the tall, large-leaved species popular as foliage plants. In my own greenhouse, I lean heavily on foliage like this to set off and dramatize flowering plants.

**Ficus pumila (Moraceae).** Another of the more than 50 species of fig, this plant grows as a creeper, clinging tightly and flat against any surface—even glass. It can also be trained on wire forms to create any number of decorative shapes. Leaves of this species, which is also known as *Ficus repens,* are dark and less than 1 inch long. The fast-growing branches should be kept pruned or they will take over large areas of your greenhouse. It is an easy grower in moist conditions with temperatures exceeding 55°, but it is subject to mealy bugs. Six-inch pieces of new growth, that have partly hardened off, will root in peat and sand in warm surroundings.

**Fittonia verschaffeltii (Acanthaceae).** Although it has an interesting flower, the leaves of this species so overpower it in importance that it has become known almost exclusively as a foliage plant. In its native South American haunts, it creeps along the floor of shaded, warm, moist, wooded areas in a soil rich in decayed organic matter. The leaves are predominantly green, but the crimson veins give it an extra dimension—as though a net were superimposed over each leaf. Too much sunshine will cause the color of the veins to fade, so keep this fittonia in dappled light, where conditions will remain fairly constant. Stem cuttings will root readily and do best if you make them at the outset of the spring growing season.

**Freesia hybrida (Iridaceae).** See Chapter 12.

**Fuchsia hybrida (Onagraceae).** This is a charming, quick-growing deciduous shrub that flowers in the summer. It lends itself to training. Cut out the side shoots for a single stem, or pinch out at every third

*The white veining of* Fittonia verschaffeltii argyroneura *creates a distinctive design.*

joint to develop a bush or a pyramid. The flowers are composed of a tube with four spreading sepals in various colors—red, white, or purple. They are propagated by 3- to 4-inch cuttings of stems on which flower buds have not yet formed. Taken in January, the cuttings should be kept in a warm, humid section of the greenhouse at 60°. Pot in a porous mixture, in 3-inch pots and shift to 4- or 5-inch sizes before they get pot-bound. When they are semidormant, replant in pots 2 or 3 sizes larger (up to 10 or 12 inches) with fresh soil. This treatment should result in colorful specimens.

**Gazania splendens (Compositae).** This South African plant provides brilliant color in the cool greenhouse. It is also a beautiful cut flower for daytime use. Like most of the daisylike flowers from the Cape region, the flowers close at night—certainly no help as an arrangement on the dinner table.

Many good hybrids are now available from seedsmen providing flowers in various shades of red, orange, and yellow.

If you sow seeds in January, flowering will begin in May. Should you take cuttings from side shoots which begin to appear in late March or early April, flowering will begin in July. But, in either case, you will enjoy flowers continuously until October.

**Gloriosa rothschildiana (Liliaceae).** See Chapter 12.

**Grevillea robusta (Proteaceae)—Silk-oak.** This delicate, silky, fernlike ornamental foliage plant originated in New South Wales. Plants can be raised easily from seed in a warm greenhouse, but afterward cooler conditions will suffice; a 50° minimum is satisfactory. Do not repot frequently—every 2 or 3 years should be sufficient. Plants can be kept to a manageable size if repotted in 6-inch pots and kept pruned back. A good potting compost consists of loam, peat, and coarse sand in equal parts; avoid lime. Keep moist throughout summer and water with care throughout autumn and winter, not allowing a soggy condition to develop. Good ventilation and plenty of light are *musts*.

To propagate cuttings of new shoots (which should be taken with a heel of old wood in spring), insert them in sandy compost and keep warm and moist until they have rooted. Pot the plants separately in 3-inch pots and later in 6-inch pots.

**Gymnocalycium saglione (Cactaceae).** See Chapter 13.

**Gynura aurantiaca (Compositae).** This perennial plant from the East Indies has purple-tinted ornamental foliage. It will grow to 3 feet in height, and needs pruning back each year after flowering. It likes a minimum winter temperature of 55°, in a shaded, but light, greenhouse. To propagate, take cuttings in the spring, strip the lower leaves, and insert the bottom 3 inches into coarse sand. Keep cuttings moist and at a 70° temperature. Water new plants freely in the summer, but very little in the winter.

**Gynura sarmentosa (Compositae).** This makes a twining plant reaching 18 inches, with leaves of slate blue and purple. It can be treated the same as *G. aurantiaca.*

**Haemanthus coccineus (Amaryllidaceae)—Blood-lily.** This interesting and bulbous plant for a cool greenhouse is from South Africa and has a bright scarlet flower that looks like a shaving brush. After it flowers in the fall, careful and moderate watering will bring on the straplike leaves (up to 2 feet in length) that lie flat on the soil. When the foliage dies down in the spring, keep the bulb dry until growth begins again spontaneously.

Haemanthus multiplies slowly and is propagated by offsets detached in the spring and placed in a pot about 2 inches wider than the new bulb. Repot occasionally (about once in 3 or 4 years) when the plant is dormant, since it does not like its roots disturbed.

**Hedera helix hybrids (Araliaceae)—English Ivy.** Although European and North African in origin, this ivy has become an accepted "native" in almost all temperate regions. From this species have developed a large number of "sports" or named varieties which make excellent potted plants. They lend themselves to all sorts of tricks from growing as pyramids on a wooden frame to training into the shape of a dog or bird upon a wire form. Grown in a cool greenhouse, ivy has many uses. Not only does it make a decorative plant, but it does well under plant benches or as an edging on top of a bench. It is perfect as a house plant or gift plant.

Those having the most compact habit are the small-leaved varieties and fortunately they are the best ones for the greenhouse, since they seem to be in the proper scale.

They should be grown in well-balanced soil of ⅓ loam, ⅓ leaf mold or peat moss, and ⅓ coarse sand. While they will tolerate areas of low light value for a while, they will begin to show the effects by their leaves becoming farther and farther apart. So, when possible, give the plants a position where maximum light is available. When watering, be certain that the moisture gets down to the bottom of the pot—not merely *through* it, but *to* it. Also, do not overlook the necessity of good ventilation to prevent fungous infections, which are more of a problem with ivy than insects.

A few of the most popular, attractive, and interesting varieties are 'Shamrock," 'Needlepoint,' 'Golddust,' 'Manda's Star,' and 'Curlilocks,' as well as *Hedera helix* var. *erecta.*

Since all of these are actually "sports" or offshoots of the species, assurance of their being true to type can only be guaranteed if they are propagated vegetatively. Therefore, make stem cuttings and root them in sand. Of course, this should not be done in the case of patented varieties. Purchase these plants through authorized commercial sources.

**Heliotropium arborescens (Boraginaceae)—Heliotrope.** This is a soft-wooded shrub from Peru with very sweetly scented flowers that bloom all summer. They are pale to dark blue and white, and are produced in umbels on a plant about a foot high. Their leaves are a rich green color and of a wrinkled texture. Prune them back hard and propagate them by cuttings or sow seeds in January in a cool greenhouse.

**Heliotropium rutilum (Boraginaceae).** Probably one of the parents of large flowered hybrids, this plant has small scarlet flowers and is more graceful than most.

*Right: One ivy plant, trained on a cone-shaped frame, will produce a crisp display in short order. Below: Ivy sculpture, trained on a wire frame, is most successful if a small-leaved variety is used.*

**Hippeastrum aulicum (Amaryllidaceae).** See Chapter 12.

**Hippeastrum hybrida (Amaryllidaceae).** See Chapter 12.

**Hippeastrum x johnsonii (Amaryllidaceae).** See Chapter 12.

**Hippeastrum prateus (Amaryllidaceae).** See Chapter 12.

**Hoya carnosa (Asclepiadaceae)—Wax Plant.** This fine climbing plant, originally from southern China, has a glorious display of clusters of fragrant, waxy, pale-pink flowers in early summer. This is the most popular species of its genus and can be grown in a border of well-drained soil in a cool greenhouse. Allowed to climb the greenhouse wall, with some support in the early stages, it will provide considerable color. It can also be grown in pots or tubs, trained on a wire frame or on 3 or 4 thin canes joined at the top to form a cone. Replace the top soil each spring and completely repot every third year in spring or summer to keep the plant healthy and free of insect pests.

*H. carnosa* thrives in a soil consisting of equals parts of loam and peat to which you have added a good sprinkling of coarse sand. Charcoal should be used freely to keep compost fresh for a long time.

Woolly aphids are likely to lodge in the axils of the leaves; if the plant is small, apply a cotton swab dipped in alcohol to get rid of them. Larger plants have to be sprayed, or inverted and dipped into a tub of insecticide solution.

**Ixora coccinea (Rubiaceae)—Jungle Geranium or Flame of the Woods.** This evergreen, a tropical, flowering shrub from the East Indies, grows to 4 feet and sports clusters of dark-scarlet, tubular flowers. It has long branches and short leaves.

Grow these plants in large pots in a compost of peat and leaf mold, with some coarse sand for drainage. When at flowering age (about 1 year) plants should be kept in a warm greenhouse at about 60°.

Take cuttings of half-ripened wood with 4 pairs of leaves, and plant in sandy compost at 70°. Any time is good but spring is best. Pot firmly in 6-inch pots at 65° when cuttings are rooted; water well, and keep humidity and temperature high. After flowering, prune back about 2 joints to encourage compact, flower-bearing growth.

Be especially careful of brown scale and mealy bugs with these plants.

**Jacobinia carnea (Acanthaceae).** A shrub in its native Brazil, the *Jacobinia carnea* is an excellent potted plant for the warm greenhouse.

The flower erupts from the tip of each stem like a pink plume above clusters of dark green leaves. After several weeks of flowering, the stems should be cut back to promote branching. Cuttings from soft new growth can be rooted in sand during April or May. Shift each new plant into a larger pot as it grows. By the time it is ready to flower, a few months hence, it should be about 18 inches high and in an 8-inch pot. When it becomes rootbound, and a larger container seems impractical or inconvenient, supply additional nutrition through a bi-monthly feeding schedule.

Soil containing ½ leaf mold and ½ loam can be loosened, if necessary, with sand. Watch out for aphids. Also, test for red spiders from time to time.

**Jasminum officinale var. grandiflorum (Oleaceae)—Poet's Jasmine.** This exotic plant from Kashmir and the Himalayas has slender, angled branches opposite small leaves and white fragrant flowers that usually bloom in clusters. The flowers are large and showy, with a delicate fragrance.

Plant in loose, fibrous soil of sand and peat moss at 70°. Keep well watered but avoid continued wetness at the roots. Plant in 3-inch pots and move on to 6-, 8-, and 10-inch pots as the plants grow. Give partial shade from spring to fall, but full sunshine the rest of the year. After propagation, keep jasmine at 50° to 60°. Beware of aphids, thrips, red spiders, scales, and mealy bugs.

**Kalanchoe blossfeldiana (Crassulaceae).** See Chapter 13.

**Lachenalia tricolor (Liliaceae).** See Chapter 12.

**Lactuca sativa (Compositae).** See Chapter 20.

**Laelia anceps (Orchidaceae).** See Chapter 15.

**Laelia cattleya Grand Gate (Orchidaceae).** See Chapter 15.

**Lagerstroemia indica (Lythraceae)—Crape-myrtle.** This is a most dependable shrublike tree. It can be kept within bounds by heavy pruning annually, before spring growth starts. Like many other native Chinese plants, it will tolerate temperatures down to 45° in winter. As winter progresses it should be given a little more heat (up to 50° to 55°) to assist the flower buds in their development. The bloom is composed of clusters of soft, pink, crinkled petals. Continuous flowering over a two-month period is not unusual.

For a plant 5 feet high, pot in a 10-inch tub using a soil mixture of ⅓ loam, ⅓ peat moss, and ⅓ sand. Water sparingly in winter and increase the quantity as spring approaches. Cuttings placed in coarse sand will root readily after a slight callus has developed. This should take about a month. Once rooted, plants should be potted, given plenty of light, and not allowed to become dry.

**Lapageria rosea (Liliaceae)—Chilean Bellflower.** The Chilean national flower is found climbing over trees in the open slopes of the Andean foothills. Four-inch-long, almost cigar-shaped trumpets are found in various shades of pink (the white form is considerably weaker in habit and flowering). The outstanding feature, however, is the heavy texture of the waxen flowers. So unusually heavy, they are certainly a botanic oddity in addition to being a most attractive climber in the cool greenhouse. They are best planted in a ground bed or a large tub, since their roots like plenty of room. Flowering will begin in September and continue for two or three months.

Propagation is somewhat difficult, but stem cuttings with additional bottom heat provided under the sand by an electric cable will eventually work. It sometimes takes six months of what seems to be suspended animation before success is achieved. Be especially careful of woolly aphids.

**Lemaireocereus thurberi (Cactaceae).** See Chapter 13.

**Lophocereus schottii monstrosus (Cactaceae).** See Chapter 13.

**Lycopersicon esculentum (Solanaceae).** See Chapter 20.

**Mammillaria candida (Cactaceae).** See Chapter 13.

**Manettia bicolor (Rubiaceae)—The Firecracker Plant.** This climber from Uruguay, with its yellow and red tubular flowers, grows very well in a cool greenhouse. If you are interested in saving space, 2 or 3 plants can be grown in a 6- or 7-inch pot with stakes used for support. Even in moist, warm conditions the plants will ramble around the stakes to produce a full, massive plant. After flowering, plants may be trimmed back into shape. Water sparingly in winter.

Cuttings for new plants can be made in May and June. New plants should be propagated in moist, sandy soil in a warm, moist situation.

**Maranta leuconeura var. kerchoveana (Marantaceae)—Prayer Plant.** This low-growing Brazilian plant has large, 6-inch oval leaves which fold upward at night, as if in prayer. The leaves are a pale gray-green with dark green blotches and are more decorative than the plant's flowers.

It grows well in a soil of 2 parts loam, 4 parts peat, and 1 part sand. It should receive shade and plenty of water during the summer. In winter the soil should be allowed to dry out occasionally, but the atmosphere should remain moist the year-round.

Propagation is best accomplished in February or March by division of mature plants. Pot them in a light but rich compost. Plenty of sand is necessary for drainage. When you water, try to keep the crown dry to minimize the possibility of rotting.

Temperature should never go below 55°; it is ideal around 68°.

**Medinilla magnifica (Melastomaceae).** This Philippine shrub is at home in a moist, warm atmosphere. While its foliage is always attractive by reason of its dark, rich green color, the plant becomes a show in itself when in bloom. The drooping coral-red flower—a foot long—is displayed against the background of a showy pink bract. Medinilla was once the pride of every collection of exotics. It is large (about 3 to 4 feet high), and, therefore, many owners of small greenhouses shy away from it. If you have the room, it is well worth growing. Cuttings root easily in a mixture of moist sand and peat moss.

**Miltonia Clown Mask (Orchidaceae).** See Chapter 15.

**Miltonia Feuerwerke (Orchidaceae).** See Chapter 15.

**Miltonia vexillaria (Orchidaceae).** See Chapter 15.

**Miltonia Wasserfalle (Orchidaceae).** See Chapter 15.

**Mimulus glutinosus (Scrophulariaceae)—Monkey-flower.** This California wild flower has been hybridized and seed is now available to produce sturdy plants with 3-inch spotted flowers in tones of yellow, brown, and orange. Sow seeds during February in a cool greenhouse. Just before transplanting to a 3-inch pot in April, pinch out the growing tip to encourage a compact habit. Once in its final 5-inch pot the plant will begin to flower and continue until fall. If you have a variety worth perpetuating, take cuttings in August, root them in sand, and continue to grow them over the winter. You will note that the stems and leaves are very sticky. Do not be alarmed; this is normal, as the name *M. glutinosus* indicates.

*The drooping flowers of* Medinilla magnifica *are well worth the space they require.*

**Nelumbium nelumbo (Nymphaeaceae).** See Chapter 12.

**Nemesia strumosa (Scrophulariaceae).** Another South African annual, this plant should be grown in mixed colors. Each is so clear and bright that a display of its white, red, yellow, blue, and purple constitutes a flower show in itself. Plants are attractively compact in habit and are about 1 foot tall. They should be started from seeds in a cool greenhouse, but do not sow an entire packet at one time. Allow 1-week intervals so that you will have flowering plants coming for several months. Nemesia will even bloom in the winter.

**Nerine sarniense (Amaryllidaceae).** See Chapter 12.

**Nerium oleander (Apocynaceae)—Rose Bay or Common Oleander.** An evergreen shrub from the Mediterranean, the oleander is large but suitable for the greenhouse. It has clusters of large yellow, pink, red, or white blooms on strong, willowy stems. Leaves are narrow and pointed.

Oleander should be grown in a medium, loamy soil and peat moss. Give it lots of sunshine, prune it after flowering, and let it rest during the winter. The greenhouse should be cool at 45°. Water just enough to keep stems stiff, or else the flower buds are likely to drop off. Cuttings from mature wood root easily in ½ sand and ½ peat moss, any time except during the winter. After cuttings root, move them into 3-inch pots of loamy soil. Transfer them to 6- or 7-inch pots as they grow. Major pests are red spiders, scale, aphids, and mealy bugs.

**Nidularium innocentii (Bromeliaceae).** See Chapter 14.

**Notocactus mammulosus (Cactaceae).** See Chapter 13.

**Nymphaea tetragona helvola (Nymphaeaceae).** See Chapter 12.

**Odontoglossum grande (Orchidaceae).** See Chapter 15.

**Odontoglossum pulchellum (Orchidaceae).** See Chapter 15.

**Opuntia pachypus (Cactaceae).** See Chapter 13.

**Osmanthus fragrans (Oleaceae)—Sweet Olive.** A shrubby tree in its native Himalayan region, it can be kept within control by hard pruning after flowering in the cool greenhouse. I have grown this plant for years solely for its fragrance. Its perfume is so delicate that it is hard to get too much of it. The tiny white flowers bloom in February and even a small plant will provide enough perfume to fill a 30-foot greenhouse. The plant is never very compact, with its twiggy branches sparsely covered with small leathery leaves, but, again, it is the fragrance that counts.

Cuttings taken of mature stems will root after they have formed a callus.

**Paphiopedilum Bromfield (Orchidaceae).** See Chapter 15.

**Paphiopedilum insigne (Orchidaceae).** See Chapter 15.

**Paphiopedilum Maudiae 'Magnificum' (Orchidaceae).** See Chapter 15.

**Passiflora caerulea (Passifloraceae)—Passion Flower.** A South American climber, the blue flower of this vine is spectacular in its intricacy. A temperature of 65° to 70° is ideal; however, a slightly cooler environment will be tolerated. Train a vine to climb along a wire forming an arch across your greenhouse. At the end of the growing season in September, you can then snip off the wire and cut the vine back. You can start over again in March. Feed these plants regularly and keep them well watered. A humid atmosphere will be helpful if leaves begin to shrivel. Examine your vines often for woolly aphids and spray occasionally with a systemic as a preventative measure. Propagate plants from stem cuttings.

**Passiflora quadrangularis (Passifloraceae).** This plant is grown in the tropics for its delicious fruit. The winged stems are exposed to view, since the foliage is sparse and this, coupled with white, purple-banded flowers, make it a most unusual vine. It is extremely vigorous and, therefore, you might do well to have new, smaller plants coming along. They are started easily as cuttings.

**Passiflora trifasciata (Passifloraceae).** This plant has a small, yellow, fragrant flower, but it is especially prized for its attractively ornamented three-lobed leaves. While basically green, these leaves are splashed with silver, bronze, and purple.

**Pentas lanceolata (Rubiaceae)—Egyptian Star-Clusters.** This small plant blooms during the winter and bears 20 or more tubular lilac flowers, which grow in a flat cluster. It grows best in a fibrous loam which has been lightened with decayed manure or leaf mold, at a temperature of 60° to 65°. Give it plenty of sun from fall to spring and shade the rest of the year. Water well during the warm months, but keep it only moist enough to avoid shriveling in winter. Fresh air in spring and summer is also beneficial.

It grows from cuttings of half-matured wood, cut early in March or April. Root at a temperature of 70°. Shade the new cuttings in 3-inch pots until they root, then use 5-inch pots and provide full sunlight. In the spring after they flower, move them into 8-inch pots.

Avoid scale and mealy bugs.

**Peperomia sandersii (Piperaceae).** This popular tropical plant does well in a dry atmosphere and, therefore, it is useful as a house plant, too. There are many variations but the appeal is always in the leaves, which are white and various shades of green. Some are striped; some are marbled. In the greenhouse, plants should be kept at a minimum temperature of 55°, watered very slightly, and kept nearly dry in winter. Use a mixture of 2 parts loam, 2 parts peat, and 1 part coarse sand. Use small pots, since their roots are not large. Pot during March in damp compost and allow to dry before watering.

Propagate plants from cuttings taken in summer and root in atmosphere of 70° to 75°. Pot the following March in 3-inch pots.

**Phaseolus vulgaris (Leguminosae).** See Chapter 20.

**Phoenix roebelenii (Palmae)—Pigmy Date Palm.** This graceful plant, found chiefly in Vietnam, is covered by feathery leaves and, although at its full height of 12 feet it bears clusters of black fruit, it is also highly suitable as a small plant in any ordinary warm greenhouse. The seeds, or *date stones*, should be soaked in lukewarm water for 1 to 2 days before you place them in 5- to 6-inch pots. When the slow-growing seedlings are about 3 inches tall, they should be transferred to 3-inch pots. If well watered throughout spring and summer, they should be decorative plants by fall.

**Pilea cadierei (Urticaceae)—Aluminum Plant or Watermelon Pilea.** This plant grows about 8 inches high and its green leaves are splashed with silvery patches. Its flowers are of little consequence, but the unusual foliage makes the pilea a valued decorative plant. Warm, humid conditions, as in its native Vietnam, are preferable when the plant is young, but slightly cooler conditions will be tolerated when the plant has matured. Light shade is required during the summer months.

It can be propagated from cuttings of young shoots in spring and summer. The shoots can be rooted in sandy soil and, as their growth progresses, they can be transplanted into 3-inch and then into 5-inch pots.

To produce a bushier plant, pinch out the growing tip of each stem. Then, after each new growth produces 2 sets of leaves, pinch out the tip once again.

**Pisum sativum (Leguminosae).** See Chapter 20.

**Pleurothallis roezlii (Orchidaceae).** See Chapter 15.

**Plumbago capensis (Plumbaginaceae)—Leadwort.** This South African plant of clambering habit, though often called a climber, cannot actually support itself. It can, however, be tied to wires or a trellis and will range from 10 to 20 feet in a few years. It will grow very well in a cool greenhouse and its phloxlike flowers of pale blue will become profuse in August and last until October. Grown in a warm greenhouse, flowering will commence at an earlier date. As long as the soil is well drained the plant will not be fussy. During the winter the plant will tolerate cold down to 40°. It will even drop all its leaves and appear dormant until heat and water are reapplied in late winter. Cuttings can be rooted in spring or, you can sow seeds in January and be assured of a 4-foot plant by midsummer.

**Poinciana pulcherrima (Leguminosae)—Dwarf Poinciana.** This spring and summer blooming plant has bright orange-yellow and red blossoms, and feathery foliage. While more often referred to as *P. pulcherrima*, it is more accurately *Caesalpinia pulcherrima*. In a greenhouse it grows well in a 6-inch pot at 60° to 65° under humid conditions. It should be grown in rich and porous soil. Watering should be heavy during active growth and lighter during winter. Give it full sun in winter and provide some shade the rest of the year.

To start, soak seeds in warm water for a few hours. Sow them in small pots with loose and relatively poor, sandy soil. Move them into 5-inch pots as soon as leaves appear. Plants will require 6-inch pots after approximately eight weeks and a still larger size as growth continues. Keep shaded until growth is strong. Cuttings are difficult to propagate, but can grow if taken when the parent plant is in its most vigorous state. Place the cuttings in a closed case at 75°.

Be on the lookout for aphids, scale, and mealy bugs.

**Primula kewensis (Primulaceae).** This variety, bearing fragrant, bright-yellow flowers, should receive the same treatment as the *P. malacoides*. Its 6-inch flower stem emerges out of a low-growing whorl of leaves. This is a natural hybrid, and it is very prolific in that it self-sows its seed on greenhouse benches after it flowers. Once you have bought the original seeds you will most likely not have to make the same purchase again! The foliage of this variety is covered with a natural white powder, which creates an unusual effect.

**Primula malacoides (Primulaceae)—Baby Primrose.** Blooming on straight, 6-inch stalks, groups of small, brightly colored flowers are surrounded by a neat rosette of green leaves. Originally from China, this species is available in an array of clear colors. For this particular variety, you can sow seeds at various times of the year to produce blooms all year-round. A cool greenhouse and rich but porous potting soil suits it well. During the summer, place the plants in a cold frame shaded from the sun, since they like cool, moist conditions. As the nights become cooler in September, return them to a cool greenhouse with a minimum temperature of 45° to 50°. Ventilate well and water sparingly when temperatures are low. Discard plants after their flowering and grow new ones from seed each year.

**Rebutia senilis cristata (Cactaceae).** See Chapter 13.

**Russelia equisetiformis (Scrophulariaceae)—Fountain Plant.** This is an excellent candidate for use as a hanging basket plant. The feathery foliage lends a very special look to the warm greenhouse and, when the small, red flowers bloom in the spring, it is a very cheerful sight. By the time a well-developed basket is formed, the branches will have reached down about 2½ feet, so you should be certain of enough headroom before you start. The space it requires is well worth it since the blooming period is of very long duration. Propagation is accomplished by cuttings taken at any time of the year.

**Saintpaulia ionantha (Gesneriaceae)—African Violet.** One of the specializations that has captured the imagination of greenhouse gardeners is the growing of African violets. However, the interest is certainly disproportionate, by all normal reasoning, to that shown for most genera. But rather than try to explain this interest, let us examine the genus and the methods of its culture.

*Saintpaulia ionantha* grows in craggy areas of tropical East Africa at low altitudes. In such an environment it grows as a perennial and readily self-sows. Violetlike flowers in either the single or hybrid form arise on short stems and are held a few inches above the rosette of fleshy, hairy leaves.

Most plants are grown best when their native environment is closely duplicated. However, for some unknown reason, saintpaulias have been cultivated in richer soil and a more humid atmosphere and in

*The variety of African violets is almost endless.*

weaker light than exists in their native Tanzania. There, they often grow virtually hanging out of crevices on wind-swept rocks. But one thing seems sure—they actually grow better in a man-made situation.

One reason for saintpaulia's popularity is the ease with which it can be propagated by leaf cuttings. Almost any mature plant will never miss a leaf or two broken off at soil level. After breaking off a leaf, trim back the leaf stem to 1 inch in length and insert it in sand so that about ¼ inch of the leaf blade is buried as well as the stem. If kept warm and moist, roots and new leaves will appear in a few weeks.

Amateur breeders have added to the already tremendous number of new crosses, so today the shades of pink, blue, purple, and white, multiplied by the single and double forms, result in almost limitless combinations.

**Salpiglossis sinuata (Solanaceae).** An annual with a great variety of available colors, this Chilean native becomes a good-sized potted plant in four months. It will tolerate either a cool or a warm greenhouse, but needs as much light as possible. Sown in February and transplanted as growth dictates, it will be ready to literally cover itself with delicately colored and interestingly veined flowers by summer.

**Schizanthus hybrids (Solanaceae)—Poor Man's Orchid.** Originally from South America and noted as one of the loveliest annuals, this plant has an extra-generous blooming of irregular, pansylike flowers in shades of either lilac, purple, pink, carmine, reddish-brown, or white.

It is easy to grow, if provided with a minimum temperature of 40°. For the large pansy-flowered strain, a 6- or 7-inch pot is advisable; however, the *Excelsior compactus* variety is a dwarf and is particularly good in smaller pots.

The best time for sowing seeds is in August or September. They will produce their richest bloom in April and May. Successive sowings can be made in February, May, and June, producing a sequential bloom until late autumn.

The seeds should be spaced out thinly and covered lightly with sifted soil. All but the February sowing can be germinated in a cold frame—the February sowing requires a little artificial warmth of about 50°. When the roots are about an inch long, they should be transplanted singly into 3-inch pots. Keep the young plants near the light and give them plenty of fresh air when possible to ensure the development of a firmer plant. Pinch the tips of main shoots a few weeks later to promote branching. Water generously in the spring, but sparingly in winter when temperatures are low. It may be helpful to stake the stems with bamboo canes (hidden behind the foliage) to insure that the flowers can be seen at their best.

**Schizostylis coccinea (Iridaceae).** See Chapter 12.

**Selaginella kraussiana (Selaginellaceae)—Spreading Club Moss.** This South African native is not a moss at all, but a creeping herbaceous plant. It forms a solid green mat no more than 6 inches high. The overlapping scalelike leaves give it a distinctive appearance and, coupled with its emerald color, this makes it desirable as a potted plant even though it has no conspicuous flowers. It requires a warm greenhouse in which it receives no direct sunlight. Therefore, it is well suited to planting along the walk and at the feet of the plant benches. Do not overwater but apply only enough to keep the soil moderately moist and, since the soil should be high in organic matter, it will not drain as quickly as a sandier mixture.

Plants can be propagated easily by cutting pieces off and pressing each into a small pot of soil.

**Senecio cruentus (Compositae)—Cineraria.** This has propably been responsible for more "oohs" and "ahs" than any other greenhouse plant. Its parentage stems from plants of the Canary Islands' hillsides and the electric-brilliant color of its daisylike blooms, the variety of hues, and quantity of blooms are no less than breathtaking. Started from seeds in midsummer and treated as a biennial, it will start blooming in the cool greenhouse in 5- to 7-inch pots (depending on the variety) in January and will continue until late March.

**Sinningia pusilla (Gesneriaceae).** This is a species that you really must try. A well-grown plant—flower and all—is about 1 inch high and 1 inch wide. It is easily grown from seed and does best in a warm, humid atmosphere. Therefore, a "thumb pot" set on pebbles and water or a small glass jar make good containers. Lavender flowers with a yellow throat are produced almost continuously as are seeds, which germinate easily. New plants spring up around the old one from these seeds, so once you start *S. pusilla* you will have it and enjoy it for some time.

**Sinningia speciosa (Gesneriaceae).** See Chapter 12.

**Solanum pseudo-capsicum (Solanaceae)—Jerusalem Cherry.** This plant from southern Brazil and Uruguay is grown largely for its ornamental berries, which it produces in winter.

*Cineraria hybrid*
(*Senecio cruentus*)

Seeds should be sown in February or March in a temperature of not less than 55°. As soon as the seedlings are large enough—generally when the first two leaves begin to appear—they should be pricked out. When transplanting seedlings into a flat, leave an inch or two between seedlings. Use a compost containing leaf mold and sand, and keep' the flat shaded from direct sun.

Transplant into individual pots, 3-inch or 4-inch, and grow outdoors in summer to insure full light and ventilation. Repot as roots become restricted. Water regularly throughout the summer, keeping the compost moist. Bring plants back into the greenhouse in late September when the berries have begun to show color and keep them at about 50° until full color is attained.

**Soleirolia soleirolii (Urticaceae)—Baby's Tears.** Originally called *Helxine soleirolii,* this subtropical Corsican creeper only grows about an inch high. It is cultivated solely for its rich green miniature foliage—each leaf being no more than ⅛ of an inch in size. If forms such a dense mat that it gives the appearance of a moss and can be grown either alone or in a pot at the base of a taller plant.

To start a new plant just pull up a small piece and plant it in its own pot. If kept well watered, it will start to spread quickly.

**Sophronitis grandiflora (Orchidaceae).** See Chapter 15.

**Spathiphyllum clevelandii (Araceae).** The crisp appearance of this South American tropical plant created by its long, spear-shaped, rich green

*Ornamental Pepper* (Solanum pseudo-capsicum), *with its decorative fruit, is ideal for the cool greenhouse.*

leaves and pure white, waxenlike flowers (actually spathes, but this is merely a botanical technicality) makes it a universal favorite. If you add to its beauty the fact that it is easy to grow in a warm greenhouse and holds up well when taken indoors as a house plant, there is little wonder why this plant is so popular.

It starts into growth in late March and by May it is in flower, continuing for six weeks or more. During active growth it should have a warm, moist atmosphere. During the winter months the amount of water should be reduced and it is at this time that new plants can be made by dividing the crown of the parent plant with a sharp knife. Pot new plants in a soil rich in leaf mold.

**Stephanotis floribunda (Asclepiadaceae)—Madagascar Jasmine.** This greenhouse climber from the Malagasy Republic (formerly Madagascar) thrives in tropical conditions, although it will grow reasonably well with a minimum temperature of 50°. Noted for its lush leaves and clusters of waxy-white, tubular flowers, it can be grown against a south-facing inside wall and trained on wires or in large pots. Rich, well-drained soil—a rough, loamy mixture with some peat—is best. Shade must be given in summer and frequent syringings are advisable, but the plants should be kept on the dry side in winter.

Watch out for insect pests such as red spiders and mealy bugs.

**Strelitzia reginae (Musaceae)—Bird of Paradise Flower.** This exotic, striking plant, reminiscent of the head of some vividly plumed tropical bird, originated in South Africa. The flowers appear in spring and early summer. Stems are about 3 feet long; the leaves are 18 inches long and 7 inches wide.

The plants may be grown in 6-inch pots in a warm greenhouse, but, as they progress, transplant them to larger pots or tubs or, preferably, into a border of good, well-drained soil. Keep them in a sunny position with almost dry soil in winter and plenty of water in spring and summer. The temperature should never fall below 50°.

To increase strelitzia, divide the plants in spring and plant divisions separately in 6-inch pots in a mixture of 2 parts loam, 1 part peat, and 1 part coarse sand.

**Streptosolen jamesonii (Solanaceae).** This clambering shrub from Colombia is colorful and makes a good subject for a hanging basket. Its clusters of tubular, bright, orange flowers bloom abundantly in June and July. It can also be grown against a greenhouse wall and, given support, in a ground bed or an 8-inch pot it will cover a space several feet across and about 6 feet high.

Winter temperatures should run about 45° to 50°. In cold weather, keep the soil dry. For a bushier pot plant, pinch out tip growth. For heavier pruning of large plants, cut the thickest stems back in January or February.

**Thunbergia alata (Acanthaceae)—Black-eyed Susan Vine.** Small in flower and restrained in habit, this is one vine that will not get out of hand. A South African twining plant, it is readily adaptable to either the warm or cool greenhouse, though best started from seed in a warm atmosphere. Its flat, yellow, 1-inch flowers have a dull purple (almost brown) center. A few plants can be grown in a 6-inch pot and trained to climb upon a pyramid of pencil-thin bamboo canes. Start seeds in midwinter for early spring flowering. Thunbergia is not fussy as to soil and has no predilection toward insects, making it an ideal plant.

**Tibouchina semidecandra (Melastomaceae)—Glory Bush.** This shrub, originally from southern Brazil, yields large, royal-purple flowers from June to October. It can be grown as a shrub, 3 to 6 feet, in an 8-inch pot. The purple flowers usually last for just one day, but they are promptly replaced, so the plant is rarely out of bloom.

Propagate by cuttings rooted in sand or peat moss. The cuttings should root in about 4 weeks, at which time they should be placed in 3-inch pots in a light, fibrous, loamy soil with sand liberally added for good drainage. As the plants progress and become pot-bound, transplant them into larger containers. Repot each fall with fresh soil. Full sunshine in fall and winter, and light shade in late spring and summer are desirable. These plants require daily and thorough watering and need a moderate to warm greenhouse of 55° to 60°. Pinch and prune when no longer in flower to provide new wood for the future.

**Torenia fournieri (Schrophulariaceae).** This close relative of the snapdragon is a native of Indochina. It is an annual, and it grows with multiple stems which make it ideal as a flowering potted plant. It is covered with pale blue and purple flowers throughout the middle of the summer, continuing into the fall. While a little extra warmth is needed for the seeds to germinate and to carry along the new plants during their infancy, the plants will do very well in the cool greenhouse thereafter. One variety, *T. fournieri* 'Grandiflora,' carries much larger flowers than the species, but is not as prolific.

**Trachelospermum jasminoides (Apocynaceae)—Confederate Jasmine.**
This Himalayan vine is one of the most fragrant for greenhouse culture. Its needs are moderate in all respects and, therefore, it can be accommodated in either a warm or cool environment. Its 2-inch, star-shaped white flowers are set off by dark green, leathery leaves.

*The very fragrant confederate jasmine* (Trachelospermum jasminoides)

**Tradescantia fluminensis var. variegata (Commelinaceae)—Wandering Jew.** This creeper from Brazil is ideal for a hanging basket. In a short time its wire container will be covered with a mass of green and white striped leaves. The flowering of this species is of little consequence, the main attraction being the attractive foliage. Grow it in a warm greenhouse in a moderately organic soil mixture. New plants can be produced easily by taking stem cuttings, stripping the leaves off the lower 2 inches and burying the bare stems in coarse sand which is kept constantly moist.

**Tripogandra multiflora (Commelinaceae)—Miniature Wandering Jew.** This West Indian native forms a complete mass of tangled stems covered with ½-inch long dark green leaves within a short time of planting. A ground creeper in the tropics, it is also excellent grown in a hanging basket. Its soil requirements are met with any mixture of medium to high organic content. Once growth is underway it should be fed once a month. It will often bloom twice a year and is then covered with hundreds of tiny white flowers. Stem cuttings will root readily in a mixture of ½ sand and ½ peat moss.

**Tropaeolum majus (Tropaeolaceae)—Nasturtium.** This Peruvian climber will brighten a cool greenhouse in a very special manner. Trained across the rafters on a few wires, the large round leaves make a solid green background for the numerous orange flowers.

Sow seeds in April. Use any of the current hybrid varieties that have larger size and richer colors than the species. The soil requirements are minimal and actually the lower the level of nutrition, the more flowers will be produced. Provide a position of full sun to insure continuous flowering from late June until early October.

**Tropaeolum tricolor (Tropaeolaceae).** See Chapter 12.

**Vallota speciosa (Amaryllidaceae).** See Chapter 12.

**Veltheimia viridifolia (Liliaceae).** See Chapter 12.

**Vitis vinifera (Vitaceae).** See Chapter 20.

**Zantedeschia aethiopica (Araceae).** See Chapter 12.

**Zygopetalum mackayi (Orchidaceae).** See Chapter 15.

# Glossary of Horticultural Terms

*Aereole*—that part of a cactus that looks like a dot or small cushion. It is from this point that new growth emanates—leaves, branches, or even spines. The *aereoles* of the cactus have, as their equivalent, nodes in the more conventional plants.

*Break*—in terms of plant growth, the development of a new stem at a node or leaf joint. Plants which enlarge themselves by means of a creeping stem or rhizome *break*, or develop, new growth along the rhizome at "eyes" or buds.

*Compost*—partially decomposed organic matter.

*Damping-down*—the process of spraying walks and under-bench areas with water to raise the humidity and lower the temperature in the greenhouse.

*Damping-off*—an entirely different matter, having no connection with the previous phrase, is a fungous disease that attacks young seedlings, causing them to rot at the soil level and quickly die. Soil sterilization (before sowing seed) or treatment with a commercial *damping-off* liquid preventive will avoid this most disappointing disease.

*Disbudding*—the removal of axillary buds so that a terminal bud may develop to its fullest potential. The terminal bud is sometimes removed to strengthen the plant.

*Dormancy*—the period when a plant has no apparent growth and is brought about by seasonal changes in temperature or humidity.

*Epiphytic plants*—those that grow on trees and have all their functional roots exposed to the air. They get their nourishment from both the air and decayed organic matter such as dead leaves that are washed down to it by the rain.

*Flaccid leaves*—those in wilted or limp condition indicating an insufficient supply of water. The leaves of chrysanthemums and poinsettias are quick to relay this information to the grower.

*Flat*—traditionally a wooden box, approximately 12″ × 24″ × 3″, into which seedlings are transplanted. Smaller flats of plastic and papier mâché are also currently available.

*Flowering*—the culmination of the growing sequence, insofar as the greenhouse gardener is concerned. In the natural scheme of things, seed production, after flowering, is the true culmination; however, for our purposes the flower is "the thing." Flowering is an exhausting drain on a plant's energy, and some bulbs that are "forced" into bloom actually cannot replenish their food supply sufficiently to perpetuate themselves, and it is sometimes necessary to discard them after flowering.

*Forcing*—an acceleration of the natural sequence of growth, rather than a change in the sequence. In some cases forcing follows an artificially induced dormancy or growth stimulus.

*Friable*—that desirable workability of the soil, when it is moderately crumbly in hand.

*Genus*—to a plant what a surname is to a person. Those plants that are closely related fall into one genus. The plural is *genera.*

*Hardening-off*—the process by which the soft plant tissue is gradually acclimated to outdoor temperatures after growing in the warmth of a greenhouse. This is accomplished by placing the plant in a protected location (such as a cold frame) which, while still covered, provides less heat, for a week or so before placing it in an exposed outdoor area. Eliminating this important step will result in a stunted plant with little success in flowering.

*Hardy plants*—those which survive the winter in a particular area. Knowing the minimum winter temperature in that area will enable you to determine its hardiness or ability to live through the winter in another location.

*Internode*—the space between the joints on the plant stem. When a plant is grown in insufficient light the internodes are apt to become elongated.

*Leaching*—the process whereby chemical ingredients in the soil are removed by the flow of water through it. This is sometimes employed deliberately to get rid of an excess of nitrogen or soluble salts but, more often, it is done inadvertently, and depletes the helpful materials, which then must be replaced.

*Nodes*—the joints on a plant stem where leaves or other stems may grow.

*Offset*—the emergence of a bulblet or a new plant from the side of the original plant. Roots form quickly and the offset can be cut apart and potted independently.

*Pan*—a shallow pot used for growing bulbs, ferns, or other plants that benefit from their roots being confined at moderate depth.

*Parasitic plant*—one that gets its nourishment from the host on which it grows. And contrary to popular belief, orchids do not fall into this classification.

*Pinching or stopping*—technique by which we can induce branching and thereby produce a bushier compact plant through pinching out the growing tip of the main stem. This should be done after the development of the second or third set of leaves.

*Plunging a pot*—in the case of bulbs, burying it over its rim in sand outdoors during the fall and winter while it develops a root system and then becomes dormant. In the summer many plants are plunged outdoors in the garden, up to the pot rim, in order to continue their growth without daily watering being required.

*Pot-bound*—a plant whose roots fill the pot and, in some cases, also grow over the entire surface of the soil. Some plants, such as amaryllis, agapanthus, and geranium flower a lot better when *pot-bound*; a greater number of plants such as chrysanthemum, fuchsia, and gloxinia need room for their active and finer-textured roots to feed.

*Potting-on*—when the plants are moved to progressively larger individual pots as growth occurs.

*Pricking-out*—the transfer of seedlings (having already acquired their true leaves) from the crowded seed pot to proper spacing in a wooden flat.

*Rest*—in bulbs, corms, and tubers infers minimal growth. While it may appear that growing conditions are ideal, the plant seems to "stand still." Often this coincides with the dormant period in the plant's native environment, and even though it is now planted in a geographically foreign situation, its internal calendar maintains a predetermined cycle. Additionally, resting seems to be part of that recuperative period, after flowering and just prior to active growth, when a complete revitalization takes place.

*Shading compound*—either a commercial preparation or a home recipe of a liquid for application to the greenhouse glass to block out a portion of the sun's rays. Whitewash mixed with a small amount of either kerosene or casein (to act as a "sticker") is in popular use. These compounds can be applied neatly with a brush or can even be spattered on, thereby creating a dappled light within the greenhouse.

*Species*—the epithet which follows a plant's generic name and refers to a plant which has enough distinct characteristics to set it apart from others in the genus. There are, however, a sufficient number of other similar characteristics to classify it within the same genus. The singular and plural of *species* are the same.

*Standard*—a plant grown treelike, trained to a single stem.

*Succulents*—those plants that are able to store water in their leaves or stems in large amounts. All cacti are succulents although all succulents are not cacti. There are succulent species of geranium, agave, begonia, haworthia, and ceropegia, to name but a few other than cacti.

*Tender plants*—those which cannot withstand frost and would, there-fore, have to be given the protection of a greenhouse in cold regions in order to carry over the winter.

*Terrestrial*—those plants that grow with their roots in the soil, as do most of our garden flowers, trees, and shrubs. A large group of orchids is also terrestrial.

*Top dressing*—the addition of fresh fertile soil to the surface of a potted plant to re-cover exposed roots and/or replenish soil leached of its nutrients by constant watering. This corrective measure is recommended annually for most plants.

*Top growth*—the production of leaves, which in turn feed the bulb or corm to replenish its energy for future flowering.

*Transpiration*—in plants, involves the loss water through the leaves caused by high temperatures or air currents.

*Turgid*—that condition wherein a plant holds itself erect with its leaves extended at the proper angle; all due to an adequate supply of water within the plant.

*Viability*—the ability of seeds to germinate. This is often measured in percentage. The age and conditions of storage play an important role in the *viability* of seeds.

# Appendix

## Manufacturers of Greenhouses and Accessories

Aluminum Greenhouses, Inc.
14615 Lorain Avenue
Cleveland, Ohio 44111

Dome East
325 Duffy Avenue
Hicksville, New York 11801

Humex, Ltd.
5 High Road
Byfleet, Weybridge, Surrey
England
*or*
E. and W. International
290 Sandringham Road
Rochester, New York, 14610

Lord and Burnham
Irvington, New York 10533
*or*
Des Plaines, Illinois 60018

J. A. Nearing Co., Inc.
10788 Tucker Street
Beltsville, Maryland 20705

Redfern's Prefab Greenhouses
55 Mt. Hermon Road
Scotts Valley, California 95060

Peter Reumuller, Greenhouseman
P. O. Box 2666
Santa Cruz, California 95060

Stearns Greenhouses
98 Taylor Street
Neponset, Massachusetts, 02122

Sturdi-Built Manufacturing Company
11304 S. W. Boones Ferry Road
Portland, Oregon 97219

Texas Greenhouse Co., Inc.
2710 St. Louis Avenue
Fort Worth, Texas 76110

Turner Greenhouses
P. O. Box 1260
Goldsboro, North Carolina 27530
   (also fiberglass greenhouses)

## Sources for Greenhouse Accessories

George J. Ball, Inc.
West Chicago
Illinois 60185

seeds, plants, rooted cuttings, greenhouse supplies

Dillon Industries, Inc.
P. O. Box 224
Melrose, Massachusetts 02176

soil pasteurizers

Florist Products
1843 E. Oakton
Des Plaines, Illinois 60018

greenhouse supplies

H. P. Supplies
Box 18101
Cleveland, Ohio 44118

lighting and watering devices

Humex, Ltd.
5 High Road
Byfleet, Weybridge, Surrey
England
*or*
E. and W. International
290 Sandringham Road
Rochester, New York 14610

automatic nonelectric watering devices, automatic capillary watering devices, nonelectric automatic ventilators, shading devices, tensiometers (devices for measuring need of watering)

Walter F. Nicke
P. O. Box 71
Hudson, New York 12534

general supplies

Al Saffer and Co., Inc.
130 West 28th Street
New York, New York 10001

chemicals, greenhouse accessories

Shoplite Co., Inc.
566 Franklin Avenue
Nutley, New Jersey 07110

fluorescent lighting supplies

X. S. Smith Company
Box 272
Red Bank, New Jersey 07701

black cloth for shading chrysanthemums

Sudbury Laboratory, Inc.
Box 1028
Sudbury, Massachusetts 01776

soil testing equipment

The House Plant Corner       general plant aids
P. O. Box 810
Oxford, Maryland 21654

## Sources for Seeds and Plants

Abbey Garden       succulents
Box 167
Reseda, California 91335

Alberts & Merkel Bros., Inc.       orchids and tropical foliage plants
Boynton Beach, Florida 33435

Antonelli Bros.       tuberous begonias
2545 Capitola Road
Santa Cruz, California 95010

Armacost & Royston       orchids
2005 Armacost Avenue
West Los Angeles, California
90025

Buell's Greenhouses       African violets, gloxinia, and
Eastford, Connecticut 06242       other gesneriads

Burgess Seed and Plant Co.       seeds and plants
P. O. Box 218
Galesburg, Michigan 49053

W. Atlee Burpee Co.       seeds of annuals, biennials, and
Philadephia, Pennsylvania 19132       perennials

Butchart Gardens, Ltd.       seeds
P. O. Box 4010, Station "A"
Victoria, British Columbia

Edelweiss Gardens       general plants
Robbinsville, New Jersey 08691

Fennell Orchid Co.       orchids
26715 S.W. 157th Avenue
Homestead, Florida 33030

Fischer Greenhouse       African violets
Linwood, New Jersey 08221

J. Howard French       bulbs
Box 37
Lima, Pennsylvania 19060

Joseph Harris Co., Inc.       vegetable seeds
Moreton Farm, Buffalo Road
Rochester, New York 14624

Alexander I. Heimlich
71 Burlington Street
Woburn, Massachusetts 01801

miniature bulbs, corms, and tubers

Margaret Ilgenfritz
P. O. Box 665
Monroe, Michigan 48161

orchids

Jones and Scully, Inc.
2200 N.W. 33rd Avenue
Miami, Florida 33142

orchids

Michael Kartuz
92 Chestnut Street
Wilmington, Massachusetts 01887

general plants

Logee's Greenhouses
Danielson, Connecticut 06239

general plants

Lyndon Lyon
Dolgeville, New York 13329

African violets

Merry Gardens
Camden, Maine 04843

general plants

George W. Park Seed Co.
Greenwood, South Carolina
29646

seeds

J. A. Peterson
3132 McHenry Avenue
Cincinnati, Ohio 45211

African violets

John Scheepers, Inc.
37 Wall Street
New York, New York 10005

bulbs

Sunnyslope Gardens
8638 Huntington Drive
San Gabriel, California 91775

rooted chrysanthemum cuttings

Thompson & Morgan, Ltd.
London Road
Ipswich IP2 OBA
Suffolk, England

seeds of annuals, biennials, perennials, and shrubs; wide variety of species

Vetterle Bros.
P. O. Box 1246
Watsonville, California 95076

tuberous begonias

# Index